D1611985

UNDERSTANDING
WITTGENSTEIN

Studies of *Philosophical Investigations*

J·F·M·HUNTER

UNDERSTANDING WITTGENSTEIN

Studies of *Philosophical Investigations*

EDINBURGH
UNIVERSITY
PRESS

© J.F.M. Hunter 1985
Edinburgh University Press
22 George Square, Edinburgh

Set in Linoterm Melior
by Speedspools, Edinburgh
and printed in Great Britain by
Redwood Burn Ltd, Trowbridge

British Library Cataloguing
  in Publication Data
Hunter, J.F.M.
Understanding Wittgenstein
1. Wittgenstein, Ludwig.
  Philosophical investigations
I. Title
149'.943   B3376.W563P53
ISBN 0 85224 497 5

CONTENTS

ABBREVIATIONS

BB
The Blue and Brown Books
Basil Blackwell, Oxford 1958

PI
Philosophical Investigations
third edition
The Macmillan Co., New York 1968

PG
Philosophical Grammar
Basil Blackwell, Oxford 1978

RPP
Remarks on the Philosophy of Psychology
Basil Blackwell, Oxford 1980

Z
Zettel
Basil Blackwell, Oxford 1967

All references without attributions are to
Philosophical Investigations

PREFACE

WITTGENSTEIN WROTE cryptically, and to make sense of his prose is always a challenge. One method of coping with this problem that I have found useful is that of working out my own way of handling a problem with which he was dealing. Sometimes when I have come, largely on my own, to see a way through his difficulty, I found I had a vantage point from which for the first time I could make some clear sense of various remarks of his that had baffled me. That is by no means a fast route to understanding Wittgenstein. One may sometimes make a half a dozen attempts before the pieces begin to fall into place, and there are all too many of his themes on which it has not yet worked for me at all. But with luck and patience, often enough it is rewarding; and when it is, I am confronted with the question whether to present the conclusions I have reached as my own views, or as interpretations of Wittgenstein. In an earlier volume, *Essays after Wittgenstein* (Toronto, 1973), I followed the former course: I presented what I had to say as philosophy, rather than as Wittgenstein scholarship; but I confessed my belief that on many points I either had a correct interpretation of Wittgenstein, or at least an interesting suggestion about how some of his deliberations might be understood.

The studies in the present volume do, or do more of, what I scarcely attempted in the earlier essays. They vary considerably in this respect, but they gravitate towards the scholar's task of focusing closely on particular passages and themes, bringing out in some detail the difficulties there are in understanding them, projecting possible lines of interpretation, and comparatively evaluating these in the light of whatever textual evidence appears relevant.

In my opinion there is not a sharp line to be drawn between philosophy and scholarship. Whatever philosopher I am reading, I find the asking of philosophical questions to be an indispensable tool of scholarship: such questions as 'If I take this argument *this* way, is it a good argument? If not, is there a better argument that can be read in the words in which this one is expressed?', or 'Does what he seems to be saying here make any sense, and if not is there any way of taking his words so that they do make sense, or make better sense?' I find that the pursuit of such questions leads me again and again to a richer understanding of another philospher's problems, and to an interpretation that not only passes scholarly tests, but gives me a new respect for the author's views and arguments.

In Wittgenstein's case I find this leavening of scholarship with philosophy to be particularly essential, because where most other philosophers make every effort to minimise the interpreter's task by careful and precise articulation, Wittgenstein on the contrary seemed to make some point of avoiding explaining what he wished to say. He prescribed work programmes, but did not explain how to carry them out, or in what way he thought their results would be relevant; he asked questions but did not answer them; posed questions he thought ought not to be asked, without saying so until much later, and then only indirectly; asked apparently rhetorical questions when it turned out he thought they called for careful answering; and (if I am right) contrived his most forthright statements in such a way as to conceal the point he wished to make.

No doubt some people will disagree with this description of Wittgenstein's philosophical practice, but if, as I believe, he does in this way systematically avoid expressing his views, clearly the interpreter's task will be a peculiarly difficult one, and there will be no way of understanding him without the philosophical activity of carrying out his work programmes, working out the significance of their results, answering his questions, deciding which of them thought deserved answers, and untangling his ambiguities and obscurities of his apparently forthright position statements.

If you wonder sceptically what Wittgenstein's motivation could be for hiding his views in the way I have described, the answer is no doubt at the end of the Preface to the *Philo-*

sophical Investigations, where he says 'I should not like my writing to spare other people the trouble of thinking. But, if possible, to stimulate someone to thoughts of his own'. The tactics I have described serve that purpose very well.

I am not entirely happy when I reflect that, if my efforts in this volume should be at all successful, they would so far defeat Wittgenstein's purpose. However, to evaluate my conclusions a great deal of philosophical thinking will be necessary, at least if the method I have sketched is accepted; and in any case I have scarcely scratched the surface of the problems with which Wittgenstein leaves us, and something might be learned from my tactics about how to make headway with the many questions that remain.

I would have liked these studies to run more consistently in the direction of sober verification of interpretive hypotheses with textual evidence. Sometimes I believe I have made out a strong case, but on other questions there is very little textual evidence, and I have been unable to get beyond projecting various interpretive hypotheses, and comparing their *philosophical* merits. Also, sometimes, I fear, I have been self-indulgent in yielding too much to the fascination of the philosophical issues that arise everywhere.

Because of the large role I assign to philosophical considerations in scholarly deliberations, I am sometimes accused of arguing as if only what is of good report philosophically can be attributed to Wittgenstein. Since I do in fact have the greatest admiration for Wittgenstein as a philosopher, and am very reluctant to attribute to him a faulty argument or an unsound distinction, I have reason to be stung by this criticism. The defence I would *like* to offer is that I employ philosophical considerations only as part of a method of *arriving* at interpretive hypotheses, and confine myself to textual considerations in *verifying* these. Unfortunately the textual considerations that are available are seldom so decisive as to relieve one of at least the appearance of relying partly or heavily on philosophical considerations. Often, although there is a good deal of textual evidence, it is itself ambiguous or otherwise in need of interpretation; and the same set of passages can be lined up in different ways to support different interpretations. Hence, while the force of the textual verification that is available varies from slight to strong, it is not in general sufficiently imposing to remove the suspicion that I rely on the supposition that Wittgenstein can do no wrong philosophically.

That being the case, I can in the end perhaps only put it this way: (a) I think I show repeatedly, but particularly perhaps in chapter 21, that I do not in fact treat Wittgenstein as being infallible; (b) whether or not I always say so, it is always my intention that the interpretive suggestions that I formulate on the basis of philosophical considerations should stand to be confirmed or falsified by textual evidence; and when, typically, that evidence is inconclusive, I have neither exaggerated its force nor concealed contrary considerations, at least as far as I was aware of them. I have indicated how much or how little I thought the evidence was worth, and left it at that. I have not said that in the absence of evidence, we must rely on other considerations. However, it will be obvious that my heart is not so much in the interpretive task as in the insights that may emerge in the course of struggling with it, and even if I am unable to decide what were Wittgenstein's intentions, I am content if something I have come upon that might have been his intention, is itself philosophically interesting. I read philosophy with no other end in view than that of gaining philosophical enlightenment, and hence if I come away from my attempts to understand Wittgenstein with a new thought I am delighted, and the only point of view from which I care whether this was the thought Wittgenstein intended is that if it is not, perhaps there is some other, even more interesting thought still to be uncovered, or perhaps there is a mistake in the thought I now have, the understanding of which would be instructive. Experience has taught me to entertain this kind of hope in Wittgenstein's case, more than in that of some other philosophers, and therefore I keep coming back, keep pressing the scholarly questions, is this right? Have I overlooked something? Might there be something else here?

When I read (*PI* §128) that 'if one tried to advance theses in philosophy, it would not be possible to debate them, because everyone would agree with them', and other such remarks disavowing theorising, I am left wondering if I may be making a silly mistake in puzzling so persistently over the interpretation of Wittgenstein. In pressing my interpretive questions, I am not asking 'What is Wittgenstein's thesis here?', and can that question be asked, if he disavows theses?

In the sense in which Wittgenstein disavows theses, my questions are not of the form, 'What was his thesis?'. Wittgenstein was radically sceptical about philosophical questions, and about the theses that are propounded as their answers, but he thought it was very difficult to *show* what is wrong with a given philosophical question, to defend his scepticism with sound and adequate arguments. Hence my questions are of the form 'What argument did Wittgenstein contemplate here?', 'How would he cope with this difficulty?', 'Why was he reluctant to put his case in such and such a way?', and so on. The fully articulated argument that might emerge as an answer to such questions could perhaps be called a thesis, but not in the sense in which an answer to a question like 'What is thinking?' or 'What is the meaning of a word?' is a thesis. As a philosophical sceptic, Wittgenstein of course rejected theses in that sense, but he was nevertheless a very scrupulous thinker, returning again and again to an issue in his efforts to avoid misrepresenting the problem even in the smallest way. We see this not only in his philosophical practice, but in his remarks on it, a particularly striking example of which is Z §460, where he says 'In a certain sense one cannot take too much care in handling philosophical mistakes, they contain so much truth'.

What I am concerned to sleuth out is not theses in the sense of answers to old-style philosophical questions, but the ways he worked out but did not spell out, of performing the difficult task of showing that these questions should not be asked.

In sum, I see Wittgenstein as making an uncommonly strenuous effort to be in a position to show clearly and explicitly what is wrong with a given philosophical question, and to handle successfully the manifold doubts that will arise owing to the inter-relatedness of our concepts, and the massive bewitching power of language. However, while he wanted to be *in a position* to do this, and presumably wanted to put *us* in a position to do it, he did not want to *do it for us*, and therefore constructed his prose in such a way as to stop short of saying how he would go about it, while still providing leads, which if pursued with cunning and diligence, would enable us to shift for ourselves in a competent manner.

For my part, I think he rather overdid these efforts to oblige us to think for ourselves, or if not that, the hints and leads he provided were in too many cases such as to call for too much persistence and cunning; but the fact remains that the task of interpreting Wittgenstein is one of sleuthing out, from the clues he provides, thoroughly scrupulous ways of shifting for oneself when one encounters conceptual difficulties. It is a demanding task, that requires us to find our own way through some very difficult philosophical territory, but also an occupation affording endless pleasure and fascination, that I would commend unreservedly to anyone with the peculiar skills on which success and therefore pleasure rely.

Taken together these studies do not begin to deal with everything that is important or difficult in Wittgenstein's later writings. Perhaps half a dozen chapters could be described as representative of Wittgenstein's most central concerns, but for the rest I have been moved chiefly by the fact that there was something, often something quite small, that was difficult to understand and about which I had something useful to say. The volume is therefore not comprehensive; but on the topics of which it treats I hope it will be found to have the merit of getting down to the fine detail of Wittgenstein's work, and of often showing, rather than merely saying, what can be made of it.

I have sometimes found that much the same point can usefully be made in more than one context. In general I would prefer not to repeat myself, but with a view to making each chapter as self-contained as possible, wherever a point that had appeared elsewhere seemed important, I have let the repetition stand.

For want of a better way of arranging the material, I have ordered the chapters in the sequence in which the main passage with which they deal appears in the *Philosophical Investigations*. If there are several passages with which I am dealing, it is the order in which the first of them appears.

I am greatly indebted to my friend Jack Canfield for his searching comments on early drafts of a large part of this material. Sometimes he persuaded me that I was wrong. More often what became clear was that I needed a much more careful argument. Since he had no power of veto, I cannot hold him entirely responsible for the imperfections that remain.

Preface

Other publications of mine in a similar vein are listed below.

'Wittgenstein's Theory of Linguistic Self-Sufficiency',
   Dialogue, 1967, 367-78.
'"Forms of Life" in Wittgenstein's *Philosophical
   Investigations*', *American Philosophical Quarterly*,
   1968, 233-43; reprinted in E. D. Klemke (ed.),
   '*Essays on Wittgenstein*', 273-97.
'Wittgenstein in Learning the Meaning of a Word',
   Dialogue, 1971, 294-304.
'Wittgenstein on Meaning and Use', E. D. Klemke (ed.),
   op. cit., 374-93.
'Why Animals Don't Talk', *Dialogue*, 1976, 243-50.
'Wittgenstein on Inner Processes and Outward Criteria',
   Canadian Journal of Philosophy, 805-17.
'Wittgenstein on Describing and Making Connections',
   Philosophical Quarterly, 1976, 243-50.
'Some Grammatical States', *Philosophy*, 1977, 155-66.
'Wittgenstein and Materialism', *Mind*, 1977, 514-31.
'Wittgenstein on Language and Games', *Philosophy*,
   1980, 293-302.
'Wittgenstein on Seeing and Seeing-As', *Philosophical
   Investigations*, 1981, 33-50.

One

DOES EVERY WORD
HAVE A MEANING?

These words [of Augustine's], it seems to me, give us a
particular picture of the essence of human language. It is
this: the individual words in language name objects –
sentences are combinations of such names. In this picture
of language we find the roots of the following idea: Every
word has a meaning. This meaning is correlated with the
word. It is the object for which the word stands. (*Philosophical Investigations*, §1)

IT IS very well known that Wittgenstein queried the final two
of the three propositions at the end of the above quotation; but
whether or in what way he was sceptical about the first – the
proposition that every word has a meaning – is a question not
often raised, and not easy to answer. Depending on how this
proposition is interpreted, he either did or might well have
had doubts about it:

i) He certainly questioned whether every word has a meaning *in the sense* of something correlated with it, for which it
stands; but that is not to say that in the ordinary sense of the
word 'meaning', there is something wrong with saying that
every word has a meaning.

ii) He would have been right to question whether nonsense
words, like 'mimsy' and 'borogroves', have meanings. Since
'mimsy' is clearly an adjective, and 'borogroves' a noun, they
are words; but while some people may say that they understand them, they at least do not have the uncontroversial
meaning that most English words have.

iii) Most proper names do not have meanings. Some, like
'Constance', 'Prudence' and 'Smith', do, but their meanings
do not generally play any role in their use. Not many Smiths
are smiths any more, and if Prudence is imprudent, we do not

1

hasten to give her another name. Anyway most proper names do not have meanings, even in this minimal sense.

iv) Some words of greeting, like 'Bonjour' and 'Goodbye', have meanings, but most people who use them do not know of their meanings, or do not use them on account of the meanings they have; and not all of such expressions have meanings at all.

However, one might well reckon that these, together perhaps with a few other kinds of word, represent minor exceptions, and that there ought to be some non-trivial way of excluding them such that it is true of the words that remain, that they all have meanings. It would be trivial to say that every word, except those that do not have meanings, has a meaning, but perhaps not trivial to say: 'Every word, except these in the following groups, has a meaning'. It may not be necessary to provide an adequate and specific formulation of the supposition. It may be enough if most words in any language are held to have meanings, and if there is some set of words that one would be prepared to treat as central. We may be untroubled if we find that 'outgrabe', Peter' and 'hello' are exceptions, but it will not be much of a supposition unless we say that there are some words – say 'shoe', 'halyard', 'whenever', 'nevertheless', 'jilt', 'hurry', 'seventeen', 'this', 'brown' and 'intend' – the exclusion of which would be ruinous to it.

Let us express this hazy idea by writing the word 'word' in capital letters, and saying that a WORD is any word not appearing on a short list of meaningless words, and in normal use in some language. Does Wittgenstein go so far as to question that every WORD has a meaning, in the ordinary sense of 'has a meaning', as distinct from the sense given to that expression in the Augustinian picture of language?

One might suppose it to be too uncontroversial altogether, that every WORD has a meaning; yet no further along than the end of §1, Wittgenstein says: 'But what is the meaning of the word "five"? – no such thing was in question here, only how the word "five" is used'. It is very far from clear, however, what his point is here.

If his question had been 'But what is the "meaning" of the word "five"?' – putting 'meaning' in inverted commas to indicate that he was playing along with the Augustinian conception of having a meaning, – there is a point that was perhaps available to him, namely that although it is not clear that there is anything here that 'five' names, it is not a meaningless word, and therefore the meaning of a word can at least not always be the object for which it stands.

However, (a) he did not, as he might well have done in that case, put the word 'meaning' in inverted commas; and (b) far from affirming that 'five' is not meaningless, as he would be best to do in making that point, he seems either to be questioning whether it is meaningful, or questioning whether it makes sense to ask about its meaning.

A second possibility that is not implausible, although it too is probably wrong, is that he was relying on a specification he had not yet made, but was to make in §§2 and 6, that the language he had described was the entire language of these people. If so the question could not arise, at least for *them*, what the word 'five' meant. They would have no way of asking or answering that question. However (a) Wittgenstein did not say whether the language described in §1 was the entire language of these people; (b) it would be too oblique a way of making the point we are considering, to say 'No such thing was in question here'; and in any case (c) there is no rule to the effect that we can ask the meanings of words in another language only if that language contains a word like our word 'meaning'. We do not need to know whether the Greeks asked and answered questions like 'What does ――― mean?', before asking about the meaning of this or that Greek word.

It seems more likely that Wittgenstein was concerned here with the central place we tend to assign to meanings, in thinking about language. We are apt to suppose that what is essential to a word is its meaning, and that everything else about it is as it is because of the meaning the word has. To attack that idea, number words, whether in English or the language described in §1, are a particularly useful example. One can say that 'five' is not a meaningless word, and that would mean it is not like 'mimsy' or like 'tenty' (which might have followed 'ninety'); but on the other hand the inference that it 'has a meaning' is not so straightforward as one might expect. While we can explain the meaning of 'five' by giving synonyms in other languages, there being no English synonym, we could not explain the meaning *that way* to a child or

3

a monolingual Anglophone. There are other ways of explaining meanings, that is, other procedures we call 'explaining the meaning', but there is no other way of expressing the meaning, of completing the sentence '"Five" means . . .'.

If someone asked what 'five' meant and we said it is the number after four and before six, we could be said to have explained its meaning (or made a contribution to doing so), but not to have said what it means. We might well have said 'I don't know what to say as to what it means, but it is the number after four and before six'.

The difficulty here is not like that of explaining the meanings of words like 'coy' or 'squeamish', where some people can manage it more readily than others. No amount of skill will enable us to *specify* the meaning of 'five'. Hence, contrary to what one might expect if the essential thing about a word were its meaning, it is an improper demand that a specification of its meaning be included, if not in the everyday teaching of a word, then at least in the philosophical elucidation of it. Wittgenstein made a point *like* this in §10 when he suggested that asking what the words in the language in §8 *signify* is demanding that the expression 'this word signifies *this*' be made part of the explanation of the words.

Still, if 'five' has the same meaning as 'cinq', does it not follow that it has a meaning? Certainly if Peter has the same job as Mary, it follows that they both have jobs, but we need more than the similarity of the expression 'to have the same meaning' and 'to have the same job', to confirm a parallelism in what they entail. The former expression might just happen to be in the same grammatical style as the latter, while functioning quite differently.

Having said that Peter and Mary have the same job, we can go on to say what it is – insurance underwriting or arc welding, but we can't *in the same way* go on to say what the meaning is that two words have. Sometimes (rarely) two words 'A' and 'B' may have the same meaning, namely C. When that occurs, we can also say that A, B, and C have the same meaning; but when we say that Peter and Mary have the same job, namely arc welding, we can't say that Peter, Mary and arc welding have the same job. And while, having said that A, B and C have the same meaning, we can ask, if rarely

4

answer, the question what that meaning is, we cannot ask what the job is that Peter, Mary and arc welding have.

When we say that A and B have the same meaning, we might alternatively have said that wherever A is used, B may be used. Here the suggestion that A and B each has something called a meaning has disappeared, and there is no longer a question *what* we are saying they have. It is not clear whether there is a parallel translation of 'Peter and Mary have the same job', and if there were, it would be disastrous if it eliminated the question what job that is.

The common expressions 'to have the same meaning', 'to have different meanings', 'to have a meaning like' and 'to be meaningless', because of their similarity to expressions like 'to have the same job', 'to have no job', and so on, generate the illusion that meanings are something that words generally have, upon inspecting pairs of which we pronounce them the same, similar or different, and on failing to find one of which, we say that a word is meaningless. That this is an illusion is shown, as above, by the differences in the ways the two kinds of expression function.

Still, the judgments we express in these words are sometimes true, even if easily misunderstood; and the question can arise, is it false or meaningless that every word has a meaning? In §13 Wittgenstein said 'When we say: "Every word in language signifies something" we have so far said *nothing whatever*; unless we have explained exactly *what* distinction we wish to make'. We can't be sure that he would say this of 'Every word in language *has a meaning*', but if he would, his view of that sentence would appear to be either that it is meaningless, or that, unlike for example 'These words have the same meaning', its meaning stands in immediate need of explanation. My argument so far would be consistent with the latter reading, and would further provide support for saying that while the sentence might be taken in various ways, the assertion made with it in each case would be either trivial or false.

We can see 'Every word in language has a meaning' as being in immediate need of clarification when we reflect that, while one may say 'This word, unlike some others, has a meaning', one can hardly say 'Every word, unlike some others, has a meaning'.

5

The sentence is false if it means that there are no meaningless words. The qualification 'in language' might, however,
be intended to exclude words like 'outgrabe' that, although
meaningless, might be said not to be words 'in the language'
or not to be 'WORDS'. So taken, the sentence would mean that
every meaningful word has a meaning, and would be trivial,
unless this in turn meant there is something that is the meaning of every meaningful word. It would then be false. It would
be false likewise if it meant that we call anything a word only
if it has a meaning; but if it meant we call anything a word *in
the language* only if it has a meaning, then since there is no
standard use of the expression 'a word in the language', it
would still be false. However if it was a proposal not to call
anything a word in the language unless it had a meaning, it
would not be meaningless, but would be *neither* true *nor* false.

I do not know whether the above possible senses of 'Every
word in language has a meaning' might be called 'explanations of exactly *what* distinction we wish to make'. I am
inclined to think Wittgenstein had in mind here, not very
general statements like these, but rather points one might
make in the course of transacting some actual linguistic business. If so, the following might be a case in which this sentence could be used: if someone has mistranslated a passage
due to paying too little attention to some word, someone
might say 'You must attend to every word in the original.
Every word has a meaning'. While we could see what he
might mean by this, it could not be said that, even in that
context, the words he used mean what we are supposing he
meant by them.

It has turned out to be a complicated question whether
every word has a meaning. I have found at least seven interpretations it might be given, and in each case have suggested
reasons for rejecting it, as being either false, trivial, meaningless or neither true nor false. I have not provided evidence
that Wittgenstein would in fact give the reasons I gave for
rejecting it, but that he would anyway not care to endorse it is
at least rendered probable by the similarity between it and
what he opposes in §§10 and 13. (Here I am using 'reject' and
'oppose' to cover any kind of avoidance on principle. Compare the contrast between denying and 'setting one's face
against' in §305.)

6

Two

NAMES, USE AND GRAMMAR

WITTGENSTEIN IS fairly persuasive on the theme, which is anyway pretty obvious, that not all words, and not even all nouns, are names. He is on to something more subtle when he shows in various ways how, even when we think we are clear about this, many of the things that puzzle us in philosophy are troublesome at least partly because we press questions which make sense only on the supposition that certain words are names. The question 'What is the meaning of a word?', when it means 'Which object is the meaning of a word?', arises under such auspices, as do the questions 'What is (which something is) an intention, a belief, an expectation?'

Still, some words are names, and Wittgenstein is neither so clear nor so well understood in the places where he seems to suggest that there is a great deal more to understanding a *name* than knowing the object, or family of objects, for which it stands. He says we must also know its use; but what is that? Most of us could not, without help, get much beyond supposing that its use is to refer to objects like this, this and this; but Wittgenstein is either sceptical about whether *that* is part of the use at all, or uninterested in the fact that it is; and he suggests that there is at least much more to the use of a name than that, but gives us very little guidance on just what he has in mind. What is this 'use', to which he alludes, but which he scarcely describes?

That problem arises from such passages in the *Investigations* as the following:

> 6. 'I set the brake up by connecting up rod and lever.' – Yes, given the whole of the rest of the mechanism. Only in conjunction with that is it a brake-lever, and separated from its support it is not even a lever; it might be anything, or nothing.

26. One thinks that learning language consists in giving names to objects. Viz, to human beings, to shapes, to colours, to pains, to moods, to numbers, etc. To repeat [§15; see also §§37, 49] – naming is something like attaching a label to a thing. One can say that this is preparatory to the use of a word. But *what* is it a preparation *for*?

27. 'We name things and then we can talk about them: can refer to them in talk.' – As if what we did next were given with the mere act of naming. As if there were only one thing called 'talking about a thing'. Whereas in fact we do the most various things with our sentences. Think of exclamations alone. . . .

In languages (2) and (8) there was no such thing as asking something's name. This, with its correlate, ostensive definition, is, we might say, a language-game on its own. That is really to say: we are brought up, trained, to ask: 'What is that called?' – upon which the name is given. And there is also a language game of inventing a name for something, and hence of saying 'This is . . .' and then using the new name. (Thus, for example, children give names to their dolls, and then talk about them and to them. Think in this connection how singular is the use of a person's name to *call* him!)

31. . . . the words 'This is the king' . . . are a definition only if the learner already 'knows what a piece in a game is'. That is, if he has already played other games, or has watched other people playing 'and understood' – *and similar things*. Further, only under these conditions will he be able to ask relevantly in the course of learning the game: 'What do you call this?' – that is, this piece in a game.

We may say: only someone who already knows how to do something with it can significantly ask a name.

And we can imagine the person who is asked replying: 'Settle the name yourself' – and now the one who asked would have to manage everything for himself.

49. . . . For naming and describing do not stand on the same level: naming is a preparation for description. Naming is so far not a move in the language-game – any more than putting a piece in its place on the board is a move in chess. We may say: *nothing* has so far been done, when a thing has been named. It has not even *got* a name, except in the language-game.

257. . . . When one says 'He gave a name to his sensation' one forgets that a great deal of stage-setting in the language is presupposed if the mere act of naming is to make sense. And when we speak of someone's having given a name to pain, what is presupposed is the existence of the grammar of the word 'pain'; it shews the post where the new word is stationed. [Compare §29.]

264. 'Once you know *what* the word stands for, you understand it, you know its whole use.'

373. Grammar tells us what kind of object anything is.

There are in these passages at least the following interesting claims: 1) In knowing what a word stands for, we do not yet know anything about how to use it. 2) It can mean nothing to us to know a name if we do not know what to do with it. 3) When we do know what to do with it, the name is unimportant. 4) The grammar of a word (whatever that is) shows the post at which it is stationed (whatever that is).

Although the four claims are obviously closely related, they are distinguishable, and there are different ways in which each of them may leave us puzzled. We may do well therefore to examine them separately.

1. What is it that we still have to learn,
when we have given a name to something?

Wittgenstein may quite possibly be playing games with us in §26 when he lists pains, moods and numbers as the bearers of names, but assuming he would not be so radical as to deny that *anything* has a name, we might take him at the end of the section to be supposing that something nameable has been named, and consider his question, what that is a preparation for?

He seems to take it to be true but unilluminating to say that it is a preparation for using the name; and (§27) he does not think it helps, to explain that using a name is talking about a thing, referring to it in talk. He says, but does not help us much to see, that there is more than one thing called 'talking about a thing'; and it is not clear whether in saying 'we do the most various things with our sentences', he means to say that some very different linguistic acts can be called 'talking about a thing' – or perhaps the additional point that not all uses of a name are cases of talking about a thing at all. His examples of exclamations are somewhat unfortunate, in that only one of the exclamations he lists uses a name, and he seems to have regressed to the question whether all words are names, where he had at least seemed to be talking about how words that *are* names are used.

It is perplexing also what the final paragraph of §27 is meant to contribute to the apparent question, of whether there

9

is anything much to using a name, or perhaps of whether knowing what object it names shows us how to use it. It is not clear, for example, whether the point of noting that there was no such thing in languages (2) and (8) as asking something's name is that although there were names in those languages, that use of them did not ensue. Those people might be taught the practice of asking and giving names, but it would be something further they would have to learn. That point would perhaps be a useful contribution to the question he was considering, but if it was his point, it was well concealed.

It is especially perplexing what is so 'singular' about the use of a person's name in order to call him. Perhaps it is this: When I shout 'Sam', I am not talking about Sam (saying something about him), and I am not referring to him (as I might be if I said I have a friend who knows seventeen languages), I am attracting his attention. He does not, by knowing who Sam is, pick himself out as the person I mean; and I do not need to say, even if that is what I mean, 'Look over to your far left': the direction from which my voice comes does that job. (Compare 'I am here': uninformative when written, but not when spoken.) Being singular in these ways, we might have to learn the language game of calling and responding to being called.

Wittgenstein clearly wants to say that using a name requires learning much more than we learn in learning what object it names, but even if he intended the last paragraph of §27 in the ways just suggested, he has then provided only two or three rather recondite examples in support of his contention. We could perhaps make his point more vividly in the following way. Some representative uses of the word 'water' are:

Nearing the end of a long journey to the sea, on coming over a hill I exclaim 'Water!'

Delirious with fever, I plaintively gasp 'Water!'

Asked what I want in my Scotch, I reply 'Water'.

Asked what *eau* means, I say 'Water'.

Asked what that is, I say 'Water'.

Asked how I enjoyed my swim, I say 'The water was very cold'.

Asked the chemical composition of water, I say 'H_2O'.

People water their plants and their horses, some dairies

10

---

water their milk, some sailors go to a watery grave, people's eyes water when they slice onions and some theologians propound a watered-down version of Christianity.

Here there are different differences from one case to the next. I am 'talking about' some water when I say it was cold, but not about any water in particular when I give its chemical composition, and I am not exactly talking about water when I identify something as water, ask for water in my whisky, or exclaim excitedly on glimpsing water. I ask for water in preference to soda or just ice in my whisky, but I did not exclaim over water as distinct from anything else on glimpsing it, or cry out for water in preference to anything else in my delirium. I water plants by sprinkling it on them, but not horses or milk, and I water milk by adding water, but not horses or plants. I have watered the whisky if I added water before or in bottling it, but not if the water is added in serving it. People's eyes water, but although it is a very similar business, their foreheads do not water, they perspire; and we do not say that a person's eyes watered when he learned of the death of his sister.

Some, perhaps all, of these observations about the examples of uses could be called grammatical propositions. They resemble the propositions of the grammar we learn in school in various ways: we could put it that it is *correct* to say that people's eyes water, but not that their foreheads water, and that it is *incorrect* to say that one watered the horses if one sprinkled them with water, or that one watered the whisky in serving a Scotch and water, or that a person went to a watery grave if his grave was flooded at the time of the funeral. The differences between propositions true of any water and propositions true of this water could be cast in the form 'The proper subject of this sentence is not "water", but "the chemical composition of water"'; and the fact that I am not talking about water at all when I identify something as water could be cast in the form 'The proper grammatical subject of the sentence is (e.g.) "the substance in this beaker", a phrase in which the word "water" does not appear at all'.

However that may be, it is very clear that just in learning to identify water one would not learn that one could express one's gratification on nearing the end of a journey by exclaiming 'Water!', or that the expression 'His forehead watered' would not be used, or that we say 'His eyes watered' when he was peeling an onion, but not when he learned of the death of his sister, and so on. All these things must be learned piecemeal, and are neither given just in knowing what water is, nor deduced from that plus the facts of a given case. The difference between 'crying', 'eyes watering' and 'perspiring' is not a difference in the chemical composition of the liquid substance they all involve. There may be such a difference, but it is not in view of it that we use different expressions.

Perhaps if one had, in learning some other words, discovered how various their uses can be, and what some of the typical variations are [compare 'having played other games' (but not having played *this* game) §31], one would be ready for the miscellany of uses, and could guess what some of them would be; but one would not likely guess the distinction between 'crying' and 'eyes watering', or that between watering horses and watering milk.

That seems clear now, clearer than Wittgenstein made it; and it is a strong point against the view that learning language consists in giving names to objects (§26). It is moreover a new kind of point against that view. The usual objection is that it does not account for words like 'if', 'but', 'and', 'however' and 'nevertheless', because we cannot find an object they name; but that objection leaves us free to retreat to the view that *much* of language is learned by learning the names of objects. Wittgenstein clearly, and perhaps with some justice, thinks that this view lingers on (§§264, 293, 304); and his objection stands out as applying even to such very common nouns as 'water': to all words, whether or not they name objects.

2. Can only someone who knows
how to do something with it
'relevantly' or 'significantly' ask a name?

Some young children quickly catch on to the idea that things have names, ask what that is and what that is, remember the answers, and can correctly name things in spite of the differences between one chair and another or one dog and another, although they cannot yet use the words they have learned to say anything about the objects named. They may then go about gleefully saying the name of various objects, enjoying the applause of their elders. What do they not know? Why, when they ask what that is, they are not 'relevantly' or 'significantly' asking a name?

One may mistakenly liken the child's performance to that of a person learning a list of nouns in a foreign language (§32). There are resemblances: both might repeatedly ask 'What is that?', and might soon come to identify a large number of objects by name; and neither would yet be able to do anything, or anything much, with the words learned. The learner of a second language however knows a great deal that the child does not know, specifically: he knows, as the child may, but need not, that these sounds are not merely locally associated, for fun or convenience, with objects, but are words and part of a language; he knows that he still has to learn verbs and their declensions, adjectives, adverbs, connectives, and so on; knows the kinds of ways nouns will string together with these other words if the new language resembles his; knows how to string them together in his own language for various purposes; knows that names are not simply associated with objects, but that some objects have the name they have because of their visible properties, some because of their history, some because of their function, and that the same object can have different names for different purposes (woman, mother, wife, sister, landlady). He does not make mistakes such as a child will often make, of thinking that 'mother' means 'the adult female of the household', and hence that 'your mother' means 'the adult female of your household', and can be used in referring to that person, no matter which other member of the household is being addressed.

The person learning a second language might not 'know' these things in the sense that he could explain them all, but having achieved some competence in one language, the corresponding things in a second language would not be new to him and would come easily; and he would also go about learning in a sophisticated way; for example he would, like the child, ask 'What is that?' of kitchen tools and items of clothing, but knowing from his own language that persons are liable to be differently described for different purposes, he would not pose just that question about a person. Rather, he would have an assortment of questions, which he would normally pose by asking for the equivalent in the new lan-

13

guage of a word in his own language, but which would be tantamount to such questions as 'What would you call her insofar as she is married?' or '... insofar as she rents rooms?' or '... insofar as she heads the government?'

The child has no conception of the niceties that are in store for him as he progresses in learning the language. His 'What is that?' questions are virtually just a noise he has learned to make, to find out which noises will be welcomed when he associates them with a certain object. Unlike the second language-learner, he does not learn a word preparatory to using it. The only use he knows for it is in the little game of *see if you can get it right* that his teachers play with him. He is of course taught a word in the expectation that he will later learn to use it, but that learning is something further, and comes later.

We can now perhaps better understand §31. Having been told about the various pieces and how they move, without being shown a chess set, one can, when the men are produced, ask 'Now which of these is the king?', that is, which of these is the piece that moves one square in any direction, cannot move into check, and so on; and one can in a different case, not yet having had the game at all explained, but knowing something about board games, ask 'Which piece is this?', meaning something like 'Which of the roles you will be telling me about attaches to this one?' One can understand the words 'That is the king' without knowing any more than that if a piece has a different name from other pieces, it will have a different role; but anyone knowing less than that will not understand. He will not have grasped the essential point that although (blindfold chess aside) there must be a re-identifiable physical object, that object is not called the king on account of its physical properties, but on account of its role in the game. (That needs some qualification: it is good practice to design all chess sets in such a way that players will not have to learn afresh with each set they use, which piece is which, but it is not as if one simply could not play using a salt shaker for a king; see also chapter 4.)

Since we are talking here about names and their use, and since Wittgenstein opens §31 by saying that '"This is the king"... does not tell him the use of this piece', it is natural to read the section as drawing an analogy: the king, the physical piece, is like a word, and its role in the game is like the use of a word. There is nothing much to show whether that is what Wittgenstein intended, but the following very different reading is possible, and is consistent with my general line of interpretation: the grammar of the *word* 'king' is simply a special case of the grammar of nouns, in which we can see more clearly than is sometimes possible, one of the variety of connections there can be between a word and an object. Whereas, starting with the model of 'dog' or 'stone', we might have been inclined to say that it is on account of properties of the object itself that anything is called a such-and-such, in this case we find that while there is an object, and it had best be easily recognisable, it is primarily because of something else, in this case its role, that we call it a king. Anything to which we give that role is therefore a king. It is different again, but more like the chess example than the stone or dog example, with 'sister' or 'landlady'. Here too there must be an object, and it is more necessary that the object should be feminine than that the king should be any particular shape, but the 'object' is a sister or a landlady primarily because of what we could roughly call relationships, rather than properties. In still other cases, as we will see later, there will be different connections between word and object, or there will be no object at all.

On this basis it is however misleading to say only someone who already knows how to do something with it can significantly ask a name. It is not true that one cannot significantly ask what that liquid is if one does not know that, whatever the answer, we can use the word in exclamations; and it is not true that we learn nothing in learning that it is called water, if we do not know what water is; but it is perhaps fair enough to say that if we did not at least know that it was called water on account of certain properties about which we could be further informed, rather than perhaps because it was in the royal bathtub – the designation 'water' would mean nothing to us.

3. Is it important what name anything has?

At the end of §31 Wittgenstein said: 'And we can imagine the person who is asked [what a piece is called] replying: "Settle the name yourself" – and now the one who asked would have to manage everything for himself'.

There is room for argument about what he might have meant by this, but the most likely supposition is that he thought the person who had asked *could* 'manage everything for himself' – that in knowing how to do something with a name, he knows all that is important for him to know. However, is that true?

It is obvious that chess could be taught and played without ever naming the pieces, and that if we were nevertheless fond of names, each player could have his own set of them without in any way affecting the play. Some awkwardness would arise when the game was discussed, or a player's record of the moves was studied, but it would be a simple business to reach complete understanding of any player's terminology. It is not so clear however what the importance of that fact is, when we remember that it is using words, not doing things with the objects they name, that we are trying to understand. It is not what corresponds to managing to play chess that we are concerned with, but what corresponds to managing to talk chess language.

It is almost too obvious to mention, that we might have had different words in the place of 'dog', 'house', 'tree' and so on, and it would make no difference. If some people knew only one of these languages, while others knew only another, there could be some problems, but that too is a boring point.

The chess players, in spite of having different words, would readily establish communication if they used their words in the same ways, for example if your 'emperor' and my 'king' were both 'the piece, whatever shape or size it is, and whatever it is made of, that moves one square in any direction, cannot move into check, and so on'; but if, when playing with various chess sets, I called something a king only if it had a crown and was the tallest piece, although I always had a piece that moved as 'kings' do, communication would be more tiresome, but still readily enough achieved.

Hence Wittgenstein's point may be that the word token is of little importance, what matters is the place, so to speak, that the token holds – whether for example the name is assigned in view of properties of the object itself, or in view of the role the object has, whatever its properties, or in view of its role, provided that it has certain properties, or even whether the name is assigned just to a role, whether or not there is anything that has it. Speakers of languages with the same or similar 'places' will readily understand one another, and to the extent that the sorts of 'place' differ, understanding will become difficult, and ultimately impossible.

Presumably the chess example is used, not as an analogy, but simply because all there is to be known about chess language can be stated briefly, clearly and fully, whereas the uses of words in natural languages are rather too indefinite and miscellaneous to be so readily described; but the following might illustrate the application of the point in the case of an ordinary word.

My friend says he calls a woman a landlady if she has a certain set of chin, and he shows me some examples, pointing out some features he treats as particularly decisive. I say 'You mean that you infer from this set of the chin that she will be a person that rents rooms?' He replies 'No. I have found to my surprise that all landladies do rent accommodations, but all I mean by "landlady" is "women with a certain set of chin". I would not withdraw the description on finding that someone did not rent accommodations'. I ask what he finds so noteworthy about this set of chin, and he says that oh, it just always strikes him very forcibly, and asks whether that isn't why so many people see fit to mention that someone is a landlady. I ask what he thinks people mean by 'my', 'your' and 'her' landlady, and he says that puzzles him, because he has never found himself attached to one landlady to the exclusion of others, and does not understand why other people would be, and so he suspects that they really mean 'the woman who rents me my accommodations', but because so many such women are in fact landladies, they make the mistake of shifting the possessive adjective to the word 'landlady'.

We might imagine that this person had some constitutional inability to suppose that nouns were used on account of anything but standing properties of their objects, and having noticed the distinctive chin of everyone who was called a landlady, has concluded that a landlady was a woman with such a chin. He might then, if he did not find such chins to be of any interest, simply file the information away and never use the word, but if he did use it, we would want some answer to the question why he finds these chins noteworthy; and if other people use the word, then as long as he stands by his conclusion as to what it means, he will have such problems as what kind of interest they take in chins, and why they employ such constructions as 'my landlady'. We fancied him answering these questions like a rational being, but in fact his answers had the lunatic quality of the woodcutters who said that when a pile of wood is spread out on the ground there is more wood and you must pay more for it.

The interest of the story lies however first in the fact that the different kinds of connection there can be between nouns and objects makes such a mixup possible, and second in some of the relations it brings out between what we assume as the nature of this connection on the one hand, and on the other what we may have to conclude is the meaning of the word, what we may have to conclude about why people use it, or the interpretation we may have to put on some of the constructions in which they use it ('my landlady').

4. What is meant by 'the post at which a word is stationed', and how does 'grammar' show what the post is?

'The post where a word is stationed' (§§29, 257) is clearly a figurative expression: what does it mean? What would be some clear examples? What is there about a word that we can usefully describe, and that it makes some sense to call its 'post'?

The post metaphor in §29 is not of much help. From it we learn (i) that a post is a 'place in language, in grammar, we assign to [a] word', and (ii) being a colour word and a number word are such places; but putting (i) together with §257 we get 'the grammar of a word shows us the place in grammar we assign to it' – and that only deepens the puzzlement; and knowing that being a colour word is a post does not itself tell us what is conveyed by calling it a post.

Perhaps we could go on from there to describe a complex of linguistic permissions and prohibitions that is entailed by anything being a colour word, and say that having that set of connections is its 'place' or 'post'. Some of the features of such a complex might be: 'The book is red' entails that it is not black, green or yellow, does not entail that it is not scarlet, light red or dark red, and entails nothing on whether it is large or small, old or new, square or oblong. Again, a colour may be pastel, strident, gay, sombre, hot or cool, but may not be square or round, large or small, soluble or insoluble in water, or divisible by two. Here we are describing some of the linguistic slots into which words like 'red', 'yellow' and 'brown' will and will not fit, and it would not be inept to say alternatively that we are describing the post at which it is stationed; but it is still not clear whether any philosophical light is cast by such descriptions of posts, and that is presumably a condition of having the right interpretation. Certainly for his purposes in §29, Wittgenstein had no need of anything so elaborate. He was bent only on saying that while it could in certain cases be useful or necessary to say 'This *colour* is called so-and-so' in giving an ostensive definition, there is no *general* need, in giving ostensive definitions, for words that show the 'post'.

Yet although there was no immediate need, in §29, for an answer to the question what it is to be a colour word, the question might be answerable, and answerable in the kind of way just indicated; and that kind of answer to the same question about other words might serve useful philosophical purposes. Let us therefore entertain the hypothesis that by 'the post at which a word is stationed', Wittgenstein meant something like 'the complex of linguistic permissions and prohibitions constituting the use of the word', and that the meaning of this in turn is illustrated by the above examples of what we can and cannot do with the word 'red'. We can then apply this model to a number of more puzzling concepts, to see whether useful philosophical purposes are served.

When Wittgenstein says (§373) that grammar tells us what kind of object anything is, it is not clear whether he means for example that the grammar of the words 'brick' and 'stone' will tell us which objects are bricks and which are stones – or that it will tell us about more general differences between 'objects', such as whether they have some size, shape, weight or location, whether they are called a such-and-such in virtue of their properties or their relations, or whether they have any identity through time.

Perhaps the answer is: both. It depends on whether such propositions as 'A brick is an artifact, whereas a stone is a natural object' are grammatical propositions. A very small number of such propositions would tell us which objects are bricks and which are stones; but most of the grammar of these words would have nothing to do with that question because it would be the same for bricks as for stones. The fact that we can ask of a brick where it is and how heavy it is distinguishes it from a thought, but not from a stone. It is in any case the second sense of 'what kind of object anything is' that is likely to be more interesting, and it is on it that I will concentrate.

One way of distinguishing 'kinds of object' in this second sense would be by whether, in respect of any X, it would make sense to assert propositions of the form 'It is not an X if it is not ———', where the blank is filled by a word for a discoverable property, as distinct from a function (e.g. 'used for cutting' in the case of a knife) or an effect (e.g. 'making us wince' in the case of pain).

Two distinctions are necessary here: i) It is not, for this purpose, a question of *what* discoverable property, function or effect fills this blank in any particular case. That would provide us with an uninteresting distinction, for example between bricks and stones. It is rather a question of whether it makes sense to fill the blank with *any* discoverable property word.

ii) One has to say it is a question of whether it *makes sense* to fill this blank, because not every object will have essential properties. It is essential to a bicycle to have two wheels, and perhaps essential that a brick be made of clay, but it is at least not very clear whether there is anything that is essential to being a car. However, if it is false that having four wheels is essential, it is at least not nonsense; whereas with the sentence 'It is not a *thought* if it is not ———', *any* filling for the blank yields, not falsity but nonsense.

Using the proposed test, we could distinguish the word 'knife' from the word 'intention'. In the former case, there are both propositions not about properties of the object itself, like 'A knife is used for cutting', and propositions identifying the object, like 'It is not a knife if the blade is not designed for cutting along its length (rather than at its end: that is a chisel)'; but in the latter case, while there are propositions like 'An intention is what you have when you are disposed to do something of your own accord, but not firmly committed to doing it', there are no propositions by which the supposed object can be identified: no propositions of the form, 'It is not an intention if it is not ———', where the blank must be filled by an identifying feature of something, for example 'a vivid mental picture of oneself acting in some way'.

There would also be intermediate cases, of which chess pieces would be a nice example. Propositions about the role of a piece would be *like* statements of the function of a knife; and there are also propositions like 'It is not a knight if its shape does not represent a horse's head'. The latter propositions would tend to establish the word 'knight' as the name of an object, were it not that they are true only of certain chess sets, and were it not that we can play chess without any object holding the knight's place, but cannot play hockey without a puck. We could perhaps say that when playing chess with a given full set of pieces, 'knight' is the name of an object, but that a role is more essential to knighthood than any physical property. When we confer knighthood on a salt shaker, we are not conferring an equine shape, but a role.

Is it worth dwelling on the fact that there are intermediate cases – perhaps of various kinds. The miscellaneous structures of the cases might provide us a sense for 'the post at which a word is stationed'. Some of the cases are as follows:

Ordinary natural objects – a dog, a stone – have their names just in virtue of standing properties, or families of them.

Some natural objects – a vegetable, a fruit – are so called partly in view of standing properties, partly in view of relations to us – we eat them. A plant that was agreeable to eat and nourishing, but eaten only by the odd hermit would not, or not clearly, be called a vegetable.

Some things have their name partly on account of their natural history (a mother, a delta) and others partly on account of current natural relationships (a planet).

The description of the *function* of an artifact (a clock, a pen) is so essential to its concept that the importance of its physical properties tends to fade. Although they say in Oxford that the reason why it is impossible to build a better mouse-trap is that anything that trapped mice but was not a sprung wire on a small piece of wood would not be a mouse-trap (J.L.Austin, class on 'Sense and Sensibilia', 1957), it would not be out of the question to call a handy kitchen laser slicing tool a knife, and atomic clocks are clocks in spite of their lack of resemblance to mantel clocks – just because they tell the time.

21

In all of the above cases there must be an object that bears the name, although there is considerable variation about how specific the type of object must be. A mother or a landlady must be human and female, but an author or a prime minister need only be human. A murderer must be human, but a killer need not; and if Austin is right, mouse-traps can perhaps vary only in such minor ways as colour, or the materials of which they are made. While none of these objects need have a specific location in order to be the object it is, it is essential to them to have *some* location. For any object, if we not merely do not know, but can make no sense of the question 'Where is it?', it is not a clock, a knight or a prime minister.

Now consider minds. They can be small, agile, powerful, inventive, and busy, and can wander and be haunted, but it is not clear that there is something of which these things can be said. If Peter has an agile or an inventive mind, we can give an identifying description of *him* in other terms ('The short red-headed fellow with the twinkling eyes'), and can say where he is; but there are no similarly identifying descriptions of his agile mind, and we can make nothing of the question where it is. This is not because minds are always in the same place. If someone said 'They are in the head. Mine is, anyway. I know that. So it is silly to ask where it is, as if it might slip down to the chest'; we would want to know how he knows this, when he does not even know what to look for. If he says 'There is something I feel very distinctly, right between the ears', we could say 'Yes, but why do you say it is in your mind? Does it drift around when your mind is wandering, or tickle and throb when your mind is busy?'

We could say that a mind is an imaginary object, the picture of which we use to say something about people's intellectual performances, an object undefined except by its output, but an object nevertheless (see chapter 17).

Now compare pains. Nothing imaginary about them. We feel them most cruelly, and not only can normally say just where they are, but require that a pain should have a bodily location. Sometimes we are not sure which tooth is aching, but we are at least in no doubt that the pain is in the jaw, not the wrist; and if someone is visibly suffering, but is bewildered by the question 'Where is it?', we suppose he may be grieving, certainly not in pain.

22

Pains can jab, throb, shoot and gnaw. In this they are like knives, in cutting, slicing, stabbing; but whereas in the case of a knife there is not only a different description of the object that does the cutting or slicing – but only slicers describable in certain ways are knives – in the case of pain there is a grammatical vacuum where these latter descriptions might have been, and hence there can be no requirement that what throbs or gnaws, to be a pain, should be of a certain type.

Pains can be ghastly or unbearable. These words, like 'deafening', express their effect on us, but do not say in virtue of what they have that effect. Moreover, where normally anything that is unpleasant might have been pleasant, that is, some objects bearing the same name (faces, paintings) are pleasant, a pain is not ghastly as distinct from delightful, but only as distinct from slight or bearable. Whereas there is no requirement that a face make an agreeable or disagreeable impression on us, nothing is a pain if it is not in some measure abhorrent. This resembles calling a man the prime minister only if he is accorded a certain position in the government; but is unlike it in that the title 'prime minister' then attaches to an object with a wealth of unrelated properties. The prime minister can be six feet tall, play the violin and go for a swim, but a pain is not anything as well as being ghastly, in the shoulder and jabbing.

The shirt I am wearing, although it is so faded and frayed now that you would hardly recognise it, is the same one that I bought three years ago. Although it has been lost and found, lent and returned, it has never been replaced with another just like it. There is a sense in which we can have the same pain repeatedly, but it is not that sense. (a) If it is hardly recognisable, it is therefore not the same pain, and (b) we can attach no sense to its having a continous history, always being somewhere during the months that I did not have it, or to its being replaced by another just like it.

Minds are imaginary objects; pains are real objects, but of a peculiar kind: they are grammatically required to have a bodily location and to be distasteful, and they do things like jab and gnaw, but they are neither grammatically required to have any properties in virtue of which they do these things, nor do they have properties unconnected with their being

23

called pains, and therefore they have nothing to sustain an identity through time. Now compare intentions.

Such objecthood as minds and pains possess is due to their being conceived as something having properties and power, and doing various things. This comes out in the array of verbs and adjectives with which these nouns can be geared: 'small', 'agile', 'powerful', in the case of minds; 'intense', 'jabbing', 'throbbing', in the case of pains, The word 'intention', by contrast, takes few adjectives, ('vengeful', 'gruesome', 'honourable' perhaps), and those it does take can readily be shifted to the person intending or the action intended. It was vengeful of him to have that intention, the intention itself was not vengeful, (as if it were getting back at him for something he had done to it); and if we say that Jack the Ripper had gruesome intentions, we are expressing an opinion about *what* he intended, not as to whether he found the having of the intentions as disagreeable.

Intentions, unlike pains, have neither location nor genuine duration. We can perhaps intend at the back of our minds, but not at the back of our heads; and we do not say it was at the back of our minds because we noticed it there, but rather assign it that location because of its irresolute character, which is itself not something we could *notice*. We can have had an intention all day, but not continuously, like a headache or a lump in the throat, or intermittently either. We may be periodically mindful of our intention, but it is not false that we are intending in the intervals between being mindful of it. We say we are no longer intending, not on finding that something that was there has gone, but when we have decided against doing something we had previously intended (or sometimes *in* deciding against it). It would make no sense to say 'Although I decided against it, the intention stubbornly persisted'. ('So I repeated the decision three times in quick succession, and then the intention finally went away'?)

Having an intention to go to Montreal, we buy tickets, but intentions do not cause us to do such things. We do not, knowing ourselves to have a travel intention, reckon that ticket-buying will surely ensue, and wonder whether it will happen quickly this time, wait for it, and see it taking shape, with pleasure or dismay. Having no location, duration, properties, behaviour or effects, intentions are no kind of object

24

at all, not a peculiar object like a pain, not even an imaginary object like a mind.

I have now reviewed salient features of the grammars of several words, trying to bring out the many different kinds of way in which they differ. Wittgenstein said (§257) 'the grammar of the word . . . shews the post where the . . . word is stationed'. This may suggest that the grammar is one thing, and the post something else, and from the grammar we can draw inferences about the post. This would make sense if there were some very limited number of 'posts', and what we had to decide was at which one of them a given word was stationed. However, in view of the very many ways in which the grammars of different words differ, it seems more reasonable to suppose that the grammar is the post, and that showing the grammar is showing the post. The post is all of the mosaic of the use that we may depict in any given case, a mosaic having some similarities and many differences from case to case.

We do derive from the grammar, conclusions for example on whether a certain word names an object; and if we treat naming an object as one of a limited number of standard jobs words can have, it will be fair to say that this is a 'post', and that posts are distinct from grammars. Yet while 'dog', 'planet', 'prime minister', 'pain' and 'mind' all name objects and 'intention' and 'belief' do not, there are different relations between word and object severally in the former cases; and the denial that 'intention' or 'belief' name objects does not set these words more apart form one name-object relation than from another.

Here it is not very clear whether I may be disagreeing with Wittgenstein, for example when he writes (§293): 'That is to say: if we construe the grammar of the expression of sensation on the model of "object and designation" the object drops out of consideration as irrelevant'. Whereas this is most naturally taken as recommending that we get away entirely from that model, what I am saying might be put 'if we construe the grammar . . . on some models of "object and designator" the object drops out of consideration . . .'. This question will be discussed in chapter 11.

Whether or not Wittgenstein would agree, however, it seems to me right to say that the word 'pain' names an object.

It is not whether *that* is true that is important, but whether this relationship is the same as some other name-object relationships. We can see in the following example how, by never doubting that it is the same, we come to the conclusion that pains are indescribable.

Knives slice and pains jab, but whereas we can describe a knife apart from its slicing, we cannot describe a pain apart from either its jabbing or something else it does. The analogy leads us to suppose however that there must be properties of the pain itself, as there are of the knife itself; and since there are no words in which we describe these properties, we may conclude they are indescribable. Whereas we might have accepted the grammar of 'pain' as simply being different from that of 'knife', we forcibly assimilate them in this way. The absence of descriptive words in a certain slot is explained as being due, not to there being no task for them to perform, but to our inability to devise words for the task.

Since only some things that slice are knives, and we need the description of the slicer itself to show whether it is a knife, we therefore suppose that not everything that jabs and is frightful is a pain. But since, in the case of pain, we cannot describe the jabber itself, we conclude that we never know whether what jabs is a pain. Then we are deeply mired in a perplexity from which we might have been saved by dwelling on the fact that the grammar of the word 'pain' includes no requirement of what features the jabber, gnawer or throbber must have if it is to be called a pain. It may be surprising that this should be so, but then grammar is full of surprises.

I am suggesting then that the 'post' is the grammar and that the grammar of one word may differ in important ways from that of another apparently very similar one. Here we can take nothing for granted, but must look and see how each word functions. Many of our philosophical problems would not have arisen if we had known that we must do this, and known how to do it.

Three

ON THE QUESTION
'WHAT HAPPENS WHEN...?'

IN THE *Philosophical Investigations* Wittgenstein tangles with no question more frequently than that of *what happens when* . . .: what happens when we attend to the shape, rather than the colour (§33), what comes before the mind when we understand a word (§139), what happens when a person suddenly understands (§§155, 321), what happens when we make an effort to find the right expression for our thoughts (§335), what is it like to say something to oneself (§361), what goes on in me when I imagine someone is in pain (§392), what goes on in us when we not merely say, but mean words (§507), what happens when we learn to feel the ending of a church mode as an ending (§535), what happens when we do not find something conspicuous (§600), what happens when I raise my arm, rather than have it go up (§621), what happened when at that moment I hated him (§642).

Although he clearly thought it a fundamental mistake to ask this question, he confuses us a good deal by sometimes asking it without comment, as if he thought it a good question, and by sometimes either sketching answers that could be true or discussing answers that he thinks false. People do not ordinarily make an effort to have the right answer to questions they think should not be asked.

Sometimes, without offering any or much justification, Wittgenstein makes such comments as that the question is badly framed, or that it is a fundamental mistake to ask it; but in general one has to dig for his arguments in support of such claims. They are neither always clearly marked as arguments on this topic, nor are they generally very explicit. For example, when he says in §316 that the word 'think' is not used to say what we notice about ourselves when we think, he

27

does not spell out either how it would have to be used, to give rise to that question, or what kind of a use the word does have.

The arguments, however, when constructed and lined up, make out a strong case: and hence one may wonder why the question is so frequently aired, and so often with little or no help in seeing what is wrong with asking it.

No doubt the reason we are often given so little help lies in Wittgenstein's stated policy (end of *Preface*) of leaving us as far as possible to work through to philosophical conclusions for ourselves. Perhaps the reason the question is so frequently aired is that no supposition is more natural than that if there are times when one is thinking, what thinking is should be part of what one notices about oneself at those times – and the same for hoping, believing, intending and the rest. 'What happens when . . . ?' will thence be the first question to ask with a view to understanding these concepts; and many of one's other questions will be further to that one: asked for example with a view to deciding whether this or that fact about oneself when one thinks is thinking or is part of thinking.

We might begin by noting some rather elementary blunders that one might unwarily commit in trying to understand Wittgenstein here:

i) It may seem astonishing to find him, of all people, suggesting in §139 that what comes before the mind when one understands a word may well be a picture. To anyone not yet turned around by Wittgenstein's arguments, that will suggest that in his view understanding sometimes is having a picture – one of the things we are always told Wittgenstein denies. Yet he is surely not saying that understanding is sometimes having a picture, but rather flaunting his indifference to *what* comes before the mind. It is neither because we do not have pictures, nor because we do not have them when we understand, nor because understanding is the occurrence of something less obvious than a picture, that Wittgenstein denies that it is having a picture, but because it is not something that happens at all: neither a happening common to all cases of understanding, nor even any one of a family of happenings. It is a natural but disastrous mistake to suppose that the 'family resemblance' doctrine applies, at least in this way, to psychological concepts (see chapter 6).

ii) In a similar way, one may be bemused and perplexed by

28

some of Wittgenstein's descriptions, for example of what happens when I turn my attention on my own consciousness – which he describes (§412) as 'a particular act of gazing. . . . I stared fixedly in front of me, not at any particular point or object. My eyes were wide open, the brows not contracted (as they mostly are when I am interested in a particular object). . . . My glance was vacant; or again *like* that of someone admiring the illumination of the sky and drinking in the light'. What it is like to *expect* is described in §444 as walking up and down the room, looking at the clock now and then, and so on. What happens when one thinks 'This pen is blunt. Oh well it'll do'. without saying it, is described in §330 as testing the point of the pen, making a face and going on with a gesture of resignation. Stubbornly persisting in intending is described in §588 as having a feeling of a certain rigidity, or of unalterable determination. In §151 we are told that when we are able to go on we may have 'the sensation "That's easy!" (Such a sensation as, for example, that of a light quick intake of breath, as when one is slightly startled)'.

From some of these descriptions one might take Wittgenstein to be a phenomenologist, advancing the view that intending, thinking, understanding, introspecting consist of myriad complex patterns of hard-to-describe experiences; but it is more likely that here again he is flaunting his indifference to *what happens when* – and also no doubt trying to make it clear, by getting down to cases, how inadequate the happenings are as an account of these concepts. When we are reminded of the actual character of what we can notice about ourselves, we readily see that for example it is *because* I was expecting him that I paced up and down, felt tense or excited – the expectation and the behaviour or the feelings are distinct, but the latter are all that *happen*; or that it is because I stubbornly said 'Now as before it is my intention to go tomorrow' that I had a feeling of a certain rigidity – the feeling was brought on by the fact that I persisted in my intention, and was not identical with it. One can easily be so sure that intending is part of what happens when we intend, that one does not bother with the mere mechanical task of describing those happenings, although had one done so it would be very obvious that in no part of the happenings could one discern the intention.

29

iii) Some of the above descriptions are behavioural: the way we stare, furrow the brows, pace up and down, and so on. If anyone is inclined to read behaviourism in this, he need only reflect that Wittgenstein almost as often mentions the occurrence of mental events as *what happens when*: feelings, pictures, thoughts. Taking the view that nothing that happens *is* the intending, understanding and so on, Wittgenstein can be as permissive about representations of what *behaviour* occurs as we saw him being about the occurrence of mental pictures. He is not stressing behaviour: just reminding us that it too can *happen when* we expect, think, imagine (see also chapter 15).

I will now review Wittgenstein's main arguments. In doing this I will be partly gathering together explicit arguments from various quarters, partly constructing the argument that may have been intended by such remarks as (§316) 'But this concept is not used like that'. Characteristically Wittgenstein treats the topic as one with manifold aspects, and accordingly will give his arguments under several different heads:

1. What we find.

Wittgenstein has a number of things to say about what we find when we examine ourselves as we X:

i) He describes much of what we will find, as 'characteristic accompaniments' of Xing (§152, p.218). He does not clearly indicate which phenomena he would so describe, but we can suggest the furrowing of the brow or the feelings of tension when we think, or the feelings of excitement or anxiety we may have when we are intending. Nor does Wittgenstein say what the import of calling anything a 'characteristic accompaniment' is; but clearly anything that accompanies something is not that something itself.

ii) He stresses (§§35, 151) that we do not always find the same thing when we X. The point of stressing this is not made perfectly clear, but for reasons already indicated it is presumably not that Xings form a family, but perhaps something like this: that we can know what a person means when he says he understands, for example, without at all knowing or wanting to know which of the things that might have happened, did happen. When a person says he played a game, we want to

30

know what game, but there is no parallel question we have when he says he understood.

iii) Wittgenstein notes (§646, p.181) that even if we did find some one thing that always happened, it would not therefore be the Xing. If we experienced a particular tickle every time we intended, the tickle would not be the intending; and if we could do something only when we had a certain feeling, the feeling would not be the capacity.

iv) He suggests that we do not always find anything that is even a possible candidate for being the Xing. We do not know, for example, of a characteristic experience of pointing to a piece in a game as a piece in a game (§35); when we try to remember precisely the experience of meaning for a moment to do something, it seems to vanish on us (§645); and when we are being guided, everything is simple and we do not notice anything special; it is only afterwards that we come to think something indescribable has happened (§175).

v) Wittgenstein does seem to allow however that sometimes, for example when the formula occurs to us (§179), or when we say to ourselves 'What time is it?' (§607), something happens which is a promising candidate for being (in these cases) the knowing how to go on, or the addressing to oneself of a question. Whether these candidates pass muster we will see later on.

2. What we fancy

Wittgenstein suggests at least three ways in which we are likely to fancy things in the course of our deliberations about *what happens when*:

i) We fasten on cases in which there is a promising candidate for being the Xing, and come back to them again and again, without asking ourselves how often really something like that does happen when we X (§§173, 592–3, 607). We are fancying that they occur much more commonly than they do.

ii) When we do not find a candidate ready to hand, we may be so sure that there must be one, that we make various suppositions such as that it is hidden in some way – a brain process (§376) or an unconscious process (§36); or that it happens so fast that we cannot make it out (§436); or that we do not notice it because we are pre-occupied with what we are doing (§456). (§374 is a comment on this, but not an argument.) Wittgenstein suggests (§153) that if we say such things there will be a problem how we know in an actual case that the process has occurred, and also one of how we know, if the process is hidden, that it has occurred, and thus that we are Xing.

iii) A more subtle way in which we fancy things is described in §369: we answer questions like 'What happens when one does a sum in one's head?' by saying 'First I add 17 and 18, then subtract 39 . . .'. Wittgenstein's comment that 'What is called doing sums in one's head is not explained by such an answer' leaves us to explain why not. The answer however is not far to seek: if there is a problem about what it is to do sums in one's head, there is exactly the same problem of what it is to add 17 and 18. The former is only a more general description of the latter. Similarly if there is a problem about what it is to think, there is exactly the same problem of what it is to do some particular pieces of thinking: to wonder whether she will come is indeed one of the things that may happen when I think, and that is why it can seem right to give that answer; but 'I wondered if she would come' does not itself tell us what kind of experience I had, exactly what happened.

3. Whether the happenings explain *the meaning of the psychological words*

If to intend, to think, to understand, to ask oneself a question is to have H happen, (where H is a richly described event, such as 'having the impression that, without making a sound, I was saying the words "What time is it?", not very loud, rather quickly in my usual tone of voice, accompanied by a feeling of puzzlement') – then to say that I asked myself what time it was would be to say that an appropriate H occurred. Wittgenstein has a number of arguments about whether Hs do explain the meaning of the psychological words:

i) The burden of §183 is not undebatable, but the following is a possible reading: it can look as if 'Now I can go on' means the same as 'The formula has occurred to me', because the verb 'to mean' has various senses, in some of which it can be used to connect these two propositions: (a) 'to mean the same' can mean 'to achieve the same', and it can achieve the same thing to say either 'Now I can go on', or 'The formula has occurred to me'; (b) we can say 'I can go on, I mean the formula has occurred to me', when we want to say that at least this condition of being able to go on is satisfied. However in neither of these cases is there an identity of meaning. (a) If I say the formula has occurred to me and you know I have some algebraic training and aptitude, you will know I can go on; or if I say I can go on and the series is one I would not likely be able to develop without the formula, you will know the formula has occurred to me; but in both cases you need further facts to get from one proposition to the other. This would not be necessary if there were an identity of meaning. (b) Where there is identity of meaning between A and B, it is contradictory to affirm A and deny B; but it is no more contradictory to say 'The formula has occurred to me, but I can't go on', than to say 'My legs are alright now, but I still can't walk'.

ii) Wittgenstein suggests in §361 (see also §§6, 375) that we do not teach a person to talk to himself by telling him what takes place. We do not, that is, treat talking to oneself as a particular experience, or even a family of experiences, which perhaps it would be a pity if people did not have, or which perhaps it had been found one had to have in just the right way, otherwise the talking would be ineffective; (the arguments propounded would not persuade or the questions posed would not lead to the search for an answer). We do not describe the right experience, or work with the student until he has it. We might teach a person to talk to himself by first getting him to whisper things he is inclined to say, then say them moving his lips but not making any sound, then do it without moving the lips, and so on; but having done this, we would not, to see if the instruction had been successful, inquire whether the student was now having a strange sensation as if he could hear his voice, but without hearing it in the ordinary sense, and without being able to say whether it was loud or soft, soprano or tenor, emotional or unemotional (or whatever other 'rich' description of talking to oneself anyone might care to suggest). We do not say 'If you are not having this experience, you are not yet talking to yourself, and you must work at it some more'; and we have no artifices to suggest he try, that have been found sometimes to achieve the desired result.

The reason for this is that it is no part of the concept of talking to oneself that it should be experienced in a certain way, or even in a family of such ways.

This could be generalised for thinking, intending, believing, hoping, expecting, understanding. Of course, unlike talking to oneself, not all of these are activities, which we might teach people to perform; but neither are they events, which we might teach them to recognise, by how they feel, the course they take, or any other such characteristics. We do not say 'You may have difficulty at first distinguishing between hoping and expecting, because the differences are sometimes quite slight. Watch out for a tinge of despair, perhaps a sinking feeling that comes and goes. That is very rare when one is expecting, and will probably show you are hoping, especially if you want what may happen. The particular experience of wanting it is always found in hoping, but only sometimes in expecting'.

Similarly with thinking, if it were a certain kind of experience, or one of a family of experiences, one might fail to notice a peculiarity of what was currently happening, and so think one was thinking when in fact one was doing something else, or doing something for which we do not happen to have a name; but if there is room for a mistake here, it is not a mistake about whether the experience one is having is one of those we call 'thinking' (§328). If nothing in particular, or no one of a family of things, has to happen when we think, hope, expect, then when we say we were thinking or hoping, we cannot mean that happenings of some familiar kind have occurred.

iii) In §316, Wittgenstein says 'In order to get clear about the meaning of the word "think" we watch ourselves while we think; what we observe will be what the word means! – But this concept is not used like that'. Like what, one wants to ask; and how *is* it used? It is not much help when Wittgenstein goes on to suggest that it is as if we were to work out what the word 'mate' meant by close observation of the last move of some game of chess.

There might be a lead however in the examples in §§674–5 of how we do not use the verb 'to mean':

> Does one say, for example: 'I didn't really mean my pain just now; my mind wasn't on it enough for that'? Do I ask myself, say: 'What did I mean by this word just now? My attention was divided between my pain and the noise –'? (§674)

Presumably the answer to both questions is no. If we had to

work out, by sensitive observation of ourselves when we say something, what we meant, we did not mean anything, and were just babbling.

'Tell me, what was going on in you when you uttered the words . . . ?' – The answer to this is not: 'I was meaning . . .'! (§675)

The words 'What was going on in you?' are not used as a way of asking what you meant or whether you meant anything; and 'I was meaning . . .' is not used at all, and *a fortiori* not used as an answer to that question.

On similar lines we can now construct a display of the kind of use of 'think' one could expect if the word referred to what happens when we think. 'I have thought about your offer' would be like 'I have been having an odd sensation in my chest': we would treat 'think' as an indication of the occurrence of a certain broad type of experience, and want to know more of the specific details. It would be normal to ask what form and order the thinking took, whether it was fast or slow, pleasurable or vexatious; and to recieve in reply such reports as 'It was a curious thing: I didn't say anything much to myself – a word here and there – but I had a dream-like feeling of knowing exactly what I would say: such things as that I could borrow some of the money from Peter, and that you might be willing to wait for the rest. There were intervals when I just felt tense and expectant, nothing else that I noticed, but when something came, it came very fast and I was amazed that I could understand it. . . .' (cf. §§319, 635, 653).

Philosophers sometimes debate whether there is any place at all for such questions and answers, but we need not enter that dispute, because even if there is a place for them, say in philosophy or psychology, they are not asked in the course of the routine use of the verb 'to think'; whereas they would be the first questions to be asked if thinking were a characteristic process or experience.

It may look as if there are at least some questions we can ask about the experience: whether we thought seriously or hard, for example. However we do not answer these questions on the basis of an examination of what happened. We do not say 'I am fairly sure I thought seriously. There was quite a strong feeling of tension, and I had that sense of being on the *qui vive* as I did it'. It can be hard to say how seriouslv one has thought, but this is not because seriousness is hard to discern – it is neither hard nor easy; rather, because more will be expected of the person who says he thought very seriously, and we can be unsure whether we will be able to deliver goods of a suitable quality (cf. *RPP* II.263, I.852).

A question that *par excellence* looks like one about what happened is the question *what* one thought. 'What are you thinking?' 'That we had better turn left at the next corner, because left turns are not permitted after that'. An account of what happened. Yes, I did think we had better turn left; but these words no more tell us what happened than 'I added 17 and 18, then subtracted 39' tells us what happened when I did a sum in my head. The question remains, what happened when I thought we had better turn left?

4.*The role of abilities, dispositions, attitudes*

Wittgenstein draws our attention to various ways in which understanding, intending, expecting, thinking and so on either involve or sometimes are abilities, dispositions or attitudes. He does not spell out the importance of this for the *what happens when* issue, but it can be suggested that its importance is that these grammatical states (as we can call them, following §572) are not phenomena, and not something that can *happen*. Here I must first document the role of grammatical states, and then justify the claim that they are not phenomena: that the answer to the question in §573, '*what* gets treated grammatically as a *state* here' is NOTHING.

A. Documentation of role. In §572, expecting. believing, hoping, knowing and being able to do something are flatly described as 'grammatically, states'.

In §510 Wittgenstein says 'The grammar of the word "knows" is evidently closely related to that of "can", "is able to". But also closely related to that of "understands".' The point is illustrated in §139 by the suggestion that if a picture of a cube occurs to us when we hear the word 'cube', still we must know how to, be able to, connect this picture with cubes and only cubes, construct cubes from the picture, and so on. In §§152 and 179 there is a similar suggestion that to continue a series of numbers someone has written down, it is not enough that the formula should occur to us, we must have a certain algebraic training and so be able to continue formulae of that kind (see also chapter 7).

In §338 Wittgenstein says that in order to want to say something, one must have mastered a language. This would presumably apply also to being about to say, or intending to say something. If I say 'What I was going to say was that it looks like rain', it is not neccessary that the words 'It looks like rain' should have run through my head, but only that I should have the elementary linguistic skill that would enable me to say this on a suitable occasion; just as, if I intend to dance a polka or recite a certain sonnet, I do not need to review the steps of a polka or say the sonnet to myself, I need only have the ability to dance a polka or recite that sonnet (§338).

On p.217 Wittgenstein suggests that two people might think of the same person by saying the same words to themselves, and adds: 'But wouldn't even these words be only a *germ*? They must surely belong to a language and to a context, in order really to be the expression of the thought *of* that man'. In this example all that *happens* when they think of him is perhaps that they say to themselves 'the tall man who came yesterday'; but for that to count as their thinking of *him*, they must further understand the words, and be able in that context to connect them with that person.

On p.188 it is suggested that when a person explains what he meant by something he said, he may be supplementing or paraphrasing the earlier utterance. There were at the time, that is, other ways he could have put it, further things he could have said; but these paraphrases and supplements did not run through his mind. He need only have a general ability to explain something in different ways, or an ability to delve further into a topic he has touched on.

Wittgenstein does not give any more examples along these lines, but with these in hand we may easily suggest further cases. We may say we have been thinking of doing something only if we are seriously interested in doing it, might conceivably decide to do it. That is an attitude we have, which need not and generally would not show in what went through our heads, and which we do not have only when the possibility of doing something is actually before our minds.

We can say we hope she will come only if we would be glad if she did, and if there is some reason to expect her; but neither of these conditions is something that *happens*, either at the time we say we hope, or at any other time.

We say 'I was intending to go home, but I will stay if you like', but at the time referred to in such remarks, one may have been wholly pre-occupied with other things. One *could have said* that one was going home soon, but what one could have done is not something that was *happening*.

B. *Justification of the claim that 'grammatical states' are not phenomena.* (a) They are not conscious phenomena. Abilities for example are excercised, and we can be aware of our exercise of an ability, but not of the ability itself. It is true of a person night and day, sleeping and waking, that he can play chess, recite the alphabet, do sums in his head, but we are not conscious of those abilities when we are asleep, having breakfast, going for a walk. We can be conscious of *the fact that* we have an ability, for example when we boast of it, or decline to admit it, but not conscious of the ability itself. It is not like a headache, or a hollow feeling in the stomach. We have abilities day in, day out, but as Wittgenstein noted [§148; note (a) p.59] not continuously – or discontinuously either.

In certain cases, we might be tempted to say that a rule or a formula, which is something of which we can be conscious, when we repeat it to ourselves, *is* an ability, since it tells us all we need to know; but as we have seen, remembering the rule, or having the formula occur to us, is not enough to explain our abilities to go on: we must also have learned to use such rules and formulae.

b) Grammatical states are not conditions of the nervous system. Few people are inclined to say they are conscious states, but it is immensely more plausible to suppose that they are states of the nervous system, that the instruction and practice that goes into acquiring an ability for example affects the nervous system until it comes to be in a condition such that at appropriate times it will so function that we play chess competently or apply an algebraic formula correctly. As long as the nervous system remains in that state, we have the ability, and when the state is disrupted, the ability is affected.

Wittgenstein's remarks in §149 can be applied to this picture: 'there ought to be two different criteria for such a state: a knowledge of the construction of the apparatus, quite

apart from what it does'. We say that someone can play chess
perhaps if he plays according to the rules, constructs plausible stratagems and recognises elementary threats. Are we
inferring, from these things he does, that his nervous system
is in some appropriate state? Wittgenstein can be taken to be
saying no, it is not like inferring from the performance of a car
that its engine is well tuned. In that case we can spell out what
condition of the spark plugs, distributor, carburettor and so
on, counts as being well tuned; but in the case of the supposed
inference to an ability, we have only the performance, and
none of what corresponds to the specification of the condition
of the spark plugs and so on. Without that, we are not inferring
anything.

'Well,' you may say, 'it is only because the science of neurology is in its infancy that we do not yet know what state a
person's nervous system is in when he can play chess or find
square roots. Wittgenstein would surely not argue on *a priori*
grounds what the findings of an empirical science will or will
not be.'

Whatever Wittgenstein would in fact say in response to
this, and that is unclear, especially in view of Z §§608–11, it is
available to him to say that he is not laying down any restric-
tions on what neurologists may discover, but only claiming
that their discoveries, whatever they may be, will not supply
the meaning of the concept 'ability'. That concept is not used
that way. Consider:

i) We are not, in using the word 'ability', adverting to an
unsolved problem. We could hardly say 'He has the ability to
play chess, but what the ability is, no one knows yet'.

ii) If there is any answer to the question what the ability is,
it consists in the description of competent chess-playing.

iii) We know whether a person has an ability without
knowing anything about neurology. We do not, on the basis of
his performance, suppose that he has it, and hope to confirm
this when we can examine his brain. We may indeed suspect
that he is more of a bungler than he looks – that he did not see
the threat his opponent made, and it was only by chance that
he responded with a good move, but that doubt is relievable
by further study and tests of his performance.

iv) 'He plays chess competently because he has the ability
to play' is nonsense; but 'He can do it because his nervous

system is disposed in such and such a way' may be true.

v) If it were found that a discreet part of the brain was uniquely responsible for our chess performances, that part of the brain might weigh a gram and be the shape and size of a bean. We would not then say that our ability to play chess had a shape, size and weight. The bean-like object would be responsible for, but would not be the ability. When we removed it, a person would lose his ability, but the ability would not now be in a bottle on the shelf if that was where the removed organ was. There is no question 'Where is your ability to play chess?'

vi) We would have to be clear what we were prepared to call an ability before we could trace the neurological state responsible for it, and hence we could not learn what an ability is by neurological research.

vii) There can be a problem deciding when to say 'He can read', 'He can speak French', and so on, or in other words a problem what these abilities are; but it is a problem of what standards of performance to require: how good his pronounciation must be, how extensive his vocabulary, whether to require that he understands the nuances of meaning and so on. This is not much of a problem, and people rarely disagree about it, because it can always be handled by saying, for example, 'He speaks French, but haltingly', or 'He is very fluent in French'.

A large source of bafflement in all this lies in the fact that if we understand, have an attitude, or have an ability, there are myriad things we would do if . . ., all of which can be attributed to us at a point in time. The use of a word, for example, can be various and complex, and if I understand the use of a certain word, I would use it here this way and there that way, would not be confused by the similarity between this and that case, and so on. The question hence seems to arise, how can I understand it now, if I do not now review all these things I know about it?

It is our inability to see how (as we fancy) a great deal can be packed into a moment, that makes us grasp at rules and other guides when we think about knowing how to go on (§§179, 189, etc.) – or makes us suppose that the complexities are all there, but concealed in one way or another, in the unconscious mind (§36), in the brain (§376) or in experiences that rush by quickly (§436) or are not noticed (§456).

Wittgenstein was very interested in this feature of the problem, and came back to it repeatedly (§§138, 188, 191, 197, 319–20, 337–8, 684; p.175). His most succinct statement of the difficulty is on p.175: 'In saying "When I heard this word, it meant . . . to me" one refers to a *point of time* and a *way of using the word*. (Of course, it is this combination that we fail to grasp)'. He did not, however, have a great deal to say directly about how to avoid the difficulty. In §197, when he said 'there is nothing astonishing, nothing queer, about what happens. It becomes queer when we are led to think that the future development must in some way already be present in the act of grasping the use and yet isn't present', he presumably meant that it is not astonishing to experience, the way a magician's trick is astonishing, or the way understanding a word might be, if it were somehow evident that its whole use flashed by in a moment, and we noted all its features as it flashed. It is in no way clear from experience that we do something remarkable when we understand a word, and the problem how we perform incredible feats in understanding arises, not from the fact that we do, but from the supposition that we must. Hence the only problem here is to explain the illusion. The illusion is explained in general by our disposition to think that to know, to understand, to hope, to expect, to intend, is to have something happen, and is dispelled by arguments such as I have been reviewing.

In detail, the illusion derives from such facts as that we say 'When I heard the word "cube", I understood it', 'When I said that, I was hoping to go to Montreal', 'When I saw him, I knew that he was very ill'. Such common expressions suggest that understanding, hoping, knowing are occurrences contemporary with hearing, saying and seeing; and if we see complexities in these concepts, we will want to suppose that the complexities are contained in these occurrences. Yet my understanding of the word 'cube' does not *happen*, either in a moment or over a stretch of time; my hoping to go to Montreal consisted in such non-events as that I would have been pleased to go and that I would have gone if it had proved feasible; and my knowing he was very ill consisted in the non-event that I would not make a mistake about the health of someone as hollow-eyed and pale as he was.

41

On the Question 'What Happens When . . . ?'

It is a wonderful question, but one for another occasion, HOW IT CAN BE that thinking, hoping, expecting, remembering are no part of what happens when we think, hope. . . . Not even Wittgenstein is going to deny that we do think, hope, understand, talk to ourselves. . . .*

* The main places in the *Philosophical Investigations* where the question 'what happens when . . .?' is asked or commented on are: §§6, 33–5, 139–40, 148, 152–3, 155, 173–5, 183–4, 187, 296–7, 305, 314, 316, 327–8, 332, 335, 347, 361, 363, 369–70, 375, 392, 394, 417–18, 422–4, 436, 442, 453, 507, 535, 545, 549, 591–2, 596, 600, 607, 621, 625, 635, 638, 642, 645–6, 651, 656, 659, 661, 666–7, 674–6, 678, 680, 690, 692; pp.174, 175, 176, 182, 187, 190, 193–214.

Four

UNDERSTANDING WORDS
AND UNDERSTANDING LANGUAGE

IN §199 of the *Philosophical Investigations* Wittgenstein says, as categorically as he ever says anything, 'To understand a sentence means to understand a language. To understand a language means to be master of a technique'.

In §33 he expresses a similar view: 'Suppose, however, someone were to object: "It is not true that you must already be master of a language in order to understand an ostensive definition . . .".' This is not so categorically expressed; but calling it an *objection* would seem to imply that the proposition objected to was one Wittgenstein would defend.

Again in §30 we read: 'So one might say: the ostensive definition explains the use – the meaning – of the word when the overall role of the word in language is clear. Thus if I know that someone means to explain a colour word to me the ostensive definition "That is called 'sepia'" will help me to understand the word'. This is even less categorical, but the words 'So one might say' can quite naturally be read as about equivalent to 'So I suggest', and thus again as marking a position Wittgenstein would defend.

This last passage, however, is also where doubts may begin, because Wittgenstein goes on to say 'And you can say this, so long as you do not forget that all sorts of problems attach to the words "to know" and "to be clear"'. This suggests that Wittgenstein may agree that an ostensive definition explains the meaning of a word when the overall role of the word is clear, but only in a sense, and possibly in a sense such that the proposition is no longer of much moment.

What Wittgenstein goes on to say may be read as a conformation of the above suggestion. In §30 he had written 'One has already to know (to be able to do) something in order to be capable of asking a thing's name. But what does one have to know?' §31 can be taken as an answer to this question, and as answering in effect 'Nothing in particular, and not very much'.

In that section Wittgenstein describes three interestingly different cases. He begins with one most favourable to the idea that you have to know a great deal to understand a definition: the case of a person who learned all the rules of chess without ever having been shown an actual piece, and was then told 'This is the king'. The ostensive definition means a great deal to him because he already knows the role of kings in chess; but it is not clear that he understands the definition any better than the persons in the other examples that follow.

In the second case the learner knows much the same, but knows it in a different sense, and learns something different from the definition. He has learned to play chess without being told the rules or formulating them to himself; and since he plays the game, he in a sense knows which piece is the king, he just does not know what it is called. Without the definition, the learner in the first case might have assigned the king's role to the piece which is in fact the queen. The second learner would not do that. He moves kings correctly, tries to protect his own and attack his opponent's, and so on; but without the definition he might make the mistake of taking the word 'king', when he first heard it, to refer to the piece which is in fact the queen. He only learns *what to call* pieces, the role of which he already knows.

The third case is the most striking. Here at the point at which the king is ostensively defined, the learner knows nothing about chess, but does know something about games in general: such things perhaps as that they may have pieces, each with its own identifying marks, name, and role in the game. He need not be able to explain this. It can be something he has picked up or got the hang of from playing other games, or seeing them played. Nor does he need to know very much: he knows nothing about chess in particular; and to know that some games have pieces, each with its marks, name and role, is to know very little. Yet it is all he needs. Given that much, he understands 'This is the king', even before the instructor goes on to say 'He moves like this, and the object of the game is to mate him', and so on.

44

Understanding Words and Understanding Language

In sum, no one kind of background is necessary for understanding ostensive definitions, and not very much is necessary. That considerably emasculates the idea that the ostensive definition explains the meaning when the overall role of the word is clear.

There is corroboration for this downgrading in §§29 and 32. In §29, having illustrated in the preceding section how ostensive definitions can be variously understood in every case, Wittgenstein goes on to consider and reject the idea that we must therefore supply background which will make the sense of an ostensive definition unmistakable. He suggests that while it may be useful in particular cases to say 'This *number* is called "two"', or 'This *colour* is called so-and-so', it would be absurd to follow this practice generally, since (a) while ostensive definitions *can* always be misunderstood, they are not generally, (b) different measures will be required to avert different misunderstandings, and (c) there will be no prospect of saying enough to avert all possible misunderstandings.

The above is an argument that *explicit* provision of background is not necessary. The beginning of §30 can then be read as an imagined objection that nevertheless the background must be there, in what the learner already knows; and as we saw §31 then cuts this down to where it is a very minor claim.

§32 can be read as capping that with a diagnosis of how this temptation arises: we may be looking on language-learning on the model of learning a new language when we have already mastered our native tongue. In learning a second language we of course already know such things as how colour words work, and only have to fit the words of the new language into the slots already provided for them by our mastery of our native language. Clearly our initial acquisition of linguistic skills cannot be explained this way; and yet the idea that we cannot understand a word unless its overall role in the language is first clear is of a piece with what can happen in learning a second language.

The question now arises, if Wittgenstein accepted only a restricted version of the thesis in §30, why does he express similar views in such an unqualified way in §§33 and 199?

There is a fairly short way of reconciling §33 with my

45

conclusion so far. In that section he was primarily concerned with the question whether one might understand ostensive definitions simply by knowing or guessing what the other person was pointing to, and focusing one's attention on that. In the very statement of this possibility there is a difficulty: how could one, without having acquired the concept of colour, know what it is to point to the colour? One must know *something* to be able to do this, but just as one need not know anything in particular or very much to understand an ostensive definition of the king in chess, one need not know anything in particular or very much to understand that he is pointing at the colour. If someone pointed to two objects and said 'Those are both saffron', the learner might either (a) know that 'saffron' was a colour word, but learn *which* colour it was, (b) not know the word 'colour', but have learned to distinguish reds, blues, greens, and so knowing how some colour words were used, be able to assign a similar role to 'saffron', (c) never have learned to name any colours, but be struck by the similarity of the two objects designated, and thereby get a toehold on the use of this colour word, which could be further refined later. Here it might help if he had learned to distinguish other aspects of objects, shape from size for example. In all these cases he does need some linguistic skills, but not always the same ones, and not such extensive skills as the expression 'master of a language' would suggest. Clearly Wittgenstein needed no more here than the limited concept of mastery that we took from §31.

I am left with the problem of reconciling my conclusions so far with the very categorical statement in §199 that 'To understand a sentence means to understand a language. To understand a language means to be master of a technique'. This claim is only similar to the earlier ones. They were about understanding ostensive definitions, while this is about understanding sentences, and is therefore at the very least more general; but that difference is not likely to affect our problem.

There is another difference: in the earlier passages the mastery of a language was conceived as *enabling* us to understand ostensive definitions. §33 for example reads in part 'you must already be a master of language *in order to* understand an ostensive definition' (my italics). In §199, by con-

trast, the relation between mastery of a language and understanding a sentence would appear to be that it is a condition
for adjudging someone to understand a sentence, that he
should understand the language in which the sentence is
spoken. Wittgenstein here, though not earlier, uses the word
'means'. In English this word can mean 'involves' and could
express an enabling sense; but the German *heisst* does not
have that sense, but has, among other senses, the sense of
'implies' or 'entails'.

Except in the very trivial sense that we could scarcely
believe that a child understood what he was saying if his first
sentence was 'The cat will not run even if the dog comes
close', it is difficult to see it as being true that mastery of a
language is a necessary condition for being adjudged to
understand a sentence. Wittgenstein probably intended §200
to cast light on this, but that section is not as helpful as one
might like. The suggestion is that if two members of a tribe
unacquainted with games were to make all the moves in a
game of chess, with appropriate mental accompaniments,
then while we might hastily say they played chess because it
looked so much as if they did, we could not in fact regard
them as playing chess, because they were unacquainted with
games in general. (Even that description of the section says a
good deal more that Wittgenstein specifically declares; but
when he says 'if *we* were to see it we should say they were
playing chess', and then goes on to imagine the game translated by suitable rules into yells and stamping of feet, his
point is probably that then it would not *look* like chess, and
we would more readily see that something was missing.)

The point might come clearer if we imagined that when
these people chewed on some weed, its effect on them was to
make them sit at a chess board, make appropriate moves, look
puzzled or intrigued at appropriate junctures, have such
words run through their heads as 'If he went there I could go
here and his queen would be in peril', and so on; but that
when quizzed about it afterwards, their answers had a strange
quality. Asked 'Why did you move there?' they would find
the question odd and perhaps say 'I just moved there. I
remember that before moving I found the words "If I moved
here he would have to go there and I would get his queen"
going through my head. Is that what you call a reason for

moving as I did?' Asked 'What would you have done if, instead of that, he had gone there?' they would be at a loss, and would perhaps say 'I have already told you all that happened'. Asked whether they were puzzled when there opponent did such-and-such, they would not see how the idea of being *puzzled* could apply to such events as these, and perhaps say 'I remember my face feeling as if I were frowning, and having a sort of lost feeling like I sometimes have when I am puzzled, but it is absurd to be puzzled about bits of wood on a board'. When they were going through the motions of moving the pieces and so on, the current facts were all just as they might be in a genuine game of chess. What is missing is not some fine point of behaviour, thought or feeling that we find when chess is being played, but various abilities: to explain why they did thus and so, what they would have done if . . .; to say what were the difficult or the intriguing parts of the game; to explain what a mate is, or a pin, and so on. The ability is neither a move they make, a feeling they have, a thought that runs through their heads, or anything else that *happens*; but if it is missing we should hardly say they were playing chess.

[The example is complicated by the fact that we might imagine that the weed they chewed had the further effect of making them answer such questions afterwards in the way a chess-player might. It might be thought that I arbitrarily restricted the effect of the weed to what happened when they were sitting at the chess board. The example could indeed be extended that way; but the effect of the weed would wear off some time, and when it did they could be cross-examined *both* about their conduct before the chess board, and about their conduct in the quiz when they were still under the influence.]

A linguistic analogue of this chess example might be mine above of a child whose very first words were 'The cat won't run even if the dog comes close'. Suppose these words were said in a lively, interested way, in the presence of a cat known to be fearless, and when a dog was lurking nearby – but then the child showed no interest or embarrassment when the cat did run, did not find it odd if the sentence were spoken when there was either no cat or a notoriously cowardly one in the vicinity, and repeated the same sentence in the same way when it was obviously a dog that was likely to stand fast. We would doubt whether the child understood the sentence, not because of anything that was clear at the time of speaking – that was all quite in order – but because of various things he proved unable to do.

His inability here cannot readily be identified with one thing he does not know. It is not like not knowing that 'saffron' is a colour word, and hence not knowing whether to attend to the colour or the shape of an object so described. In that kind of case there can be something one does, in view of something one knows, that enables one to understand. Knowing that 'saffron' is a colour word, one attends to the object's colour, and thereby comes to understand the word. Here understanding is delayed; but in the ordinary case in which we hear a sentence and understand it, we do not at first not understand, and proceed to where we do understand. There is no period of time, even so little as a split second, between hearing and understanding, and hearing and understanding do not occur simultaneously. The hearing occurs, the understanding does not. It is true of us timelessly, night and day, sleeping and waking, that we understand most of the sentences we do understand; and that is not like the timeless truth about a smoker that he smokes. In *that* case, there are necessarily times when he is engaged in smoking; but there are no times when we are engaged in understanding sentences that we understand.

If understanding, in these cases, is not something that comes to pass, there could be nothing that brings it about; and if the thesis considered in §§30 and 33 concerned an enabling condition, while that in §199 did not, Wittgenstein could consistently hold a strong form of the latter thesis, while accepting the former thesis only in the weakened sense that was described.

He could *consistently* hold a strong form of the thesis in §199, but whether or not he did take such a view is another question. His official disavowal of philosophical theses (e.g. in §128) gives us a right to be sceptical; and recognising this, we could perhaps pare the apparent thesis here down to a point where it is one of those which it is impossible to debate, because everyone would agree (§128).

It hardly needs saying, that to understand a sentence, we do not need to understand a language in the sense in which some linguists and some philosophers may understand this or that language. It is also fairly obvious, not only that we do not need to understand a language in the sense of having an elaborate vocabulary, but also that we do not need to understand sentences which differ in kind from a given sentence. In most languages there are ways of explaining what words mean, or what one meant by a word on a given occasion; but someone who had never been introduced to that part of a language might still be adjudged to understand at least a great many orders, questions, assurances or reports; and similarly someone might understand orders and reports without understanding pleas or assurances.

It is less clear whether a person who would do the right thing in reponse to requests that he bring two slabs or two blocks, but was at a loss when asked to bring three slabs, understood the sentence 'Bring two blocks'; or whether a person who returned just as confidently with red slabs as with blue ones when given the order 'Bring two blue slabs' understood that order.

We could schematise the different forms such sentences can take this way;

Bring	one	blue	large	slab(s)
Take	three	green	small	block(s)
Send	some			pillar(s)
Mark	all the		clay	
Cut			stone	

—and say that while a person need not know all the words that will go in any column, and perhaps need not know any of the words that will go in the third and fourth columns, he will not be said to understand a sentence of this kind if he does not (a) know at least two of the words in each of the first, second and fifth columns, and (b) know what to do differently, given the substitution, at any place in the sentence, of another word he knows for a given word.

Something like this is suggested by §20: 'I think we shall be inclined to say: we mean the sentence as *four* words when we use it in contrast with other sentences such as "*Hand* me a slab", "Bring *him* a slab", "Bring *two* slabs", etc.* Wittgen-

---

*Wittgenstein himself makes the connection I am making here at *PG* p.131. See also *PG* p.153.

stein goes on to consider whether using a sentence in contrast with others consists in having the others hover before one's mind, and if not that, whether there is not *something* different going on in the person who knows the sentence to contain four words. He rejects both suppositions, but does not reject the suggestion about using a sentence in contrast with others; and argues that having a mastery of this language is sufficient to explain our using a sentence in contrast with others, and that this having a mastery is not something that *happens* while one is uttering a sentence.

The issue in §20 is different from that in §199, but we can see that parallel things can be said in the latter context. We can say that a person understands a sentence if he uses it in contrast with some other sentences that can be constructed on a schema like that set out above; and that using it in contrast with these other sentences does not consist in having any of them come before his mind, or in anything else that happens at the time, but in the fact that he *could* correctly use the other sentences. That is something that is true of him at the time he uses a given sentence, but not more true than at other times, and does not consist in anything *happening*.

If it requires some argument to show that this is true, it is at least not highly controversial, and to that extent it fails Wittgenstein's test in §128 of being a 'thesis'. If there were only one sentence constructable from our schema with which a person could do anything, for him it would certainly not be a sentence, or part of a language, but rather an (excessively) complex sound, to which he had somehow learned to react appropriately. It only begins to take on the character of a sentence as he learns the technique of making the various substitutions available in the schema.

Not only is the point not *very* contoversial, I have pared it down to where it is not an imposing contention. The language of which a person must be a master is not for example the whole of English, or even large swatches of it, but just that of the alternatives to a given sentence as provided in such schemas as I constructed; and it does not even include all the vocabulary that might be given in any of the columns of the schema, but only whatever minimum vocabulary would enable a person to learn the technique of making substitutions.

The contention is clearly confined in this kind of way in §20. Wittgenstein says 'Of course you have a mastery of *this* language' (my italics), and the expression 'this language' clearly refers to a given sentence together just with the sentences in contrast with which it is used. In §199, when we read 'To understand a sentence is to understand a language', there is no reason to suppose that the words 'a language' refer to anything more extensive than a sentence together with the other sentences that may be used in its place.

It seems likely therefore that Wittgenstein intended his observation that 'To understand a sentence means to understand a language' in some such restricted sense as that to which we have pared it down – a sense, given which he would regard it as scarcely controversial.

It is probable too that he was less interested in this than in the further contention that 'To understand a language means to be a master of a technique'. What is interesting about this, as suggested in §20, is that this mastery is not something that *happens*. Exercises of the mastery can happen, but not the mastery itself. Not happening, it is not a mental process; but neither is it a behavioural one; and it is no other kind of a process either.

Five

A PROBLEM ABOUT THE IDEA
OF FAMILY RESEMBLANCES

IN §65 of the *Philosophical Investigations*, in the course of introducing the idea of family resemblances, Wittgenstein writes:

> Instead of producing something common to all that we call language, I am saying that these phenomena have no one thing in common which makes us use the same word for all, – but that they are *related* to one another in many different ways. And it is because of this relationship, or these relationships, that we call them all 'language'.

Here both the words 'which make us use the same word for all', and the final sentence, suggest that Wittgenstein thought it is *in virtue of* various resemblances, of a kind he went on to describe further, that we call various things by the same name, or in other words, that we do or can use family resemblances as a criterion of class membership. Is this what he did intend? As I will explain later, it is in many ways an unsatisfactory doctrine, and there is an alternative to it that is more philosophically defensible, and also more consistent with some other things Wittgenstein said.

The alternative is that there is another criterion of class membership, and when, using this criterion, we assemble some members of any class, we will generally find on surveying them that there are significant resemblances among them, although not generally and certainly not necessarily any one resemblance running through them all.

On this interpretation, the family resemblance doctrine does not provide a new answer to the old question why we call all bedsteads 'bedsteads', but might come as some relief to anyone who could not live with the idea that we should sometimes call things by the same name that resembled one another in no way, and still not class that word as ambiguous.

This reading however seems to conflict with the parts of §65 I began by noting, unless we suppose that it is a sociological remark that 'it is because of these relationships that we call them all "language"', a suggestion that in the evolution of language the extension of a concept may have been gradually enlarged, here to include this, because of such and such a similarity, and there to include that, because of a quite different similarity. Wittgenstein could have used 'because of', not in a criterial sense, as it is natural to suppose, but in this kind of sociological sense.

There is a sort of model for the alternative reading in family relationships themselves. We as a matter of fact very often find that there are resemblances between one member of a family and another, and different resemblances between different members; but we do not take these resemblances as settling which persons are the McTavishes of Dalkeith Road: there can be more marked resemblances between certain McTavishes and certain Gordons than there are among the McTavishes themselves; and the criterion of McTavish-hood has nothing to do with resemblances, but is biological – whether two persons are father and son, or share one or more parents.

Part of the cunning of the idea of family resemblances might lie here, if we were supposed to see from the very analogy used, that the resemblances, while often there, had nothing to do with the criterion of membership.

The alternative reading is further exemplified in what we do to satisfy ourselves that there need be no feature common to everything having the same name: in the case of the word 'game', we set before ourselves various games, and check them over to see what resemblances there are. We do not assemble them by whether they have criss-crossing and overlapping resemblances, still less by whether they all share one or more features. That would make our findings a foregone conclusion. Our guide, if we use a guide, about whether chess, tennis, and canasta are all games is whether they are routinely so called.

Some activities we do not call games resemble games more markedly than many games resemble one another. Figure skating and hockey resemble one another more than do

54

hockey, backgammon and solitaire, but the last three are games and figure skating is not. One can of course say 'That is because there is no winning', or 'because there is no team-work'; but there is winning in figure skating contests, and teamwork too, and yet they are not games. The hard fact is that we simply do not call figure skating, boxing, skiing, swimming 'games', and do so describe hockey, ski-tag, parcheesi and old maid.

There are at least three sorts of consideration that can incline one away from the alternative theory as so far propounded:

i) When new things come along (are discovered or invented) it will be necessary to decide what to call them; and we could not decide to call a new activity a game by whether it is called a game, but could and (it might be thought) generally would decide by how far it resembled games.

ii) There are analogical and metaphorical uses of many words, sometimes just as common as their standard uses; and hence if common use is the criterion, there will be no way of distinguishing between the standard and the metaphorical cases; whereas we *could* distinguish these by the extent and character of the resemblances.

iii) Similarly, ambiguous words, like 'bank', are perfectly standardly used in both their senses (or all their senses, if they have more than two), and therefore standardness of usage will not distinguish one sense from another, while a rundown of similarities and differences will.

There are confusions underlying all these difficulties:

i) We could divide things that do not yet have a name according to whether there is any problem about what to call them. If I invent a variation of chess, in which queens can sometimes make a knight's move, there will be no problem either whether it is a game, or whether it is chess. It is a game, and it is not chess. We can of course say that the reason it is a game is that it resembles chess, which is certainly a game, in so many important ways, and differs from it in such a slight way; but this is overkill: there is just no problem about whether it is a game, and no necessity for reasons. In so describing it we are routinely applying our acquired ability to use the word 'game'. Having been shown a number of cases of games, we can right away say whether backgammon, if we have never encountered it before, is a game. We do not need to be informed specifically for each activity whether the community calls it a game; but neither do we need to review how far it resembles anything we know to be a game. An activity that is new to everyone and not just to us is not different in principle.

In the case in which there is a problem, on the other hand, it seems absurd to suppose that an activity either is or is not a game, and that whether it is can be ascertained by a review of its similarities to games – as if God knew, but we had to figure it out. Suppose that prisoners were made to engage in an activity the guards called the game of bonkers. The prisoners would stand in two large closely packed groups. A member of one group would throw a heavy steel ball at the other group, the members of which would scramble to get out of its way. If it hit no one, these men would have to re-group while another ball was thrown. If it hit someone, it would be their turn to throw the ball. The guards would say 'Now we are going to have a nice game of bonkers this afternoon', while the men referred to it as 'the so-called game of bonkers'. Since it is just because this activity is both like and unlike a game that the problem arises, there will be no possibility of deciding if it is a game by reviewing its similarities and dissimilarities. It is not as if something depended on whether something is a game, and we therefore had worked out a set of principles for deciding. In that case, while the decision would often be obvious and require no calculation, we could if need be get out pencil and paper and work it out by careful observation and listing; but as things are we have no guidelines with which to make such calculations, and can say nothing else than that it is like a game in these ways, and unlike one in those.

ii) Metaphorical and analogical uses of words are indeed often standard ways of talking; but not standard in the sense in which it is standard to call chess a game. The predicate 'is just a game' is standard in the sense that it is one we have all heard many times applied to various things – philosophy, politics, the writing of examinations. It is not new or puzzling to us, and we know what to make of it. However it is only the predicate that is standard, not its application to any particular subject; whereas it is the standardness of propositions like 'Chess is a game' that is the criterion of class membership on the alternative theory.

'Chess is a game' is a grammatical remark, whose primary use is in teaching language. It does not express an opinion or an attitude, but conveys an item of uncontroversial information about how these words are used. From it we learn for example that if someone says he feels like a game of something, chess is among the things we may suggest without revealing linguistic incompetence (whereas boxing is not); but if someone says philosophy is a game, we take him to be expressing an opinion, and in no way expect that if at another time he says he feels like a game of something, he will accept 'How about philosophy?' as at least a competent, if perhaps not a welcome suggestion. He has noticed certain things about philosophy that he dislikes and expresses by calling it a game; but one can no more notice that chess is a game than that bachelors are unmarried.

We neither need to check over the similarities between philosophy and some games to find out if 'game' is being used analogically here, nor would that method be even one way of finding out. If remarks like 'Philosophy is a game' have any substance, there will of course be similarities. There will be differences too, but not more than there are between one game and another; and we have no guidelines with which we could go on from there to settle the question.

There will be few English speakers who do not know without inquiry how to take 'Philosophy is a game', 'Harry is a vegetable', and so on; but should the question ever arise, and should we for some reason not wish to settle it just by asking the speaker, or someone else, it would be settled, not by comparing the phenomena, but by studying the use of the relevant words. Is philosophy described in dictionaries as a game? Would it be accepted on a list of six games as routinely as tennis, hopscotch, old maid? Do people treat it as an important question whether it is a game, and disagree over it?

All this is more obvious in the case of Harry's vegetable-hood. We would hardly set out seriously to compare Harry with potatoes and leeks, wonder if he is better boiled or baked, or whether he goes well with spaghetti. We *know* that he is not in that sense a vegetable. It is not even a matter of its being obvious that we do not need to make the comparison in detail: if we did not know vegetables from non-vegetables before the inquiry began, we might list, if not Harry, at least Peter and Martha, amongst the objects to be compared with Harry as being vegetables.

iii) Much the same considerations apply to words that have two or more different senses. It is very easy to see, in the case of words like 'bank', that have altogether different senses (a) that if we did not already know what objects to list as banks in each of the senses of that word, we could not form two groups to be compared, and (b) that we are playing a fool's game if we start solemnly ticking off the differences between hillsides and financial institutions.

It is not such plain sailing if we take words that have subtly different senses. The word 'game' has a different sense in 'Olympic games' on the one hand and 'Chess is an absorbing game' on the other; and a different sense again in 'How about a game of chess?' The difference here could not be explained by comparing the objects referred to. How could one compare the game of chess we played this evening with the game of chess? What objects would one select if one wanted to compare Olympic games with polo or hockey? Olympic games are not a species of game, the way board games and card games are. The activities that go to make up board games are all games, but Olympic games are mostly non-games: sailing, skiing, swimming, high-jumping. That Olympic games are not a species of game is not a fact about the set of phenomena we call 'Olympic games', but about the use of the expression 'Olympic games'. We do not notice on reviewing them that they possess a characteristic that we call 'being Olympic', whereas we notice on reviewing scrabble, backgammon, chess, and snakes and ladders that they are all played on a board.

Olympic committees may have criteria for deciding what activities to accept for inclusion in the Games, but something is an Olympic game, not if it satisfies those criteria, but if it is acceptable by the committee. We can say that such and such *should* be an Olympic game if it has the necessary characteristics; but we cannot say just on that basis that it is one. The special sense that 'game' has in 'Olympic games' is shown, not in the nature of the activities at Munich or Montreal, but in such features of our language as that we do not call all Olympic games 'games', that Olympic games are 'held', not 'played', that they are not contrasted with field games and aquatic games as the latter are contrasted with one another and with board and card games.

The main intent of the argument so far has been to show that it is philosophically preferable to regard the family resemblance idea, not as an account of how we do or might decide which activities are games, or which objects are vegetables or horses, but as claiming that, having determined in other ways which objects belong to a given class, we will not necessarily find that they share one or more features, but will generally find that there is the kind of network of resemblances that there is often amongst the members of a family: A and B have similar eyes, B and C similar chins, A and C similar mannerisms, while perhaps D resembles B only in some way in which B resembles no other family members, and therefore there is no resemblance between A and D.

I suggested that the criterion of class membership was linguistic: anything is an X if the linguistic community routinely so describes it. This is a serviceable criterion, and the one we implicitly use when we rely on our own linguistic competence in saying for example 'Bridge, polo and hopscotch are games; now let us see in what ways they resemble one another'. We may be wrong here, but we are not generally; and if we are, it will come out in the fact that other people are surprised that we should call such and such a game. They may give reasons for their surprise, such as that this is rather too unlike anything they have learned to call a game, but (a) this relies on their simply having learned to call *a* to *n* 'games' and (b) it is not a good argument, because generally one or more of *a* to *n* will be just as unlike the others as the disputed activity is unlike them all. The hard fact will be that they have not heard this activity matter-of-factly called a game on all sides. If they had, its difference from some other games would not bother them.

If we did not have some way, apart from their resemblances, of setting the right objects before us, we would have no way of surveying them to find out if they have common features or family resemblances or whatever. If we choose objects because they have common features, or because they have family resemblances, it will be no discovery, but a foregone conclusion, that they are related in those ways.

A Problem about the Idea of Family Resemblances

Three kinds of cases have been considered in which there are special reasons for saying that we must distinguish senses of words on the basis of the extent of resemblances and differences, and in each case it was shown that these comparisons will not do the job, while reference to the way words are used will.

If all this shows the alternative view to be preferable, it does not show it to be what Wittgenstein intended. For an answer to this question there is not a great deal on which we can rely. The sentence quoted at the beginning is a contrary indication; but as I suggested, not decisive, in view of the possibility of reading 'because of these relationships' in a historico-sociological sense.

There are two features of Wittgenstein's presentation that support the alternative view, although not strongly:

i) The very obvious fact, which however was not specifically noted by Wittgenstein, that resemblances are in no way a criterion of family membership; and

ii) The equally obvious, though equally unmentioned fact that to carry out Wittgenstein's survey of games, we would need some way other than their resemblances of determining which activities to survey.

Perhaps the only other prominent piece of evidence that can be offered is that our various references to the ways a word is used are just what one would expect of Wittgenstein, given what he says about meaning and use in *Philosophical Investigations* §43 and elsewhere. For the rest, was anything said with which Wittgenstein would clearly not agree?

Six

THE SCOPE OF THE IDEA
OF FAMILY RESEMBLANCES

S I N C E Wittgenstein never specifically cautions against doing so, it is natural to assume that his idea of family resemblances was intended to apply very generally, not of course to connectives, definite and indefinite articles, pronouns or auxiliary verbs, but to nouns regardless of whether they name physical objects, activities, processes or psychological phenomena, and very widely at least to verbs, adjectives and adverbs. The assumption here need not be formulated with great care, because it would not generally be spelled out in being made. One would just not doubt that according to Wittgenstein thoughts, efforts, colours and sins form families as much as do games, tools, vegetables and diseases.

It would be a very large project, and not clearly very useful, to work out for every kind of word whether it is a family resemblance concept. I will confine myself to the philosophically important question whether the family resemblance idea applies normally to what are sometimes called psychological concepts. If this was Wittgenstein's intention, he would characteristically diagnose our puzzlement about these words as being due to demanding, but failing to find, some one feature running through all instances of thinking, hoping, believing and so on, and would represent our problems as being solved when we realised that it was enough if there are family resemblances, and he might remind us how we learn to identify cases of believing, for example, by their experienced properties, in spite of the fact that there is no feature common to them at all.

While he never denied that the idea of family resemblances applied to psychological words, and while, in the *Blue and Brown Books* he sometimes (not always) spoke as if he did hold this view, there is nothing in *Philosophical Investigations* or in *Zettel* that shows him to hold it, and much that is inconsistent with so interpreting him. It will make a very important difference to our understanding of his work, on which side of this issue we take his philosophical performance to lie.

There may be other considerations that bear on the question, but I will concentrate on the following two:

1. In the case of any particular psychological word, does he represent it as being used to designate a phenomenon? These words may vary in this regard, but in the case of any word that does not designate a phenomenon (an event, a process, a state,) there will *a fortiori* be no family of phenomena, one of whose members is being spoken of when the word is used.

2. When a psychological word *is* represented as designating a phenomenon, is it characteristics of the phenomenon so designated that show it to be a case of for example thinking, or being in pain? While, as argued in the previous chapter, the final arbiter of whether something is a game is whether the linguistic community routinely so describes it; in spite of there being nothing that all games share, we all soon learn to identify activities as games by their properties. Without knowing whether a particular activity is called a game, we will nearly always be right about whether it is; and when we are wrong it will often be a failure to notice features of the way the activity is carried out that led to our mistake. If Wittgenstein says we cannot in this way tell whether we have been thinking, or whether we are in pain, then thinking and pain are not family resemblance concepts.

1. To begin with the first of these questions, Wittgenstein clearly holds that some psychological concepts do not designate anything. In Z 487, he says this in no uncertain terms about joy: 'But "joy" surely designates an inward thing. No. "Joy" designates nothing at all. Neither any inward nor any outward thing'. And what he says about believing in *PI* II, ch.x can without great contrivance be taken in the same way.

> How did we ever come to use such an expression as 'I believe
> . . .'? Did we at some time become aware of a phenomenon (of
> belief)?
>
>   Did we observe ourselves and other people and so discover
> belief?

The Scope of the Idea of Family Resemblances

Wittgenstein does not answer these questions, but his answer would almost undoubtedly be negative. We did not for example notice an experience we had when thinking about a proposition, having had which we found ourselves declaring that proposition true, and decide to call that experience 'believing'.

There is a similar thought lower on the same page. We do not say, as we might if believing were an identifiable experience, 'I believe it's raining and my belief is reliable, so I have confidence in it'. Someone could say this who had found that almost invariably when she had had the experience called believing, the proposition in respect of which she had it turned out to be true. She would be in a position to infer from the experience the truth of a new proposition in respect of which she had the experience. We do not make such inferences, because there is no experience of believing, and hence no family of them either.

When Wittgenstein says 'One can mistrust one's own senses, but not one's own belief', he does not mean that we are somehow incapable of distrusting the experience of belief, but that there is no such experience, to be either trusted or distrusted. 'Moore's paradox' would indeed be a paradox if believing were an experience. Then one could say 'It is raining, and I don't believe it (or I believe it is not)', when, to one's surprise, one found the belief that it was not raining occurring during a rainstorm. If that never happened, it would be providential, and would put us in a position to infer from the occurrence of believing to the truth of the proposition believed.

Similarly Wittgenstein seemed to think that intending is not an experience. If it were, the main candidates for the title of the experience of intending would be formulating the intention, aloud or to oneself, acting on the intention, and thinking about the intention. But in Z §49 he says:

There might be a verb which meant: to formulate an intention, in words or other signs, out loud or in one's thoughts. This word would not mean the same as our 'intend'.

There might be a verb which meant: to act according to an intention; and neither would this word mean the same as our 'intend'.

Yet another might mean: to brood over an intention; or to turn it over in one's head. [He no doubt means it to be taken as read that this word too would not mean the same as our 'intend'.]

Moreover if intending were an experience, it would occupy some time, however short. But (Z §50): 'One may disturb someone in thinking – but in intending? – Certainly in planning. Also in keeping to an intention, that is in thinking and acting'.

There are other cases, for example that of fear in *PI* p.188, but these should be enough to show that in Wittgenstein's view not all psychological words designate something. There cannot therefore be family resemblances among their various designata.

2. Some such words clearly enough do designate something, however, – either that or at least something must have happened or be happening to make their use appropriate. One can be interrupted in thinking (*Z* 50), and a pain can intensify or fade (*PI* §154). In these cases there is something going on that is the thinking or the pain. Here the question whether we have a family resemblance concept will be one of whether we can identify what happens as thinking or as pain, by its observed properties. Do we learn to identify thinking or pain in ways like the way we learn what a game is, being shown how all sorts of other games can be constructed on the analogy of these, being told that this and this would scarcely be called games, and so on? (*PI* §75) Or better, to avoid the suggestion that we do learn these identifications in *some* way, do we learn to identify thinking or pain?

With regard to thinking, Wittgenstein expressed scepticism about the latter question in *PI* §328:

> If I say I have a thought – need I always be right? – What *kind* of mistake is there room for here? Are there circumstances in which one would ask: 'Was what I was doing then really thinking; am I not making a mistake?'

In asking what *kind* of mistake there is room for here, Wittgenstein probably means to suggest that there *is* a mistake we can make, we *can* misuse the word 'think', but there is no misuse involving the misidentification of what has been happening. We do not ask 'Was what I was doing then really thinking?', or we do not, if that means 'Did what happened have properties that would make it correctly describable as thinking?' There is no common knowledge of what to look for with a view to answering that question. There is however a similar sounding question, one of whose forms is 'Should I here have described myself as thinking of doing it?' If I wonder sometimes if I might write a book on nonsense, I can describe myself as thinking of doing that only if I am quite seriously inclined, might very well set about it. 'I have been *thinking of* doing it' means roughly 'I have *thought about* it, and might very well do it'. To say that one might very well do it is not a report of what has been happening, but the expression of an attitude towards the project one has been thinking about. We have made a mistake in our use of the expression 'to think of doing such and such', not if the detail of the mental process failed sufficiently to resemble any of the family of processes we have learned to call thinking, but if, whatever the detail was, we do not care to say that we might well embark on the contemplated action.

Wittgenstein does not say that the kind of case I have discussed would be an example of the kind of mistake there is room for, but it is moderately clear he thinks there is no room for the other kind of mistake, and also that he does think there is room for a mistake of some kind; and mine seems a plausible suggestion about *what* kind. It is also a plausible interpretation of Z §§114–16:

> 114. One learns the word 'think', i.e. its use, under certain circumstances, which, however, one does not learn to describe.
> 115. But I *can teach* a person the use of the word! for a description of those circumstances is not needed for that.
> 116. I just teach him the word *under particular circumstances*.

The word 'circumstances' here suggests that it is not the character of the mental process itself that decides whether the word was correctly used, but something in the neighbourhood of the process; and whether one would care to say that one might well embark on the contemplated action would be a circumstance in that sense.

Similar points can be made about the word 'pain'. Consider Z §380:

> A tribe has two concepts, akin to our 'pain'. One is applied where there is visible damage, and is linked to tending, pity, etc. The other is used for stomach-ache for example, and is tied up with mockery of anyone who complains. 'But then do they not notice the similarity?' – Do we have a single concept everywhere where

there is a similarity? The question is: Is the similarity important
to them? and need it be so? And why should their concept 'pain'
not split ours up?

Here in spite of a similarity between the sensations themselves, they are not both called by the same name. Rather, it is
something extrinsic to the character of the sensations themselves, the connection with visible damage, that leads to the
use of one of the tribe's words rather than the other, and to
pity or mockery.

I see no way in which this example brings out anything
about *our* concept of pain. It was probably not meant to serve
that purpose, but rather to show that it need not be on the
basis of similarities between the sensations themselves that
we call them pains. We are likely to suppose that it will of
course be such similarities that entitle anything to be called a
pain. That is why we are inclined to say that we never know
whether what another sufferer has is a pain, exactly. We know
that they detest what they are feeling, but we never know
whether *what* they detest sufficiently resembles what we
detest, and therefore (we reckon) don't know whether it is
pains that they are finding so deplorable. If only we had a
common language to describe the feel of our sensations, we
think we could soon settle that question.

Wittgenstein is perhaps saying that it is not on the basis of
properties of the sensation itself that we call it a pain, when he
writes in *PI* §290: 'What I do is not, of course, to identify my
sensation by criteria, but to repeat an expression. But this is
not the end of the language-game: it is the beginning.' What
would it be like for it to be the end, and what is the game of
which it is the beginning?

It would be the end if what I was trying to settle was
whether what I have is a pain or not. If there was such a
question, then before it was settled, I could be in doubt
whether what I had was a pain, but (*PI* §246) 'The truth is: it
makes sense to say about other people that they doubt
whether I am in pain; but not to say it about myself'.

The language-game of which 'I am in pain' is the beginning
is perhaps one in which I am asked how long I have had it,
when it principally occurs, how intense it is, whether it jabs
or gnaws, and so on. An important thing about these questions is that they do not contribute to deciding whether I am

in pain. That is either not in doubt, or if I am suspected of dissembling, this is not a question to be settled in that way. If, when we say we have a pain, we have not applied criteria to the sensation we have, then whether anything is a pain does not depend on whether its properties show it to belong to the family of sensations called pains.

To understand this point, it is important either to agree with, or to accept for the sake of argument, the point that the adjectives we apply to pains do not describe the sensations themselves. When we say they are nasty, bearable or excruciating, we are describing our reaction to them, or their effect on us; and when we say they are jabbing, throbbing or gnawing, we are saying what they do, but not what it is that does it. When we say they are diffuse or localised we are not saying what it is that is spread out or concentrated. It is as if there were patches of various colours on a page, and some of the orange patches were small and round, while others were much larger, and shaded off into their surroundings. Here we want to liken the pain to one of the colours, and say that just as we call a patch orange because of its distinctive colour, and treat the dimensions of the patch as inessential to whether it is orange, so we call a sensation a pain because of its indescribable feel, and treat it as inessential whether what has that feel is localised or diffuse, whether it is steady or pulses, and so on.

We do not need to suppose that Wittgenstein himself held this view, but only that he treated holding it as part of the way we are thinking when we say that we never know whether what another person has is a pain. We are looking at pains on the model of typical physical objects, that are identifiable by their properties, independently of their effects, or their connections with other things. Thus we look for properties other than our abhorrence of them that identify sensations as pains, and finding none, say that we never know whether a disagreeable sensation is a pain.

A pain, unlike a belief or an intention, is not 'a nothing'. If these non-nothings were identifiable by their properties, there might be a family of such properties, any one of which might show a sensation to be a pain, but if there are no properties we use to identify sensations as pains, there will not be families of them either.

The Scope of the Idea of Family Resemblances

If I have interpreted Wittgenstein correctly on these aspects of the topics of believing, intending, thinking and pain, only carelessness and inattention would allow him to say that these were family resemblance concepts.

Seven

KNOWING HOW TO GO ON

THE SUBJECT of knowing how to go on, like most other topics treated by Wittgenstein is somewhat of a labyrinth. There are aspects of it that Wittgenstein handles more darkly than others, but because various strands of the subject are woven together in his discourse, it can be difficult to disentangle even the aspects that are in themselves comparatively clear. One important path through this forest will be traced in this chapter.

A writes down a series of numbers. B is supposed to continue the series. For a time he is unable to do so, but then he says 'Now I can go on', and does. How did he know he could go on? What did he mean when he said this?

Our first inclination may be to ask ourselves what happened just then. It may not be clear to us what we will do with the answer to this question, whether for example we will be able to say that he means that this happened, or whether he meant something else, for which what happened might be his justification for saying he could go on, but it seems fair to suppose that something must have happened that will somehow be vital to anwering any other questions we may have about his saying he can go on.

An obvious thought is that what happened here is that the formula of the series occurred to him. After all, if that happens we can normally continue a series, and for most of us with most numerical series, we could not continue if that did not happen.

Wittgenstein can be read as offering two rather different objections to this obvious thought. In §151 he suggests that we may know how to go on without the formula occurring to us – for example (i) if we hit on the series of numerical

69

differences, (ii) if we recognise it as a series we are familiar with, or (iii) if we suddenly feel it is easy.

We might not be much disturbed by the first and second of these cases. They might only require that we give a more cautious answer to the question what happens, such as 'Something occurred to him that showed him what to do: he hit on the formula, noted the series of numerical differences, or recognised the series'. The third case might cause us some difficulty though, because there is no way having the feeling that it is easy can show him what to do. It is too unspecific – could be the same for any series. So we might hesitate to believe that he could go on if that was all that happened.

Wittgenstein would not have to claim that the third kind of case does in fact occur – although he showed some interest in calculating prodigies, and in people learning to play chess without ever learning the rules, cases about which it is natural to have the same sort of reservation. He might argue that no matter how astonishing the third kind of case would be, if B did have the feeling that it was easy and then continued the series correctly, (and perhaps also if he did similar things repeatedly), there would be no doubt that when he said 'I can go on', he could. The third case may have been included as a way of making the point that we should not confuse the question *whether* a person can do something, with the question how it is that he can.

Wittgenstein's second objection (§152) is that the formula may occur to us without our being able to continue the series. 'I can go on' can be false when 'The formula has occurred to me' is true. Thus he asks (§154) 'in what sort of case, in what kind of circumstances, do we say "Now I know how to go on", when, that is, the formula *has* occurred to me?' The question is expressed in a cumbersome way, but we may take it to have the same sense as 'In which of the cases in which the formula has occurred to a person could he be said to know how to go on?'

Wittgenstein makes rather a point of it being a matter of the 'circumstances', whether I can go on when the formula has occurred to me. In §154 he writes: 'If there has to be anything "behind the utterance of the formula" it is *particular circumstances*, which justify me in saying I can go on – when the formula occurs to me'. In §179 he says 'And in this case too we should say – in certain circumstances, – that he did know how to go on'. Yet while he thus emphasises that it is a question of circumstances, and in §154 asks what the circumstances are, one has to search a little to find his answer to that question.

Antecedently there will be at least three possibilities, the first two of which perhaps do not deserve any serious attention.

1. The first is that by 'circumstances' is meant certain current facts about oneself or one's situation, in view of, or upon noticing which one was justified. It is not easy to suggest what facts might be canvassed here, but if we had to offer *something*, the occurrence of a peculiar feeling that it is easy, the special way in which there was a slight intake of breath (§154), or perhaps the fact that one felt clear in the head and confident, might be such circumstances. In §§152 and 153 Wittgenstein fairly clearly rejects such 'more or less characteristic accompaniments or manifestations of understanding' as being relevant circumstances. He suggests that they, as much as one's thinking of the formula, could occur without one's knowing how to go on.

2. From §323 one might glean the idea that the circumstances intended might be any that justified one in expecting not to be interrupted – the children being at school, perhaps, or the phone being disconnected. If one is interrupted, one may not be able to continue; and in certain circumstances one can confidently expect not to be interrupted. Yet a claim that one can go on is not a claim that one *will* go on. Even if I have a heart attack and die, it may still have been true just before my death that I was able to continue a numerical series.

3. The word 'circumstance' is perhaps unfortunate here. It makes us look for current facts about ourselves or our situation of a kind that we could notice; but no such facts seem capable of justifying the assertion that we can go on. The word is used in a somewhat offbeat way in the passages that fairly clearly show what Wittgenstein had in mind.

In §179 he writes: 'The words "Now I know how to go on" were correctly used when he thought of the formula: that is, given such circumstances as that he had learnt algebra, and had used such formula before'. In §198 he says 'Let me ask this: what has the expression of a rule – say a sign-post – got to do with my actions? What sort of connection is there here? –

Well, perhaps this one: I have been trained to react to this sign in a particular way, and now I do so react to it'. In §320: 'This certainty [that I shall be able to work out the values of an algebraic function for the arguments up to 10] will be called "well-founded", for I have learnt to compute such functions, and so on'. Here we see that the circumstances Wittgenstein has in mind are not currently noticeable facts, but such facts as that one has a certain training in the activity in question, and has done similar things before.

If in the past we have learned to do something, the fact that we can now do it is a day-in, day-out fact about us, and does not show any more when we are on the point of doing it than when we are having breakfast or taking a nap, although at those times too it is true of us that we know how to do it. Abilities may come and go, but while they remain, they are with us always – yet not *continuously*, like a persistent pain. They are not something we can be aware of, whether continuously or intermittently (§148, notes p.59).

Although when we have hit upon the formula, we may be justified in saying we know how to go on, we do not generally give the justification; but if it were given, it would have the form 'Look, I am not a beginner. I had good teachers, and have done a lot of this kind of thing'. This is not in itself controversial, but it has some interesting consequences:

i) It relieves any need there might have been for the kind of alternative accounts Wittgenstein considers and rejects in such sections as §§197 and 198. We do not need to say such things as (§197) that the whole development of the series appeared to me in a flash when I suddenly understood, or (§198) that if I have the formula, I have enough: it will tell me what to do at each step as I proceed.

ii) It may be surprising that the justification does not have more *specific* connections with the task. It is not like justifying a claim to know that the bird at the bottom of the garden is a bittern by listing the characterisitcs of bitterns and checking them off against those of the bird we see, but rather like saying 'I see it quite clearly', or 'I was brought up on the fens', that is, by claiming to be a person who does not have to work out, or who does not get confused about such things.

iii) Connected with the fact that there are no current observations about ourselves that we are relying on, is an interesting contrast between two concepts of training. When we jog, spar and do push-ups to get in shape for a boxing match, the training has noticeable effects: our weight is down, muscle tone good, and so on, and it may be on the basis of these effects of the training that we say 'I think I can win this one'. By contrast, the training we are talking about has no other noticeable effects than that we do things of this kind correctly. Continuing a series correctly is not the kind of thing one does better or worse depending on the shape one is in, and certainly not the kind of thing one could do better than anyone else if one were in superb shape. People with a bit of training all get it right, and by being in good shape they can excel only in such things as the speed with which they do it or, if it is in writing, in the legibility of the script.

iv) The training here is not a training *for* doing it, as it might be if it were perfectly clear *what* we had to do, but it was a task one had to be agile in order to perform. We do not, as it were, limber up the mind, perhaps by doing chess problems and crossword puzzles, or struggle to achieve the detachment the task requires, perhaps by doing difficult things while rock music is playing or children are squabbling. It is just a training in performing correctly. We work with a student until he does the right thing on his own initiative, and take no interest in the shape he is in, but only in his performance. Hence to advert to our successful training in justification of a claim to know how to go on is not to cite facts about ourselves, known by experience to be conditions of a good performance, but the credentials we have acquired. We have become one of the people to whom you would apply if you were in doubt about the correct way to go on.

Something like this may have been the point of some curious remarks of Wittgenstein's in §§143–5. At the end of §143 he suggests that if a student makes a mistake, and also makes mistakes in the application of the corrective measures one offers, his capacity to learn may come to an end at that point; and in §144 goes on: 'What do I mean when I say "the pupil's capacity to learn *may* come to an end here"? Do I say this from experience? Of course not'. He adds that he wanted to change one's way of looking at things, but indicates neither how he thinks we might have been regarding it, or how he wants us to regard it. It does not cast new light when, in §145, he similarly writes: 'And now at some point he continues the series independently – or he does not. – But why do you say that? *so* much is obvious! – Of course; I only wished to say: the effect of any further *explanation* depends on his *reaction*'. [It is probably better to translate *Wirkung* here as 'production', rather than 'effect', and then the sense of the closing comment would be that we terminate that part of the teaching when he reacts, performs, as we wish. ('Whether we produce any further explanation depends on his reaction.')] Not much is clear here, but (a) the words 'Do I say this from experience? Of course not' are in line with what I said about the training not having an eye to the shape he is in, which we might have learned from experience to be a condition of a good performance; and (b) (given the amended translation) the final remark similarly stresses that it is the correct performance that we are angling for.

It is of course the fact that in formal disciplines we must proceed in a certain way that makes for this difference. While it does not matter how a runner does it, or exactly how fast he is, as long as he excels; and while a dancer must perform with grace and style, but there is no one style that is required of him, there is only one correct way of continuing the +2 series, and it is that, that we must insist on.

v) However the concept of correctness takes a special turn in terms of the picture of training that has been described. The pupils acquire their credentials through coming to do things the way the teacher does, but the teacher knows what to insist on only through himself being a graduate, having acquired the credentials. It is not as if we were all being drilled in something, the specifications of which were fully set out, say in an old statute, and the teachers were people who had memorised the statute. There is no way of setting out fully what we learn, and hence no other concept of getting it right than that of doing as competent practitioners do. Being human, they can of course make mistakes, but there is no other concept of a mistake than that of a departure from what a competent practitioner does when he is being careful and double-checking.

We are much inclined to think that there must be some concept of correctness that is independent of what the practitioners do: that their aim is to discover what, independently

74

of all of them, is correct; but there is no mathematical practice or technique that reflects this belief. Except in school books, there is no place where, having calculated, we can look to see if we have got it right. If we have doubts, we calculate some more, perhaps in a different way, and if we are still uncertain we may ask someone else; but the person we ask is himself fallible, and must himself calculate, and when he has doubts, calculate some more.

The idea of an independent standard is a picturesque expression of the care and precision that is demanded of us in the training. We are taught to proceed diligently as if God's eye were upon us; but if that were true, the eye would be that of someone who has learned our mathematics, gets his answers by calculation and gets them right if he does as we do; but perhaps is not so prone to the blunders we sometimes inattentively commit.

A picture like this can be pieced together from a number of different things Wittgenstein says. In §145 for example 'Now, however, let us suppose that after some efforts on the teacher's part he continues the series correctly, *that is, as we do it*' (my italics). Similarly §190: 'What is the criterion for the way the formula is meant? It is, for example, the kind of way we always use it, the way we are taught to use it'. In §198: 'a person goes by a sign-post only insofar as there exists a regular use of sign-posts, a custom'. The custom, however, is nothing but what people always do, what they are taught to do. It could not be enshrined in the form, say, of an arrow pointing the way we are to go when we see an arrow (§§85, 185).

Versions of the idea that the correct development is there independently of the person continuing a series are rejected in §§187–9, and 218, 352, 426, 516.

The idea that, independently of us, a rule prescribes a definite way in which it is to be followed is rejected in §§211, 217, 219, 228.

There are two points that should be mentioned in concluding. The first is that, while Wittgenstein lays some emphasis on the role of acquired abilities in knowing how to go on, he does not say that they represent the only condition on which we are justified in saying we know how to go on. In §320 he says 'This certainly will be called "well-founded", for I have learnt to compute such functions, and so on' – but then he adds: 'In other cases no reasons will be given for it – but it will be justified by success'. [Probably this last sentence would be better translated 'In other cases there will be no reason for it ...': the reason is not generally given, although there often is a reason, even when it is not given.]

The second point is that we are generally in no way mindful of the justification when we say we know how to go on: '"Now I know how to go on!" is an exclamation; it corresponds to an instinctive sound, a glad start' (§323). In §180 Wittgenstein suggests that we might call these words a 'signal', and perhaps he means that they are like a light that is rigged to go on in certain circumstances, and in those circumstances lights automatically. Whether the light's going on means that the circumstances prevail is a question not to be settled by the signal analogy, because clearly we could have signals that meant that the circumstances in which they lit prevailed, and others that meant something else – that we should do something perhaps. (If there was a signal light on a car that lit either when we were exceeding the speed limit or when there was too much strain on the engine, what it would mean would be neither of those, but 'Slow down'). But clearly 'I know how to go on' means something like 'If I were to go on, I would do it correctly', and although I can say this if the formula has occurred to me and I have a training in the use of such formulae, it is not an assertion that those things are true.

Eight

THE HARRIED

MATHEMATICS INSTRUCTOR

IT IS initially bewildering why, in the course of his discussion of knowing how to go on in the *Philosophical Investigations*, Wittgenstein introduces the following example:

> 185. . . . Now we get the pupil to continue a series (say +2) beyond 1000 – and he writes 1000, 1004, 1008, 1012.
>
> We say to him 'Look what you've done!' – He doesn't understand. We say: 'You were meant to add *two*: look how you began the series!' – He answers: 'Yes, isn't it right? I thought that was how I was *meant* to do it.' – Or suppose he pointed to the series and said; 'But I went on the same way.' – It would now be no use to say: 'But can't you see . . . ?' – and repeat the old examples and explanations. – In such a case we might say, perhaps: It comes natural to this person to understand our order with our explanations as *we* should understand the order: 'Add 2 up to 1000, 4 up to 2000, 6 up to 3000, and so on.'
>
> Such a case would present similarities with one in which a person naturally reacted to the gesture of pointing with the hand by looking in the direction of the line from finger-tip to wrist, not from wrist to finger-tip.

There need perhaps not be much argument what Wittgenstein is asking us to suppose here. We are to suppose, not merely that the student makes this mistake, but that he takes everything we say by way of showing him that it is a mistake, as confirmation that he has proceeded correctly. Like a rational person, he stays to talk about it, and has something to say in response to any point we make; and what he says is said with apparent earnestness and because it seems right to him; but whether he is rational in the further sense that what he says, although wrong, is nevertheless such that (a) we can understand someone thinking it right, and (b) given it, he had proceeded correctly, is an important question on which Wittgenstein gives us no explicit guidance. When the student says 'I thought that was how I was meant to do it', and 'But I went on in the same way', he has perhaps promised, but certainly not provided, an explanation of how he sees 1004 as 2 greater than 1000. Since it seems impossible to do this without making such fanciful suppositions as that, after 1000 and without noticing it, he starts grouping numbers together in pairs and treating them as one number, it may be our soundest policy just to suppose that, although this student is attentive to arguments, and does not treat them as irrelevant, for some reason they are all wasted on him, and we will make no progress with him that way.

If this was Wittgenstein's intention, the fact that it was is important, because then mathematical relativism is no part of the issue here. If the student's position had been meant to be intelligible, but just different from ours, it might have been part of Wittgenstein's problem, whether there could be any reason for preferring ours to his, since the reasons that first come to mind are all taken from within our system; but if the student is not supposed to be an innovative genius (and he certainly does not sound like one), then whatever the problem is, it will not be that one.

What is the point of the example then? This student is a most curious and improbable fellow: it is unlikely that the problem was that we might encounter such pupils, and not know how to go about teaching them. It is not pedagogical theory that Wittgenstein is at work on, intended to prepare teachers for every emergency.

Characteristically, there is no specification of what the general problem is in the stretch of the *Philosophical Investigations* in which this passage occurs, but the following is at least one problem that can be seen in those sections: how is it that we are able, after a comparatively small amount of instruction, to do quite complicated things that take us beyond the examples used in the instruction, and do them correctly? What does the student derive from the instruction, that enables him to go beyond it?

Clearly that question could arise in connection with §185: the student has been specifically drilled in doing various series, but the instruction has never taken him past 1000, and it is when he tries to go beyond this point, to proceed on his own using the instruction he has recieved, that we find him making this annoying mistake.

Wittgenstein mentions various possible answers to the question how good students do it, but there is only one of these that he dwells on extensively. He mentions that we might have a new intuition at each step, and that we might take a new decision at every stage (§186); but he is most interested in the idea that we are guided by a formula or a rule we have been taught or have hit upon. It is all we need, because it will tell us what to do at every juncture.

This, or something like it, is certainly the most popular and tempting account, and therefore the most deserving of extensive scrutiny. Wittgenstein does not deny that we do use rules and formulae in mathematics, but does deny that their use can explain our ability to go on independently. Why he denies this is not the chief concern of this chapter (see chapter 7), but his main point is that a rule does not itself spell out what to do – we must learn how to apply it – and if there were rules telling us how to apply the rule, the application of these rules would not be contained in them, but would have to be learned. When mathematical instruction is successful, we have no doubt what to do with a formula, and in that sense it tells us, but we have yet to bring out what the instruction does that makes it so clear to us what to do (*PI* §§139, 141, 143, 145, 151, 154, 179, 189).

In the context of this rejection of the rule-following theory of mathematical competence we can begin to make some sense of the story of the deviant student in §185. In arguing with him, we reiterate various rules, but they are of no avail. The student knows and accepts the rules, but still proceeds incorrectly; and he is not just a blunderer who, as soon as he is reminded of the rule, sees his mistake, is embarrassed, and can develop the series correctly. Even when mindful of the rule, it seems to him he has followed it correctly.

Wittgenstein may have described us as rather frantically sputtering 'But can't you see!' to suggest that we are at our wits' end because we can think of no other way of showing the student his mistake than that of reiterating rules, the application of which is so clear to us, yet he blithely takes anything we say as confirmation of the correctness of what he has done. This seems to confront us with an impossibility. What we take to be the only method of showing him what to do fails utterly.

That the reading so far is along the right lines is confirmed by the final paragraph of §185, since we seem to be confronted with a similar impossibility in the case of the person who takes the gesture of pointing in the direction of a line from finger-tip to wrist: if we imagine that our only resource in correcting this mistake is to point in the direction in which the gesture of pointing should be taken, obviously it will be of no use, because he will of course misconstrue the further pointings in the same way.

Wittgenstein leaves us to shift for ourselves on where the example might lead, but one interesting way we might go from there emerges from reflecting on the man who misconstrues the gesture of pointing. While we might, if we thought the only way of explaining the gesture is by pointing, reckon that it is unteachable, and there must be some happy genetic adaptation that makes people construe it in the way we wish, it is not so clear that in fact we would have either to abandon anyone who lacked this happy adaptation, or in any case not correct his mistake in any way that we could call 'teaching' or 'showing'. It would not *have* to be done, even if it could, with drugs, radiation or psycho-analysis: there are dozens of things we could try, none of which is sure to work, but any of which might succeed. We could tell him to fetch something we pointed at, and rap his knuckles every time he fetched what was on a line from finger-tip to wrist; or ask him to bring that apple (pointing), when there were other apples, but none of them on the line from finger-tip to wrist; or draw a picture of someone pointing, with an object at either end of the line of pointing, and then erase the object at the wrong end and heavily encircle the one at the other end, and so on.

We only fancied we would be in a fix if we encountered someone who misconstrued pointing, because we did not doubt that pointing would be the only way of setting him right; and similarly perhaps we only fancy that we could do nothing with the deviant mathematics student, if we do not doubt that citing various rules is the only way of showing him how to proceed correctly. Are there not other ways?

The teacher in §185, perhaps lulled by the fact that the pupil was not a rank beginner, or by the fact that, unlike beginners, he talked back, attempted to argue with him. He would not have done that had it been a question of whether 6 was the next number after five, or the number after 2 in the +2 series was 4. If we explain to a student how to construct the natural number series after 9, 19 and 29 we may, if he gets it wrong when we ask him 'Now how about 39?', rehearse the explanations and examples already given, and so appear to be arguing; but we could scarcely countenance any counter-argument. If the student objects, then unless there should be some useful insight to be communicated by looking into his objection, we should rather say 'Look, don't argue about this. Do it this way'. We would *tell* him what to do, and insist on it. The meaning of any rules or guidelines we may have given him consists in the fact that they are applied precisely that way.

When we had occasion to *do* anything that had been learned just by its having been insisted on, drilled into us, we would have no mathematical reasons for doing it that way, we would just do it. Hence:

> How can we *know* how he is to continue a pattern by himself – whatever instruction you give him? – Well, how do I know? – If that means 'Have I reasons?' the answer is: my reasons will soon give out. And then I shall act, without reasons. (*PI* §211, see also §§217, 219)

One thing we could do with the deviant student then is leave off arguing and insist: tell him 'Look, this is what you do here. Anything else is wrong. Do it this way', and perhaps keep him in after school unless he does. If this were merely a fine point of pedagogical practice, how to cope with a very rare breed of student, it would be of no particular philosophical interest. Its importance lies in what it may show about the nature of mathematical competence.

It has already been suggested how very prone we are to suppose that this consists in knowing a set of rules that tell us what to do. Getting things right consists in doing what the rules prescribe. It is not difficult to see why this thought is so attractive:

i) We want to be able to explain how it is that we are able to go beyond the examples canvassed in the instruction, and do it correctly; and rules, being of perfectly general application, seem capable of advising us what to do in every case, not just in the few cases our teachers show us.

ii) When we are trained in the use of a rule, it is transparent to us: we apply it with utter facility and without a tremor of doubt. It therefore seems to be our guide and source of information about what to do.

iii) When we are learning, we are often perplexed for a long time by the examples that are shown us, until suddenly something happens and it all comes clear. If we ask *what* has happened, it seems fair, in view of the power of rules to take us beyond the examples, to suppose that we have either hit on a rule or come to understand the rule that had been propounded to us.

From the tale of the harried teacher we can derive at least the beginning of an alternative theory. The instruction by insistence that seemed to be the way out of the impasse depicted in §185 suggests two important points:

i) That whatever rules the teacher may cite in pressing his case, the hard fact about him is that he is simply not prepared to brook any other continuation of the series than 1002, 1004 . . . . He may adduce various rules in his desperation, but his colours show when the rule proves useless and he simply insists. I did not earlier go into just what rules he might adduce, but when we get down to cases here we may find that what we have been calling the rules by which he proceeds are in fact quite *ad hoc* teaching devices. He might for example say 'In this series you take the sequence of natural numbers and write down the even numbers in the order in which they appear. Hence (putting parentheses around those omitted) 1000, (1001), 1002, (1003), 1004. . . .' Now, *if* the student followed this procedure he would continue the series correctly, but it is neither the only procedure that could be followed, nor is either it or any other procedure followed by the teacher, who would (in this kind of case at least) simply write out the series.

ii) What the student primarily learns is what the teacher insists on: to do it this way – this is what we do here. The practices that he learns in this way can be symbolised, and various of them can be represented in a formula that he comes to be able to use as he advances, but the bedrock of his understanding consists of those things he has simply been *told* (or, if he has proved recalcitrant or careless, the things that have been insisted upon or drilled into him).

Once we are shaken loose a little from our fascination with the rule-following theory of mathematical competence, we can begin to show how large a role simply 'being told' plays. We are simply told the order of natural numbers in decimal notation, and drilled in it until we reproduce them in that order. If we should make certain kinds of mistake, rules may be introduced: if it emerges as our natural inclination to write 1, 0, 3, 2, 5, 4 . . ., we may be told to write them that way and then reverse each pair along the line (§143); but (a) the rule itself will probably have to be explained to us with examples, and (b) such rules are not part of mathematics, but only serve for a time to get individual students over some difficulty. It may appear that there are rules for developing the number series past 9, 99, or 999, in as much as, if we applied ourselves to the task, we could compose such a rule; but most of us were never told, do not know, do not use and would have difficulty composing such a rule. We go right on from 9 to 10 or from 99 to 100; and would not know where to turn for a justification of that practice.

I could go on to explore, develop and justify this kind of alternative to the rule-following account of mathematical competence, but it would take me a very long way from §185; and it is perhaps enough if it has been shown how these might have been the issues underlying Wittgenstein's introduction of this most curious and bewildering example.*

* The problems here are more fully explored in my essay, 'Logical Compulsion', in *Essays after Wittgenstein* (Toronto 1973).

Nine

SENSATIONS AND BLOOD PRESSURE

BEGINNING AT §256 of the *Philosophical Investigations*, Wittgenstein is pondering the case of a man who has no 'natural expression' for his sensations, but only has the sensations. In §258 he supposes that, to keep a diary of the recurrence of a certain sensation, this person associates it with the sign 'S', and writes this sign in a calender for every day he has the sensation. Wittgenstein notes a number of awkward features of this supposition, but nothing very clearly ruinous, and then considers this possibility:

> 270. Let us now imagine a use for the entry of the sign 'S' in my diary. I discover that whenever I have a particular sensation a manometer shows that my blood pressure rises. So I shall be able to say that my blood pressure is rising without using any apparatus. This is a useful result. And now it seems quite indifferent whether I have recognised the sensation right or not. Let us suppose I regularly identify it wrong, it does not matter in the least. And that alone shews that the hypothesis that I make a mistake is mere show. . . .
>
> And what is our reason for calling 'S' the name of a sensation here? Perhaps the kind of way this sign is employed in this language game. – And why 'a particular sensation', that is, the same one every time? Well, aren't we supposing that we write 'S' every time?

There is something incoherent about this case, at least the way it is presented. One can hardly say 'I discover that whenever I have a particular sensation . . .', and then go on to say or imply that it does not matter whether I have that particular sensation. That cancels the supposed discovery; and not only that, it leaves us mystified why Wittgenstein should so confidently say, as if the point were perfectly obvious, that it is quite indifferent whether I have recognised the sensation right or not. If I say I discover that whenever I eat an apple I get indigestion, it is not obviously indifferent whether it is an apple or something else I have eaten.

The incoherence would disappear, and Wittgenstein's point would be obvious, if the second sentence of the section were re-written: 'I discover that whenever I routinely or sincerely write "S". . .'. Then, whereas it had previously appeared that we just had two things between which connections might be made, the sensation and the blood pressure, we would now have three, the sensation, the writing of 'S' and the blood pressure. It would clearly be between the latter two of these that we had discovered a connection; and clearly either it would not matter, or there would be room for doubt whether it mattered, whether the sensation was correctly identified.

It is clear from the final two sentences of the section that it is indeed between the writing of 'S' and the blood pressure that Wittgenstein is supposing a connection to have been discovered; but then (a) why did he not say that in his initial description of the case? and (b) is it not mystifying what would make anyone write 'S' with such interesting regularity, if not the occurrence of the same sensation?

It is unlikely that Wittgenstein wrote 'I have a particular sensation', rather than 'sincerely write "S"', inattentively, in as much as he unmasks the error of the former way of putting it later in the same section. Hence we must suppose that he deliberately presented the case in a misleading way. Why would he do this?

The answer may be that whereas he might have *described* the mistake we are apt to make here, he preferred to lull us into making it ourselves; but to set it up so that if we were on our toes, we would see for ourselves the silly thing we had done. Not everyone will be 'on his toes', but a point is driven home more forcefully when we see it for ourselves and catch ourselves making the mistake it concerns, than when it is spelled out for us, cast as a possible mistake that other, less sagacious people might make.

When we read 'I discover that whenever I have a particular sensation . . .', there may seem nothing wrong so far, in spite of the warnings we have been given in §§257 and 261. 'To have a particular sensation' is an ordinary expression, normally quite in order, but we forget that it is being used here in the special context set up in §256, and that in that context it is no longer clear what will count as having a particular sensation.

The foregoing hypothesis on why Wittgenstein presented the case here in such a misleading way gets some support from a possible reading of the first two sentences of the second paragraph of §270. It is admittedly debatable what Wittgenstein meant when he answered the question 'And what is our reason for calling "S" the name of a sensation here?' by saying 'Perhaps the kind of way this sign is employed in this language-game'; but he might have intended this as something *we* might think: that in setting up the context in §256, the supposition was made that we did not have the natural expression of sensation, but only the sensation, and that we are now using the word 'sensation' the way it was used there. To this imagined thought of ours he might, given his objections in §§257 and 261, respond that it has not yet been specified how it was being used in setting up that context, and therefore it is empty to say that we are now using it in the same way. We were not worried about our use of the word 'sensation' in §§256 and 258, because it is an ordinary word used in a perfectly grammatical way; and no more did it worry us to say in §270 'I discover that whenever I have a particular sensation . . .'.

I will now turn to the question of how strong a point it is, that there being a connection between someone's writing 'S' and his blood pressure being high shows nothing about whether he has the same sensation. Wittgenstein seemed to take it that once (a) a wedge had been driven between having the same sensation and writing 'S' and (b) it was clear that it was the latter that had been found to be connected with rising blood pressure, it would be obvious without further argument that it was indifferent whether one had the same sensation; and indeed it *is* obvious: one would still be able to say that one's blood pressure was high without using any apparatus. If God said 'But the sensation was different!', one could reply 'I don't care. It seemed the same, and it is between its seeming the same and high blood pressure that I have discovered a connection'.

Against this however it might seem fair to suggest that

while there may be room for a kind of Cartesian doubt whether the sensation is the same, the remarkable connection surely would give us an imposing reason for thinking we are having the same sensation. After all, it is our avowed intention to write 'S', not when we suspect a rise in blood pressure, or when we are angry, but when the sensation recurs. [Here I keep using the suspect word 'sensation'. What can one do? Emit an inarticulate sound? (§261) Wittgenstein raises a question like this in §339.]

Here it should be noted that Wittgenstein does not need to say that it is actually doubtful whether we are having the same sensation when we write 'S'. He is only saying that if the sensation were different, it would make no difference. It is like saying 'Whenever I suspect it is raining in Peking, a manometer shows that my blood pressure has risen'. In that case it would clearly make no difference whether it was indeed raining in Peking. Quite independently of that, I would have a way of telling that my blood pressure was high.

However, it is conceived as mattering for other purposes whether the sensation we have on several occasions is the same: we are supposing that if it is different on various occasions, it can not be a pain on more than one of them; and we may want to suppose that the connection with rising blood pressure shows or is evidence that it is the same.

We must remember that we are operating here in the highly artificial context set up in §256, in which the sensation remains, unaltered, but there is no natural expression of it. We have gone through the ceremony of focusing our attention on something and saying 'S', and we want to know whether this piece of engineering has brought it about that we recognise this object of our attention when it recurs.

For the normal sufferer, there is no particular problem of reidentifying sensations. If, last year when I had an ulcer problem, I had leaden pains of moderate intensity, and what I now feel is describable in the same way, I am having the same pains, and may suspect a recurrence of ulcers. By contrast, in the special context in which we are now operating, we may pronounce a sensation the same as last week's or last year's, or different, but we cannot enlarge on these judgments or relieve doubts about them with further description. The doctor cannot say 'Now are you sure? Were they both steady, leaden pains, that fell short of being unbearable, but were extremely uncomfortable?' They can neither be slight, bearable or ex- cruciating, because those words express our reaction to them, which is ruled out by the supposition in §256.

When we thus rule out all the normal ways in which we would think about whether our sensations are the same or different, it is no longer clear what the issue is, or whether indeed there is an issue; but whatever it is, we are trying now to settle it in a peculiar way: not by comparison but by infer- ence. 'What else', we think, 'could explain the remarkable connection between its seeming to us that we are having the same sensation, and our blood pressure?'

Inferences somewhat like this are made in the case of normal suffers. If X-rays show ulceration, a doctor may expect that a patient will describe his pains in much the way others have done in similar cases, and similarly descriptions of pains lead doctors to suspect ulcers.

These inferences work for two connected reasons: (i) our descriptions of pains are normally accepted as being reliable, and therefore (ii) general truths such as that pains of such and such a description are a symptom of such and such can be established, and form the basis on which inferences are made in particular cases.

These conditions do not obtain in the case we are consider- ing. (i) Far from it being the case that descriptions of pains are accepted as being reliable, what we are trying to establish is whether they are reliable. Someone says 'I am having the same sensation again', and we want to know whether that is true (*and so does he*). (ii) Since the same doubt arises in every case, we are never in a position to reckon that since in general when people's blood pressure is high and they say they are having the same sensation, they *are* having it, therefore in this case that is probably true also. The diarist in §258 is not an unknown quantity among known quantities. In a world in which *everyone* simply associated 'S' with a supposedly characteristic sensation, we would have the same difficulty with everyone else's claims to be having the same sensation as on some previous occasion.

Might we say then that it must simply be accepted that when people think they are having the same sensation, they *are*? If it were indeed important that they should be right about this, if for example at least one of two sensations would not be a pain if they were different, there might be no recourse but to say some such thing. But if it does not matter whether the sensation is the same in the relevant respect, we could live with the supposition that mine might be different in this respect from day to day and from one in the head to one in the knee, and that all of mine might be different from all of yours. Does it matter?

Pains do differ widely without therefore not being pains. Some are mild, others excruciating. Some jab, others gnaw. Some are searing, others leaden. The respect in which we are demanding that they be the same can be none of these, or any other way in which they are *describable*, and must be the possession of some quality or feel that we are not able to describe. But now if this quality is indescribable, it cannot be part of the concept of pain that if a sensation is not (something), it is not a pain. This is a language-game we cannot play. And we do not try to play it. If people say they have a pain, we do not grope for a way of enquiring whether their sensation has a peculiar quality, and even in our own case, where we do not need an established nomenclature, we do not sift through our nasty sensations and call pains only those having a certain distinctive feel.

For my own part, there seems to be something right about saying that my pains resemble one another, in the possession of a quality I find hard to describe, and if other people are like me in this particular, this might partially explain our resistance to Wittgenstein's scepticism about whether pains have an indescribable quality. But he need not and does not deny that there is something about the feel of a pain that is indescribable. He need only deny that it is in virtue of the possession of this quality that sensations are called pains.

Ten

THE CONNECTION BETWEEN PAIN AND LIVING HUMAN BEINGS

> 281. 'But doesn't what you say come to this: that there is no pain, for example, without *pain-behaviour*?' – It comes to this: only of a living human being and what resembles (behaves like) a living human being can one say: it has sensations; it sees; is blind; hears; is deaf; is conscious or unconscious.

I WILL NOT go into the hard questions, i) how Wiitgenstein can deny that he is saying there is no pain without pain-behaviour, and ii) how what he represents himself as saying instead of this can be seen as what the preceding discussion 'comes to'. I will concentrate on questions having to do with what the latter *means*.

The most basic point to be noticed is that except in the case of having sensations, there are *pairs* of (opposite) attributions: 'sees or is blind', 'hears or is deaf', 'is conscious or unconscious'. This argues that 'sees', 'hears' and 'is conscious' are not being used transitively, and that what is at issue here is what we may call 'category attributions', questions of whether *either* of these opposite predicates is applicable. If we say of a human being or a horse that he can't see or hear anything, it follows that he is deaf or blind, but if we were to say of a chair that it never sees anything, or of a flower that it never hears anything, these implications would not hold. When 'never sees' entails 'is blind' or 'never hears' entails 'is deaf', the living being to which the predicates are applied belongs to a species, members of which normally see or hear. When we say the chair doesn't see or the flower doesn't hear, we could conclude that they were blind or deaf only given that some chairs see, or some flowers hear.

Presumably the same holds of 'having sensations'. It is

meant as a 'category attribution'. Perhaps the reason it is not paired with an opposite is that there is no word or expression commonly used as its opposite. Or, since Wittgenstein might have said 'has or does not have sensations', perhaps the reason is that he did not want to make it too easy for us to see that we are dealing here with category attributions.

We might have taken 'it has sensations' to be a generalisation from 'it has an itch', 'it has a pain', 'it feels the cold', and so on, in the way 'it sees', as used in opposition to 'it is blind', is a conclusion from 'it sees the table', 'it sees the blue jay'; but just as we do not ask whether a living being sees this or that or is blind, unless we take it to belong to a species – members of which do see – we do not ask whether anything has a pain or an itch unless we take it to belong to a species, members of which are sensate. We do not ask whether the chair sees the table or the hydrangea hears the chickadee, not because, never having known chairs to see anything or hydrangeas to hear anything, we think it unlikely in a new case, but because we do not know what would count as the supposedly unlikely event occurring.

When we take the questions 'Does it see this?', 'Does it hear that?', 'Is it in pain?' to be applicable to a particular living thing, normally there is no difficulty answering them. We are not raising both the question 'Might it X (see, hear, have pains)?' and 'Is it Xing now?' If Rover stirs eagerly when Johnny's footstep is to be heard, there will be little doubt that he heard it, and if he yelps when his tail is caught in the door, there will be no doubt that he is in pain. It is when there is uncertainty whether the *questions* are applicable, that it is perplexing how they are to be answered. When we wonder whether a fish feels pain, if we had no doubt that fish sometimes are in pain, there would generally be no problem in a particular case. It is our uncertainty whether the question is applicable, not the behaviour we see, that makes it difficult to answer.

If in this particular, attributions of pain presuppose that the being to which they are attributed belongs to a species, members of which sometimes have pains, and this presupposition is not based on having found members of that species to have pains, how do we know whether the presupposition is in order?

When Wittgenstein says 'only of a living human being and what resembles (behaves like) a living human being can we say: it has sensations [etc.]', does he mean that we know it by analogy?

It is important to notice that in the case of other human beings there is no hint of an analogical argument: if it is a living human being we are dealing with, there will of course be questions of whether it has a pain now (or sees this or hears that), but there is no question whether it may either see or be blind, hear or be deaf, have pains or be insensate. I will return to the question why there is no problem about this, but clearly Wittgenstein is saying there is none, and no need to resolve it by analogy or in any other way.

It does at least appear that it is by analogy with human beings that he says we take other living things to be proper subjects of questions like 'Is it in pain?' It is not past doubting however, whether that was his intention. If there is an analogical argument, it is almost certainly not one about whether any of a dog's or horse's sensations have the indescribable quality in virtue of which supposedly we call one of our sensations a pain. That is not, in Wittgenstein's view, what is at issue when we wonder whether anything *human or otherwise* is in pain. However it might be a question, not of whether dogs have sensations with much the same indescribable quality our pains have, but of whether to extend to dogs the care and concern that is accorded to human beings when they are taken to be in pain. ['(Pity, one may say, is a form of the conviction that someone else is in pain)' (*PI* §287).]

If something like the latter were Wittgenstein's view, he might well say that it is not that we are driven by the force of the analogy between dogs and people to include dogs in the community of beings about which we care in this way, but rather we do treat dogs as having pains, and in fact there is enough similarity between aspects of their behaviour and aspects of ours to make the complex pattern of thinking and action that is connected with attributions of pain to human beings, applicable to dogs. [The relation between the attitude and the behavioural similarities may be like the relation I suggested between our calling an activity a game, and its resemblances to other activities we call games. We can't conclude that it is a game because of such similarities. We have

Pain and Living Human Beings

no rules to determine what similarities are sufficient, but when the linguisitic community comes to call anything a game, it will be found that there are in fact similarities between it and some other activities we call games (see chapter 5).]

Let me now return to the question raised earlier, why there is no doubt that the question 'Is he in pain?', when it is in no part a question whether he is a being who may have pains, is applicable to a human being. If we do not argue by analogy with our own case, that when anything behaves as we do when we are in pain, it too will have a pain, is this a conviction we have? Could we say we do not *know* it to be true, but either we accept it on faith, or we take a strong stand on it, and will not tolerate anyone raising any doubts about it? Such a view of the matter would make a kind of sense if whether a person had a pain were a question whether the sensation he has has the indescribable quality that mine has. If it were clear that it is essential to being a pain that a sensation should have a certain property, while at the same time we never knew whether another person's sensations had this property, it would be possible to say we *trust* that the sensations people have in certain circumstances have this property, or to say we *declare* that they have it, we close ranks on this issue, and jeer at anyone who questions it.

I will take it to be clear that Wittgenstein did not suppose the question whether someone has a pain to be one of whether the indescribable qualities of his sensation are the same as one's own, and correspondingly clear that he would reject any suggestion that we accept this on faith, or that we will not stand for any questioning of it. It is not that the supposition that other people's sensations are the same as ours has some other status, but that whether this is the case is not the issue when we ask whether other people have pains.

What entitles us to presuppose that the question 'Is he in pain?' is applicable to any human being? I suggest that the answer is similar to the answer to the comparable question in the case of horses and dogs: we attribute pain to people primarily because that is the way we have learned to use pain language. People are the prime beings to whom pain is attributed, and when we ask whether a person is in pain, while the question may be ruled out of court by the fact that he shows no

93

sign of it and is not a Stoic, no difficulty arises of the kind we encounter when we raise the question whether a fish is in pain. When a human being is wounded and moans, and there is no reason to suspect fakery, the linguistic community raises no question whether he is in pain, but when a fish convulses when the hook is taken from its mouth, although there will be no suspicion of fakery, the judgment that it is in pain is not routine. If fish were everywhere included among the beings who may have pains, there would be no doubt in a particular case. It is the category attribution, not its consequences in particular cases, that is the problem.

The difficulty here is that whereas we have ways of deciding whether anything we suppose may have pains has one now, there is no established procedeure for deciding the category question.

It might seem fair to suggest doing it by analogy; but if we try that, the problem will be that there will always be differences, more numerous and greater in some cases than in others, and we will have no way of deciding when the differences are too great. Normally when a similarity leads us to suspect something, our suspicion can be confirmed in other ways, and the differences thereby shown not to have been too great, but in this case there is no prospect of what an analogy leads us to suspect being confirmed.

We treat dogs as having pains, and in fact there are more similarities than differences between dogs and people in this connection. It is often clear where a dog's pain is, what sort of a pain it is, and how acute. Dogs tend the affected part of their anatomy, and the gingerness with which they will use an affected paw varies from case to case. On the other hand there is no question of their faking pain, or being stoical either, and it is not clear whether their demeanour can ever be such as to make us wonder whether they are suffering or grieving. In these latter ways they are unlike people. With fish the want of fit is more marked: their convulsing is not so expressive as the yelping of a dog; they do not, perhaps because they cannot, attend to the offending part of their anatomy; we would not know what to count as their looking miserable; and if we saw a fish in the water convulsing as if in pain, say after lightning had struck, we would be disinclined to take remedial measures. If some people show more concern about the welfare of fish than others, and *would* take remedial action in such a case, they might still not know whether to say that they believed the fish to be in pain, rather than that they supposed the fish would prefer not to be driven to convulse that way.

I have been saying that category attributions are not something we can figure whether to make or not, but rather something the linguistic community comes to make in one case, not in another. This is not to say that there may not be considerations that make a particular kind of attribution more livable in one case than another, but only that the practice *emerges*, rather than being decided upon. And to repeat, it is not a question of whether the members of a species have sensations that are like ours in ways in which ours are indescribable, but of whether to apply to members of that species the pattern of thoughts and actions that is applied to human beings in supposing they are in pain.

I read Z §380 as an illustration of this point. There Wittgenstein described a tribe that had two different words for nasty sensations, depending on whether they were connected with visible bodily damage, and showed concern about one of these sorts of sensation, while mocking anyone who complained of the other kind, although they recognised similarities in the way the two kinds felt. We could perhaps conjecture that their practice reflected their inability to do anything about sensations not connected with visible bodily damage. If they had no drugs or surgical procedures with which to treat stomach ailments, they might have fostered a stoical attitude towards the sensations associated with them. But whatever the explanation of the structure of their language, or of ours, the justification for a member of their own community using its language in the standard way would not be in terms of any propositions that might be false, such as that everyone's nasty sensations feel the same, or that the dog's nasty sensations feel pretty much like those of humans. If the question arose why I say he is in pain when he is wounded or writhing, the answer would not be 'That's what we all assume, rightly or wrongly', but rather for example, 'That's a paradigm case in which we say a person has a pain', or 'If that's not a case in which to say that, nothing is'.

I have treated questions about the pains of fish as undecidable owing to the fact that we have not come to make the category attribution of pains to fish, given which it would be routinely decidable in particular cases whether a salmon or a perch was in pain. It is important to add that we do not make the contrary attribution either. We do not say that fish are *not* the kind of beings that may have pains, whereas we do deny that hydrangeas, pine trees and buses may have pains, and do not wonder whether any of these things is in pain. Is this view consistent with §284, where Wittgenstein says 'And now look at a wriggling fly and at once these difficulties [about ascribing a sensation to a *thing*] vanish and pains seem able to get a foothold here, where before everything was, so to speak, too smooth for it'? I think this is not a problem. If there is no wriggling or squirming, the category attribution is out of the question, but it does not follow that when there *is* wriggling or squirming, we are right if we make the category attribution. It only follows that it is not out of the question to do so. If it is not absurd to wonder whether this fly or this salmon has a pain, the question gets a foothold; but that is not to say that when a fish convulses we can conclude that it is in pain, the way we could if the category question were settled.

If questions about the ethics of hunting and fishing are primarily questions about whether animals have pains, anyone who treats that question as undecidable in the case of some animals may appear to be supplying a justification for these sports or industries. Yet whichever view of the logic of pain attribution one takes, there is much the same doubt whether fish have pains; while there is a twist to the view that I have proposed that may be of some importance in this connection. The expression 'not in pain', as applied to human beings, relieves us of the immediate need to be concerned, to sympathise, to tend, but we can say no more of a fish that it is not in pain than of a chair that it doesn't see the table. 'Not in pain', with its responsibility-relieving implications is predicable only of beings that can have pains. If we cannot say of this perch that it is in pain, we equally cannot say that it is not, and so be relieved of responsibility; but pain or no pain, a fish clearly does not care for being hauled from the water, having a hook torn from its mouth, or being left to flop in the bottom of a boat.

If the question is thereby changed into one of whether to respect a living being's wish to go its own way intact and unmolested, it may not be more readily answerable, but if, in the worst event, it involves taking an ethical stand, we at least get rid of the bogus pretence that the stand is required by something we know about fish.

Eleven

THE BEETLE BOX

> 293. Suppose everyone had a box with something in it:
> we call it a 'beetle'. No one can look into anyone else's
> box, and everyone says he knows what a beetle is only by
> looking at his beetle. – Here it would be quite possible for
> everyone to have something quite different in his box.
> One might even imagine such a thing constantly chang-
> ing. – But suppose the word 'beetle' had a use in these
> people's language? – If so it would not be used as the
> name of a thing. The thing in the box has no place in the
> language-game at all; not even as a something: for the
> box might even be empty. – No, one can 'divide through'
> by the thing in the box; it cancels out, whatever it is.

THIS FAMOUS passage in *Philosophical Investigations*
conceals a multitude of subtleties and mantraps, as we will
see if we press questions like the following: (1) Why does
Wittgenstein say 'everyone *says he* knows what a beetle is
only by looking at his beetle', rather than just 'everyone
knows what a beetle is [that way]'? (2) Why does he say, as if
it were a new feature, 'suppose the word "beetle" had a use in
these people's language'? Has he not already described its
use? (3) What is it to be the name of a *thing*? (4) If we can
'divide through' by the thing in the box, is that supposed to
show something about the use of the English word 'pain', or
only to draw a consequence of a use attributed to it by philosophers?

1. It *may* have been excessive caution that made Wittgenstein say 'everyone *says he* knows . . .' rather than just 'knows
. . .'. In §§246 and 295 he raises objections to saying similar
things about pain, and so would not want to be caught saying
the same things himself. But is his objection just to a certain
way of putting it? Might he say that, however exactly one may

express it, there is something about these boxes and their owners that makes it not all wrong to say 'I know only from my own beetle . . .'? Did he mean to describe something exceptional about beetle boxes, or only something exceptional about people's attitude to them? Do his conclusions rest on that attitude, or on the properties of beetle boxes? These last questions, it will be seen, are another way of asking our question '(4)' above, and their answer will have to await the consideration of that question: but we can make some progress with the question of whether Wittgenstein means to imply a peculiarity of beetle boxes by considering the question what it is going to mean to know what a beetle is?

i) In saying 'I know only from my own case what a beetle is', they imply that they do know; but while in general 'to know what an X is' is to know something about any X, that cannot hold in this context. If God told me there were identical things in these six boxes and they were called 'beetles', but permitted me to look in only one of the boxes, I would know from (a) what I saw in that box, plus (b) God's assurance, what beetles in general were; but if I lacked anything doing the job of God's assurance, what I saw in one box would tell me nothing about what beetles were. One could not say there must be something in common between this and other beetles: that would introduce something doing the job of God's assurance. Even to assume that a beetle was some kind of material object because there was one in my box, or some kind of mark on the bottom of the box because my box had such a mark, would be to allow something these people *say* they cannot know. (For that matter, if they did not know what a beetle was, then even if the box only contained a mark on the bottom, they would not know that the mark was their beetle.)

ii) It is not clear in what sense they can know what a beetle is, or even what *this* beetle is, if they cannot say; and yet there is a fairly clear implication that these people *cannot* say, in the fact that (they say) they only know from their own case. If they could say what their beetle is, they would know about other people's beetles from what they said. 'Mine is round and gold-coloured'. Now you know something about my beetle, unless, that is, we suppose either that these people are a shifty lot, or that there is some reason to be sceptical about whether they use the words 'round' and 'gold-coloured' in the usual way; but we could find out if they were shifty or used words eccentrically.

iii) There might be an off-beat sense of 'to know what a beetle is' – a sense like the sense in which we know what 'having' is when we know that one can 'have' money, debts, an empty till, a broken leg or a toothache. However for this sense we would have to know that my beetle was round and gold-coloured, yours a red squiggle and his an acrid smell; and this is what these people say they cannot know.

Here we have three reasons, in addition to those Wittgenstein offered in §§246 and 295, for doubting whether what these people say about their knowledge of beetles is even intelligible; but in raising these doubts, I have in no way relied on supposed peculiarities of beetle boxes. It was entirely on the basis of what Wittgenstein supposed them *saying* that I drew the conclusions that they could draw no inference from what they saw in their own box about what a beetle was, or that they would have no reason for saying this or that in their box was a beetle, and so on. This can serve as a model for how we can manage in our deliberations about this passage without making any suppositions at all about the existence of a state of affairs such as to *justify* these people in saying they know only from their own beetle; indeed no state of affairs would justify them in saying something unintelligible.

2. Why does Wittgenstein say, as if adding a new feature to his example, 'But suppose the word "beetle" had a use in these people's language'? Has he not already described its use? What further feature is he suggesting? He is surely not supposing that it has *another* use, in the way the word 'beetle' in fact has an entomological use in English, because he goes on to say that it would not be used as the name of a thing. He is making an inference here, but he has not yet laid down any basis for this claim *other* than the use he has already described. It must be a use connected with what he has already said, otherwise he would have to stipulate, rather than infer, that it would not be used as the name of a thing.

There are perhaps two possibilities here. The first is that he was asking us to suppose that not only in their philosophical moments did these people say such things as that they know only from their own beetle what a beetle is, but also the word 'beetle' played a role in their day-to-day affairs – just as

English speakers use the word 'pain', and also philosophers say such things as that we know only from our own case what pain is.

If we consider the (then) parallel case of the relation between our pain language and our philosophical pronouncements about pain, we might notice that we describe and compare our pains, and sympathise when we hear that someone is in pain – proceeding, that is, as if we knew something about what pain is. We regard ourselves as knowing from what other people say that pain is not necessarily jabbing, even if our own always jabs, it can also be throbbing or gnawing; we also regard ourselves as knowing whether another person has the same pain as ours from the fact that he says 'Mine jabs too'. If we are to resolve the apparent contradiction between this and our philosophical urge to say that we know what pain is only from our own case, something further will be needed. It will not help to suppose that we cannot trust other people, or that their use of words like 'jabbing' and 'throbbing' may be different from ours, because these are empirical hypotheses which, while they may be true in some cases, will not turn out to be true sufficiently generally for our purposes. But we *could* resolve the conflict by supposing that pain is *what* jabs or throbs, is in the shoulder or the tooth, and so on, and noting that no one ever describes the thing that *does* the jabbing. When you ask people what pain is, they may tell you that it is what is jabbing now, or what makes them moan so, or what they have when there is a cavity in a tooth; but they never say *what* jabs, *what* makes them moan, except to say that it is pain, which we already know.

This would be an interesting line of development, but there are at least three reasons for doubting whether it is the road intended. (a) We have not yet constructed an ordinary use for 'beetle', and it is not easy to see, from what we have seen so far, how such a use would run. (b) If we were to construct it, it would be on the analogy of ordinary pain language, and not as an inference from the description of the beetle box owners; whereas (c) Wittgenstein showed that he thought the use could be constructed just from the description of the case when he said the word 'beetle' *would* not be the name of a thing.

101

Hence perhaps it is preferable to suppose the suggestion to be that we should try to be specific about what the ordinary use of 'beetle' ought to be, given what beetle box owners say about beetles. One possibility is that they would use the word as we use the expression 'what is in your box', or 'the contents of your box'. Their 'I can't see your beetle' would come out in English 'I can't see what is in your box'. Their 'My beetle is red' would be unlike our 'My brooch is red', in that they would not, whereas we would, be saying *what* is was that was red. They would have some (to us) odd expressions, like 'My beetle is nothing just now'. They would say *that*, where we would say 'My box is empty just now'; but to us it would sound as if they were referring to a very different sort of object which, without ceasing to be, could sometimes be nothing. If in their language the noun 'beetle' was unusual in having this kind of role, and most of their nouns, like ours, were such that one could ask and say what a '——' is, they might hastily assume that one could also ask what a beetle is; and their philosophical puzzlement about beetles would express their despair over not being able to answer that question. We would not share their puzzlement, however, because we would right away see that the question what a *what is in your box* is, makes no sense. In the case in which what is in my box is a cockroach, there is a question what *that* is; but even in that case the expression 'what is in your box' does not *mean* a cockroach. One could say the expression points to a place, but is utterly indeterminate on what is there, or whether anything is.

The fact that this line of development can be built on the specifications of the example, together with the fact that it displays the use of 'beetle' as not the name of a thing, and also that in the following section Wittgenstein says 'Isn't it as if I were to say to someone: "He *has* something. But I do not know whether it is money or debts or an empty till" ' – provide strong confirmation that something like this is intended.

3. It is now easy to answer the question what it is here to be the name of a thing. It comes out when we see that, in the ordinary use I have constructed for the word 'beetle', whatever the box had in it, whether it was a cockroach, a mark on the bottom or an acrid smell, 'beetle' would not be the name of that thing. A 'thing' therefore is whatever could bear a name,

The Beetle Box

be it a physical object, a smell or an empty space.

4. The analogy was no doubt supposed to show something about pain, but it is not yet clear what is analogous to this in pain language, or in philosophical deliberations about pain. There are two broad possibilities about the intended application: (a) that Wittgenstein is suggesting that 'pain' is not the name of anything, but has a use like that of the expression 'what is in your box', and that since the word is rather unusual among nouns in having that function, we make the mistake of pressing the question what a pain is, as we might press the question what a car or a tree is. There is of course no answer, and when we realise this we are driven to say incoherent things, such as that we know only from our own case what pain is. (b) The other possibility is that §293 says nothing about ordinary pain language, but is entirely a commentary on the things we say philosophically about pain: in particular a suggestion that they lead to the absurd result that one can 'divide through' by what is in the box.

a) There is not much case for saying that the word 'pain' has a use like the expression 'what is in your box'. When we talk non-philosophically about pains it does not at all seem to us that the word 'pain' as it were points to a place, but gives no indication what is there, or whether anything is. We are often in no doubt that someone has a pain; it is sometimes quite clear that his pain is the same as ours, or different; and it does not appear to us at all that pain is something mysterious or indescribable, and that we can have no grip at all on the question whether mine is the same as yours. Hence Wittgenstein at least ought not to have been making his claim about the ordinary use of the word 'pain', but rather about the ordinary use it would have, given some of the things we are inclined to say about it when we think philosophically. We say we know what pain is only from our own case, and if this were reflected in our use, we would not ask about pains, describe them and draw conclusions about whether they are like or unlike our own, and it might seem to us that 'pain' was a funny word, that should not be a noun, because as a noun it seems to say what is there, while in fact all it does is point to a place where there may be anything or nothing.

b) We may thus do better to explore the second possibility, according to which Wittgenstein is offering it as an *objection*

103

to the things we say philosophically, that given them, the ordinary use of the word 'pain' would not be to name something, and we can 'divide through' by the thing in the box. It does seem absurd, in the case of pain, that what we feel should drop out as irrelevant; but there is a grave difficulty for this line of interpretation when we come to the end of the section, where Wittgenstein says 'That is to say: if we construe the grammar of the expression of sensation on the model of "object and designation" [It surely should be 'designator'] the object drops out of consideration as irrelevant'. The difficulty is that it is not by doing *that* that we have driven the beetle box theorists to an absurd result, but rather by building their grammar on the model of a word pointing to a place.

There is a way out of this difficulty, whether or not it will seem contrived or over-subtle. We do not need to cast the actual use of pain language on any model at all. We can describe it, and perhaps recognise its affinities to object and name language, and also its differences. It is like that language in that in both, descriptive adjectives modify nouns; in both we accept the adjectives as informing us of the properties or character of something, and in both, the expression 'the same' and 'different' have an application. It is unlike object and name language in that while we can talk of encountering the very same dog on different days, we cannot in the same sense have the very same pain (as if in the meantime it had been somewhere); we can paint a red car green and move it to Holland without its being a different car, but a pain cannot change from dull to sharp or from the shoulder to the hip and be the same pain; my house can become yours, but if my headache goes away and you get one, it cannot be my headache you have – not because everyone starts with a fresh headache and used ones are carried off by the wind, but because what throbs is not, apart from its throbbing, something that could do other things, go other places. *Things* can change properties, locations and so on, and remain the same thing, but pains cannot; and that is what is meant by saying that the word 'pain' is not the name of a thing.

I made a point of saying earlier, that the grammar of 'pain' is 'object and name' – like to a degree, and that is important; but we now see that it is not 'object and name' *simpliciter*. It is by forcing it into that mould that our philosophical difficulties arise; but we are making as big a mistake if we therefore shift to an *entirely* different model.

We do not need to take Wittgenstein here to be rejecting every kind of object and name relationship. In §244 he registered no scepticism about whether a connection between a name and a sensation was set up; and if, as is likely, in the present section he regarded it as absurd, in the case of pain, that the object should drop out as irrelevant, we can infer that he thought there was an object, and that it was the object to which the word 'pain' refers. His point would have been clearer if he had said something like 'If we construe the grammar of the expression of sensation on *the typical model* of "object and designator" . . .', but he never went out of his way to make things easy for us; and we do not have to proceed very far on our own from where the end of this section leaves us, to see that if we do not want the object to drop out of consideration as irrelevant, we will need to construe the grammar on *some* 'object and designator' model, if not the typical one.

Twelve

THE PICTURE POT

296. 'Yes, but there is *something* there all the same accompanying my cry of pain. And it is on account of that that I utter it. And this something is what is important – and frightful'. – Only whom are you informing of this, and on what occasion?

297. Of course, if water boils in a pot, steam comes out of the pot and also pictured steam comes out of the pictured pot. But what if one insisted on saying that there must be something boiling in the picture of the pot?

ON A HASTY reading Wittgenstein might be taken here to be saying that there is no more anything accompanying our cry of pain than there is water boiling in the picture of a pot with steam coming out. This would be a very madcap and almost certainly false claim, – unless it were read as an objection to the exact formulation, an objection perhaps to describing pain as 'something', or as 'accompanying' cries of pain. Wittgenstein does elswhere (§304) object to conceiving pain as '*a* something', and he might well object to the idea that it exactly *accompanies* cries of pain; but there is presumably a difference between being 'something' and being 'a something'; and there is nothing in these sections that even hints that there is an objection to the formulation. On the contrary, Wittgenstein seems to be agreeing that there is something right about saying there is something accompanying my cry of pain – when he says '*only* whom am I informing of this'. 'Only' is used there in the way we use the words 'yes, but ...' – to concede what was said, while going on to object to something else – the significance of it, or its relevance.

If there is any suspicion remaining that Wittgenstein denies that there is pain as well as pain-behaviour, it is put to

106

rest in §304, where he says there could be no greater difference than that between pain-behaviour accompanied and not accompanied by pain.

Then what is going on here? What are we supposed to take from these sections?

It is important to notice first that in §297 we have both water boiling in pots, and picture pots with picture steam. The analogue of the former is perhaps a person (the pot) feeling pain (the water) and crying out (the steam); of the latter it will perhaps not make much difference whether we say that the analogue is our noticing a person crying in pain, or our describing him as crying in pain.

The person who says, either of someone crying out pitifully, or of someone described as so crying, 'That man is in pain', is like the man who says of the picture pot with steam coming out 'There is water in that pot', and is doing something to which Wittgenstein takes exception. The objection we have seen, is not that what he says is false, but then what is the trouble? The only lead we have is in the question 'only whom are we informing of this, and on what occasion?' It will make a difference whether we read these as rhetorical questions, the indicated answers to which are 'No one, and on no occasion', or as having as answers some person and some occasion which we are left to specify ourselves. If the questions are rhetorical, we would have reason to suppose Wittgenstein was saying that it is true but uninteresting that there is pain accompanying a cry of pain, comparable perhaps to saying of someone alive that his blood is circulating or that he is breathing. In ordinary circumstances it would come as no surprise whatever that there is something accompanying cries of pain, and a person who earnestly went about reminding us that there would be a figure of fun. That is no doubt part of Wittgenstein's point: the laughable things we find ourselves earnestly saying when we are bound up in philosophical puzzlement.

However if that were all he wanted to say, the picture pot metaphor would be substantially wasted. Hence we should perhaps consider the question, is there anyone on any occasion whom we might inform that there is something accompanying people's cries of pain? The answer that will be suggested is yes, if we were teaching someone pain language.

The elaboration and justification of this answer will take us rather far afield, but we will return eventually to picture pots.

People do not usually learn pain language by being taught, but if we were to teach it, we might say: 'When people cry out as this man is doing, that is one of the cases when we say they are "in pain". Saying that however does not *mean* that they are crying out. We are adverting to something accompanying that kind of behaviour, which we call "a pain". Pains have a bodily location, are disagreeable, last over a stretch of time, have some intensity or other, and can be shooting, jabbing, gnawing, leaden, throbbing; but they are not physical things – not like tumours or gall stones, or even like wounds. They do not have weight, colour, taste, smell, and they cannot be removed by surgery or healed by medication. When you see someone crying out like that, you can ask where the pain is, how long he has had it, how bad it is and whether it jabs or gnaws or what, but there is no use looking for it or feeling for it. It may be *where* there is a lump or a cut, but it is not the lump or the cut'.

Here one would have said a number of things that have very much the ring of necessary truths: nothing is a pain if it has not a bodily location, is not disagreeable, does not have an intensity; or if it has a colour, a weight, a shape. Are we thereby informing the language-learner of the existence of something?

i) If we are so informing him, it is an atypical way of doing so. For that we do not generally say what properties a thing necessarily has, but what properties it in fact has. I may say there is a red flower with six petals in my garden, but hardly that there is something necessarily gaily coloured and necessarily having some number of petals (if those would be necessary truths about flowers).

ii) What we did was rather more like saying which of the things he knows exists is a pain, than informing him for the first time of the existence of pains.

iii) It is not true that whenever someone cries in pain, there is in fact a pain – unless we take 'cries in pain' to mean 'cries when he indeed has a pain', and then it is analytically true. In saying there is something accompanying cries of pain, we are not saying that people are so constituted that they cannot cry that way unless they have a pain, but saying what we are entitled to expect given a cry of pain. It is as if someone had said 'When there is a flag on my gate there will be a flower in my garden'. When he has said this there will not necessarily be a flower, but something will be amiss if there is not. On seeing the flag, we will not be making a mistake in expecting the flower, or enquiring about its properties.

The sufferer in §296 who did not want us to deny that there was something frightful was presumably not telling us something about himself personally, such as that he could not or would not sham pain; but what remains is that he is telling us what we are entitled to expect when he cries in pain.

We have now seen something right and something ridiculous about saying there is something there accompanying my cry of pain. Treated as part of a lesson in the grammar of the word 'pain', saying this is quite in order, but treated as information it is absurd, because it only repeats what we already know if we understand the grammar. It is similarly both right and wrong to say earnestly, pointing to the picture pot, 'There is water boiling in that pot'. The man who says this is right in that of course there would be water (or something) boiling in such a pot. It could hardly be a picture of steam coming out of an empty pot. He is wrong in that there is no water there, nothing but canvas and paint, or paper and silver nitrate.

He is like the man who reads a story in which we come upon two people playing chess, and says 'This game must have had a beginning'. It is not the story of two people pretending to play chess, and therefore *of course* their game had a beginning; and yet the story contains no account of the beginning, and it being a story only, there is no *other* instantiation that the start of the game could have had. In this sense the game had no beginning (*PI* §365).

Or again he is like the man looking at a picture of a peasant sitting in front of a cottage and wondering if the peasant owns the cottage. The man who posed for the picture might in fact have been the owner, or the artist might have depicted him as the owner; but the picture peasant could no more own the picture cottage than go inside it or burn it down (*PI* §398).

In all these cases there is something right and something wrong, and about what is right we can say 'of course'. There is no new information provided, nothing we might not have suspected. We are reciting what everyone knows, and not *facts* we are all apprised of, but connections: what one may expect or can look for. We are milking the concept of a game when we say that the game we found Adelheid and the Bishop playing had a beginning, and we are milking the concept of pain when we say that, if you see someone crying in such and such a way, you are entitled to suppose he has a pain. If it turns out that you were wrong, you can charge him with faking.

On this reading, Wittgenstein has engagingly used the picture pot metaphor as a way of bringing out what we may call the flip-flop character of certain propositions, which sound as if they told us something about the world, while in fact they only record features of our grammar. Having the latter function, there is something right about these propositions, and so we are drawn to them; but if we do not realise that they are grammatical truths, then taking them anyway to be true, we will construct pictures of the states of affairs that we suppose make them true.

There is something right about 'Only you can know if you had that intention', and recognising this we paint a picture of intentions as being present to the mind of intenders, but hidden from everyone else. Yet nothing of which a person is conscious when he has an intention is his intention and, according to Wittgenstein, the proposition 'Only you can know if you had that intention' expresses some feature or features of the use of the word 'intend' (*PI* §247).

There is a problem however about nearly all Wittgenstein's examples of this turn of thought, and this proposition about intending illustrates it as well as any. The problem is that 'Only you can know if you had that intention' does not itself have the form and style of grammatical proposition, and it requires some ingenuity to find some other proposition, which is clearly one about the use of the word 'intend', and of which we could say that 'Only you can know . . . etc.' is a crude expression.

To fill this bill I somewhat hesitantly suggest the following: 'We use the word "intend" in contexts in which we recognise another person's right to decide'. Illustrations of this might be that a sergeant may say to a private 'You are going on a route march today', but he could not, except as a joke, say 'You are intending to go on a route march'; and if he asks 'Are you intending to do such and such?', he is not facing up to the inaccessibility of the private's intentions, but rather according him the right to decide.

Whether or not Wittgenstein had this point in mind, we can see it as a possible point about the use of 'intend', and as one which could be expressed, albeit crudely, by saying 'Only you can know if you intend'. Thus it is an example that might at least illustrate how his thinking might be running.

It is even more difficult to fill the bill in the case of 'Sensations are private' in §248. In inviting us to compare this proposition with 'One plays patience with oneself', Wittgenstein presumably means to suggest that just as we do not call a game patience if more than one person plays it, we do not call anything a sensation if it is public; but whereas there are games played by two or more people and others played alone, there is nothing that may be either private or public, and is called a sensation when it is private. Hence, although 'We do not call anything a sensation if it is public' is a grammatical proposition that might be what we are expressing crudely with the words 'Sensations are private', it appears to be an unacceptable grammatical proposition.

A better candidate might be what Wittgenstein said in Z §134: '... in the use of the word "sensation" there is no such thing as exhibiting what one has got'. This would mean that 'Show me your sensation' is not an allowable construction – and not because we all find ourselves incapable of such exhibiting, but because we make no sense of the *project* of exhibiting our sensations.

Wittgenstein might appear to be contradicting his *Zettel* remark in *PI* §313 when he says 'I can exhibit pain, as I exhibit red, and as I exhibit straight and crooked and trees and stones'. He perhaps has in mind pricking someone with a pin and saying 'See, that's what pain is!' (§288); but clearly here one would not be exhibiting the pain one has, but just pain; and if there are ways of exhibiting the particular kind of pain I have, for example gnawing pain, one would still not be exhibiting one's own gnawing pain. That makes no sense.

The difficulty I have been illustrating, of finding a clear grammatical proposition having the requisite flip-flop character, is just the difficulty that arose at the beginning of this chapter, with the remark that there is something there accompanying my cry of pain; and in particular cases it may make the suggestion that someone is confused in this way an ineffective device, difficult to sustain. It can sometimes be an effective point, however, for example in the case of 'Another person can't have my pains' (§253). This is false if it is supposed to mean that you and I cannot both have jabbing pains in the shoulder, but it is true in a sense if it means that another person can't have this particular pain. What is right here is not that pains cannot migrate from one person to another, but that we have no concept of identity for pains, of such a kind that it would make sense to say, 'He now has my pain'. Pains are not like physical objects, of which we can be confronted with the very same one on different occasions, or a different but exactly similar one. It makes sense to say 'This chair is exactly the same as the one you sat on yesterday, but it is not the same one', but not to say 'This pain is just the same as I had yesterday, but it is not the same pain' (§253). This is not because if it is indistinguishable then it is the same pain, but because we make no sense of the idea of a pain being the very same one, or not the same one either.

Thirteen

THE PICTURE AND
THE IMAGE OF PAIN

300. It is – we should like to say – not merely the picture of the behaviour that plays a part in the language-game with the words 'he is in pain', but also the picture of the pain. Or, not merely the paradigm of the behaviour, but also that of the pain. – It is a misunderstanding to say 'The picture of pain enters into the language-game with the word "pain".' The image of pain is not a picture and *this* image is not replaceable in the language-game by anything that we should call a picture. – The image of pain certainly enters into the language-game in a sense; not only as a picture.

301. An image is not a picture, but a picture can correspond to it.

THERE ARE many dark passages in the *Philosophical Investigations*, but few as dark as those above. What distinction is intended here between an image and a picture? Can we credit the idea of there being *either* an image or a picture of *pain*? What could be meant by saying that the image of pain enters into the language-game with the word 'pain'?

We could begin with the third of these questions, which divides into two: what is it in general to 'enter a certain language-game'; and in what sense can the image of pain do this?

Since Wittgenstein neither explains the expression 'to enter a language-game' nor uses it often enough to enable us to sleuth out what it means, one can only guess; but clearly there would be a difference depending on whether it was the image of pain or the expression, 'the image of pain' that did this:

1. In the former case 'entering the language-game' might mean something like 'being as a matter of fact something that has to go on when the language-game is played'. If it were a

psychological fact that the word 'pain' seemed just a noise to people until they experienced an image of pain, and the image showed them the meaning of the word, that would be one illustration of this possible sense. It is quite clear however from, for example, §§6, 449 and 450 that Wittgenstein did not think either pictures or images entered language-games in this sense.

2. If 'the language-game with the word . . . ' includes the various ways the word is used, the various grammatical constructions with the word, then 'to enter the language-game with the word . . .' might mean 'to be one of the ways that word is used'. Then to say 'the image of pain enters the language-game' would be to say that we do have uses for the expression 'the image of pain'. If this is what Wittgenstein meant, he would certainly have been better to say 'The expression, "the image of pain" enters . . .', but since he was not always careful in that way, that is not a strong point.

Since it is false that the expression 'the image of pain' is used, it would be preferable not to have to attribute to him the view that it *is* used; but there are no other very obvious objections to this second interpretation; and if we distinguish between the general interpretation of 'entering the language-game' and its application in particular cases, we may find in the end that we can accept the former without attributing this application to Wittgenstein, and thus remove the only clear obstacle to this interpretation.

The hardest question about §§300 and 301 is what distinction can be intended between 'the picture' and 'the image' of pain? When Wittgenstein says 'The image of pain is not a picture', and 'The image of pain certainly enters into the language-game in a sense; only not as a picture', he certainly seems to be making a distinction between an image and a picture; but he does not explain what it is; and it is peculiarly difficult to guess what it might be, when one would not have thought there could be either an image or a picture of *pain*, as distinct perhaps from *people in pain* – of which, in any ordinary sense, there could be both pictures and images.

In the most familiar sense of these words, an image would be something like a reflection in water or in a mirror, while a picture would be something like a photograph or a painting; yet there seems no very interesting difference between pictures and images in those senses. While some images may be more detailed or have truer colours than some pictures, the converse is also true, and in general there seems little to choose between pictures and images in this regard. There are some differences that could be significant in some contexts: pictures can be schematic or impressionistic, while images can scarcely be either; pictures can be moved about, turned over or cut into pieces, while it is not clear whether, when we move or break a mirror, we are moving or breaking a mirror image; and pictures fix a scene, while images can change as the scene changes. However, since we could hardly have *that kind* of a picture or image of a pain (as distinct from a sufferer), these differences are unlikely to be significant.

Philosophers sometimes use the words 'picture' and 'image' in a non-visual sense, such that there can be 'images' of smells, flavours and sounds. These will generally be mental likenesses, supposed to exist for example when we remember or imagine the taste of beer or the sound of a clarinet. Wittgenstein was not in general sceptical about whether there could be such likenesses, but when likenesses were not visual he did not call them pictures or images; and when they were visual he drew no distinction between pictures and images.

It is possible that in §§300 and 301, if not elsewhere, he meant by 'image' a mental likeness, and by 'picture' a physical likeness; but elsewhere he does not make that distinction in that way (*BB* 36, 53; *PI* §§139, 663); and if this were the intended distinction, he would come out as admitting that there could be mental likenesses of pain, and denying that there could be physical likenesses. The latter hardly needs saying; while he can be seen as denying the former in §302: '. . . this is none too easy a thing to do: for I have to imagine pain which I *do not feel* on the model of pain which I *do feel*'. The pain that I do feel hurts, while the likeness of pain that I may have before my mind does not. I do not wince when I imagine pain, or if I do, it is not the pain likeness I am entertaining that makes me wince. I may wince as a routine part of depicting suffering, not because I am in fact suffering. However what I have before my mind can hardly be a likeness of pain if it does not hurt.

I have now tried all the ready-to-hand ways of making sense

115

of a distinction between images and pictures of pain, and they have failed. Hence there is a case for considering more radical measures.

The word 'image' is clearly at the heart of the trouble. It is Miss Anscombe's way of translating the German *Vorstellung*. That word is sometimes correctly translated 'image', but there are other available translations we might try. An illustration of one of these is in §367: '*Das Vorstellungsbild ist das Bild, das beschreiben wird, wenn Einer seine Vorstellung beschreibt.*' – 'The mental picture is the picture which is described when someone describes what he imagines.' Here *seine Vorstellung* is quite properly translated 'what he imagines'. This is not just a stylistic variant of 'his image'. If we are inclined to think that necessarily what is imagined is an image, the two expressions would be interchangeable; but we do not use them in the same way. If we are asked what we imagined, we do not say 'An image of such and such', but rather perhaps 'I imagined him approaching her bashfully and saying . . .'; and if it turns out that we did not have an image of this, it does not follow that we did not imagine it. To say we imagined it is not to say we had an image of it, but might be to say that we put it forward under imaginative auspices, that is, as being an interesting fancy, whether or not it is true.

'What he imagines' here is what he puts forward under imaginative auspices; and given that sense, we can make something interesting out of the otherwise curiously flat or trite §367. It will mean something like 'When we say what we imagined [for example when we say "he approached her bashfully and said . . ."] we are painting an imaginative picture'. On this reading the description is not read off from the mental image, but the production of it as a creative act, done under imaginative auspices. To get this reading, (a) for 'describe' I wrote 'paint' that is, I took 'describe' to be used in a sense like its geometrical sense, and (b) for 'mental picture' I wrote 'imaginative picture'.*

---

* One might compare §367 with §560, which has a strikingly similar structure: ' "The meaning of a word is what is explained by the explanation of meaning".' Again an apparently flat and trite remark, out of which Wittgenstein presumably thinks something interesting can be made.

I can now suggest how expressions like 'what is imagined', so used that they stand in, not for an image, but for some imaginative description, can be fed into §§300 and 301 in the place of the word 'image'.

The sentence 'The image of pain is not a picture and this image is not replaceable in the language-game by anything we should call a picture' will read 'What is imagined when we imagine pain is not a picture [or more economically 'We do not imagine pain in pictures'] and this imagining is not replaceable by a picture [although some imagining is]'.

The sentence 'The image of pain certainly enters into the language-game in a sense; only not as a picture' will come out 'There is such a thing as imagining pain [or: 'the expression "to imagine pain" has a use'], only it is not done in pictures'. The sentence 'An image is not a picture, but a picture can correspond to it' will read 'To imagine is not to picture, but we can sometimes illustrate what we imagine with a picture'.

Clearly we have to be a little unmechanical in our translation here, but we are taking no great liberties with the language, and the result is both Wittgensteinian and intelligible, whereas what we had before was utterly baffling and (though not perhaps for that reason) the last thing one would expect Wittgenstein to say.

The point is primarily about imagining, not about pain; and while it might have considerable intrinsic interest if it was elaborated further and substantiated, I will not embark on that project because doing so would not be essential to relieving bafflement, for example, how there can be either an image or a picture of pain. Wittgenstein does not mean to imply that there can be either an image or a picture of pain. He is only saying that we can imagine someone in pain without picturing anything.

The reading proposed can be shown to be consistent with other things Wittgenstein says in at least the following ways:

1. I have him denying that there can be either an image or a picture of pain (the troublesome distinction between images and pictures disappears), but not denying that pain can be imagined. This parallels a move he makes in §306, five sections later, with regard to remembering. There he points out that anyone who is disposed to think that remembering is a mental process will take a denial that there is such a process

to be a denial that anyone remembers, but says that he can deny the former without denying the latter, by severing the supposed connection between the two. He similarly denies that we can have an image (or picture) of pain without denying that we can imagine it, by saying that to imagine is not to picture.

2. That he thinks we can imagine pain, and can do it without the help of anything picturable like pain behaviour is moderately clear from §393, where Wittgenstein is not in the least sceptical whether we can imagine that a person who is laughing is really in pain, but where he rules out doing this by picturing pain behaviour, because the laughter specified in the example is supposed to exclude pain behaviour. Here indeed we *might* take him to be arguing that since the behaviour cannot be pictured, there is nothing left to picture but the pain, but such a view would be extremely uncharacteristic, whereas it is not surprising at all to have him saying that we can imagine without doing any picturing, or indeed anything else.

Further development of the conception of imagining that has been sketched here will be found in chapter 15.

Fourteen

ON BEING 'A SOMETHING'

'But you will surely admit that there is a difference
between pain-behaviour accompanied by pain and pain-
behaviour without any pain?' – Admit it? What greater
difference could there be? – And yet you again and again
reach the conclusion that the sensation itself is a *nothing*.
– Not at all. It is not a *something*, but not a nothing either!
The conclusion was only that a nothing would serve just
as well as a something about which nothing could be
said. We have only rejected the grammar which tries to
force itself on us here. (*PI* §304)

It positively seems to us as if pain had a body, as if it
were a thing, a body with shape and colour. Why? Has it
the shape of the part of the body that hurts? One would
like to say for example 'I could *describe* the pain if I only
had the necessary words and elementary meanings'. One
feels: all that is lacking is the requisite nomenclature.
(James.) As if one could even paint the sensation, if only
other people would understand this language. (Z §482)

THE REMARK that pain is not a something, but not a
nothing either is one of the many Wittgensteinian offerings
that make us sigh and pass on, hoping perhaps that someday
these mysteries will be resolved, or anyway that there will be
other things that prove less bewildering, and reward the
fearful struggle to understand. It seems perplexing how anything can be neither a something nor a nothing. One might
have thought that something and nothing exhaust all the
alternatives; and one stands trembling at the gate of the un-
written metaphysics in which there is anything in between.

Although Z §482 clearly expresses a similar thought, it
does not prove to be much help, partly because most of us
could honestly plead not guilty to the charge of regarding

pains as having bodies, especially bodies with shape and colour; and partly because Wittgenstein asks but fails to answer the question why pain would appear that way to anyone. We would *not* say that pain has the shape of the elbow or the appendix that hurts; and the fact that we say we lack the nomenclature for describing pain is at least not self-evidently connected with whether we think of it as having a body.

Let me begin by describing what it might be to regard pain as a something, as having a body. Suppose there was a tradition in a certain community of regarding the world as being populated, among other things, by blobs of an odious material that was presumed to be gaseous, but the exact nature of which was regarded as a matter for advanced study. The tradition was clear, however, on various points: that these blobs, while they could linger anywhere, had a predisposition to reside in sentient beings; that while they may disintegrate, they would otherwise retain their identity, and two of them would no more meld together to become a larger or different blob than would two people; and that blobs, while they might at times relax and not do much of anything, were generally busy things: they shot about, jabbed and gnawed, and they could spread themselves out like a jellyfish and pulse, or make themselves compact for streaking and jabbing. On other points there was disagreement. Some people believed that blobs could survive for a very long time, and that it was possible that one of them that had ached in John Locke's stomach should now be afflicting my shoulder – while others thought they were created anew all the time: everyone started with a fresh one, and when one of them was ousted from the body its composition was so affected that it could no longer take up residence in another sentient being.

Some of these people would be very careful to keep clear of anyone who had recently taken aspirin, for fear that the blob that had lain in his head might, on being evicted, move to their head, or perhaps foot. If a man was standing in a crowd when his headache went away, it would not surprise these people if as it went one person after another could be seen wincing.

If a disagreement arose among them about whether you could have my blob, it would be treated as a disagreement about the characteristics of blobs – about whether everyone started with a fresh one, and they were for some reason incapable of migrating; and they would take the assertion 'I have had the same blob for a week now' to mean that the blob I began with has not left and been replaced with another or a series of others very like it. If anything like this is what it is to conceive pain as a something, clearly we do not so conceive it; and since we obviously do not conceive this awful torment as a nothing either, it is not after all so very mysterious what Wittgenstein could mean by saying that it is neither a something nor a nothing.

However, we are still a long way from understanding why Wittgenstein saw fit to attribute this remarkable error to us.

The following is a somewhat roundabout way of answering that question. When a person good-heartedly makes a philosophical assertion that Wittgenstein regards as nonsensical, the fact that the point was offered in all seriousness, together with the fact that, being nonsense, it cannot be shown to be *false*, makes for a peculiarly difficult problem of how to display its absurdity. One way of doing this is to describe a context in which the assertion would make a kind of sense, which context however is itself nonsensical. When it seems that, in order to maintain something one is inclined to say, one may have to accept a context which is clearly absurd, one's confidence in the proposition may be eroded, if not destroyed. (The transition from disguised to patent nonsense, *PI* §464.)

It is not clear whether this procedure is intended as an argument, or as a sort of therapy. To be an argument, it would perhaps have to take the form: 'To say this, you would have to say such and such; but the latter is absurd, and therefore so is the former'. Wittgenstein does not usually, and perhaps could not, represent his points as being so conclusive. Rather, we may suppose, he in effect says: 'I don't understand you. What you say would make a kind of sense if such and such, or if such and such, but I presume you would not care to say these further things. Do you see my difficulty?' – That is, he applies a kind of sceptical pressure to the assertion by showing the kind of step that might have to be taken to render it intelligible. He reckons that if, unable to accept his suggested implications, we can be set to work trying to supply a more acceptable context, we will find out for ourselves how difficult the task is, and thereby come to sense the peculiarity of what we wanted to say.

The suggestion then is that when Wittgenstein said it positively seems to us as if pain had a body, he was not so much alleging that anyone holds that view, as suggesting that he could make a kind of sense of various other things we say or accept, in the context of the absurd view that pains have bodies.

There is, when you think of it, an imposing list of things philosophers say or accept (or what comes to the same thing, as far as their meaningfulness is concerned, disagree with), that would make a kind of sense if pains were somethings. When, as most of us do at first, we readily accept the supposition that we might have no natural expression for sensations, but only have the sensation (*PI* §256), our supposition would make sense on the blob theory: there would be a blob there, with all its properties intact, that was prevented from affecting us by our having turned off our sensitivity to it. Similarly if we do not balk at the supposition that we might turn to stone and have the pain to go on (*PI* §§283, 288), a condition on which this would make sense would be if there were a blob there that could not make us miserable because for the time being we were not sentient.

To say I can't have your pains is as absurd as to say that I can only blush my blushes; but a condition on which it would not be absurd would be if, as on the blob theory, when it comes and goes it comes from somewhere and goes somewhere, but in fact never journeys from one person to another – as some of our blobbists believed.

There are various senses in which two people can have the same pain: if they both have jabbing pains in the chest, for example, or if they both have labour pains. When in the face of this, we doubt whether they can have the same pain, our doubt would make sense if it were a question of whether a single blob can be large enough to reach two bodies at the same time, or of whether it can leave one body and enter another, still retaining its odiousness (compare *PI* §253). When it seems to us that another person might enjoy or at least not mind what we find ghastly – that we do not know whether what another person finds ghastly is the same as what we do, this would make sense if the blobs had properties quite distinct from their effects on people, and so might affect different people differently.

When, in spite of the fact that we neither always disbelieve people nor find what they say unintelligible when they describe their pains as jabbing or leaden, we say we only know from our own case what pain is, that would make sense if we thought of the fact that it jabbed or lay heavily in the stomach as merely the current behaviour of something whose identity is constituted by other properties – if we thought of 'The pain jabs' as telling us nothing about *what* jabbed. The believers in blobs, you will remember, had only the sketchiest concept of the blobs themselves, and what they did have was handed down in the tradition. What they *knew* about blobs was confined to their effect on people. They jabbed, throbbed, and so on. It was a question for advanced study, *what* had those effects.

When we regard pain as indescribable, and wish we had the requisite nomenclature, that would similarly make sense if we made a distinction between the jabbing or the frightful-ness, and *what* jabs or is frightful, regarding the latter as what we must describe if we are to say what pain is. This distinc-tion is standard in the case of material things. If we say 'It swooped and buzzed and was most annoying', we can say what did these things and had this effect, – describe its hairy body, its wings and its mean little eyes. When we regard pain as indescribable, we may be expecting but not finding a corresponding description of a something that throbs, aches or is ghastly.

In these various ways, although of course we find the blob theorists laughable and do not believe that pain is a some-thing, features of our philosophical thinking would make a kind of sense, and also paradoxically would be revealed as nonsense, if we were supposing pain to be a kind of some-thing with defining properties distinct from its current states or behaviour, and an identity through time. We can ask wha swoops, dives and is annoying, or what a mosquito is; an similarly we want to know what is in the shoulder, jabs and i frightful, or what pain is. We are thus treating pain on th analogy of a something, and it is from thence that most of ou philosophical perplexity about it arises.

Why do we do this, when we would immediately reject the idea that it is a something, at least in any sense like that illustrated by the tale of the blobbists? — No doubt partly because 'pain' is a noun, and generally nouns name objects having defining characteristics and an identity through time. If 'X' is a noun, there will normally be an answer to the question 'What are Xes?' — so we expect there will be an answer to the question 'What is pain?' Not that we *reflect* on the fact that 'pain' is a noun, and reason that there should therefore be an answer to the question what it is: we are just in the habit of asking and being told what an X is, and go right on to ask what a pain is.

There must be more to it than that, however, because there are answers to that question. We can say that a pain is a disagreeable sensation, having a bodily location, usually connected with a bodily disorder, lasting over some stretch of time, and variously throbbing, jabbing, gnawing, leaden and so on. These things represent a good deal we can say about pains: why do they not satisfy us? How do we ever come to say that pain is indescribable, and that if anyone were to contrive a language in which to record its properties, other people would not understand it?

The words with which we just now described pain can all seem non-essential, as if we explained what a bicycle is by saying that it can be seen on streets and in garages, comes in various sizes, styles and colours, is sometimes in good and sometimes in bad repair, and so on. Here we have omitted to say *what* it is, of which all these things are true; and we can similarly seem to have omitted to say what is frightful, has a bodily location, can jab, gnaw or be leaden and so on. If there is nothing we can say about pain that cannot be seen as merely describing its current behaviour, its connections with other things or our attitudes to it, the pain itself will seem indescribable.

Here we are already in the grip of the idea of it as a something. It is characteristic of somethings that they have essential and non-essential properties. If a contrivance has more or less than two wheels or is designed for other than human propulsion, it is not a bicycle; but it need not be capable of rusting, be any particular colour, or be kept in any particular place. In applying the essential/non-essential dis-

tinction to pains, we are assuming that they are like somethings in this regard.

We may also be doing this in treating having a bodily
location or jabbing and throbbing as non-essential to pain.
Comparable properties are non-essential to somethings.
Knuckles, pencils, marlin spikes and swords can jab, and
hence we do little to define anything by saying that it jabs. We
thereby distinguish it from pillows and floors, but leave it
entirely open whether it is a curtain rod or a car key. Similarly
having a location does not distinguish bicycles from trees,
elbows or planets, and being usually kept in a garage does not
distinguish them from cars, lawn mowers or bags of fertilizer.

Pains, however, are rather unusual amongst things that
have no weight, thickness, smell, taste or colour in having a
bodily location, and are thereby distinguished from
memories, sorrows, fears, thoughts, beliefs – if not from itches
and pulsing sensations.

Similarly being abhorrent is not something that happens to
be true of pain, as if our bodily constitution, while it did not
give us all the same taste in music or food, did happen to give
us all the same taste in sensations. We can say 'I dislike
oysters', but not 'I dislike pain' – not because no one has ever
been known to like it, but because we would not call anything
a pain that was not in some degree distasteful. We do not
know what to say about masochists. Do they enjoy pain, or for
some reason does it please them to suffer? Would they enjoy
themselves if they were not in pain, really suffering? That is a
problem for us just because we treat it as essential to pain that
it should be disagreeable, and therefore we do not know what
to do with an apparent counter-example.

Again, if a person was mystified when asked if his pain
jabbed, throbbed or was leaden – as he might properly be
when asked if his belief jabbed – that would show that he did
not understand the concept of pain. We come to think of pain
as indescribable through treating the descriptions we give of
it as non-essential and, on the model of a something, looking
for essential properties, certain that they are there, but unable
to say what they are; but in fact it is essential to pain to have a
bodily location, to be disagreeable, and to be describable by
some or other of such adjectives as 'leaden', 'throbbing' or
'jabbing'. There is not an indescribable something that may or

may not jab and that we are unanimous in disliking: pain *is* a disagreeable jabbing in the shoulder or a disagreeable throbbing in the head.

Why then can we say 'I have had a most disagreeable pain'? Given what I have just said, that ought to mean something like 'I have had a most disagreeable disagreeableness', and that is an implication one would want to avoid. The answer is not difficult. In saying that pain is necessarily disagreeable, I was giving the word 'disagreeable' a somewhat artificial sense. There does not happen to be an English word for the range of distastefulness that would include 'bearable', 'nasty', 'frightful' and 'excruciating', but I co-opted the word 'disagreeable' to indicate that range – and then inevitably encountered a conflict with its normal use, which covers, not the whole range, but a stretch somewhere in the middle-to-lower reaches of it. Had there been a word that stood to 'nasty' and 'frighful' as 'coloured' stands to 'green' and 'pink', or had we assigned that role to a newly coined word, there would not be a problem.

The metaphysically-minded might wish at this point to reach some conclusion about what sort of an ingredient of the world pain is, if it is not a something, and emphatically not a nothing either. My deliberations so far have had no metaphysical purpose. I have not been *contesting* the view that pains are somethings. I did not suppose anyone made that claim, and treated its absurdity as requiring no argument. However, if anyone felt he must assign pain a place in the scheme of things, it might seem fair enough to suggest that pains, rather than being somethings, are properties of something: that 'pain' is not a word like 'man', 'book' or 'planet', but like 'colour', 'shape' or 'weight'.

Certainly the weight of an object is neither a something nor a nothing. It does not have a shape, size, colour, or even a weight. There is no problem about how two things could have the same weight. We are not inclined to ask 'How could the same weight be in two different objects at the same time?', nor to answer that it could not – that two things can at most only have exactly similar weights. Yet weight is not a nothing either. Things do have weights.

Weight is a property, and clearly not a something. Pain is

not a something either, but is not therefore a property. Further considerations may be needed to decide about this; but the grammatical indications do not support the hypothesis:

i) 'Pain' is a noun, but prime property words are adjectives: 'red', 'round', 'heavy'.

ii) There are property nouns: 'colour', 'shape', 'weight', but 'pain' does not have the role these words have. We ask what colour something is, but not what pain it is; and it is a grammatical truth that red is a colour, but there is no corresponding truth of the form '——— is a pain'.

iii) 'Red', 'round' and 'heavy' are properties of *somethings*, but we would have to invent turns of speech in which pain was grammatically connected in the same way with somethings: 'My shoulder is empained', 'My tooth is enached', and so on. A jabbing pain in the shoulder would come out as the shoulder being jabbingly empained.

iv) We say 'Tom has a pain', and similarly 'The chair has a colour', but Tom does not *of course* have a pain, whereas the chair of course has a colour; and we can ask where Tom's pain is, but not where the chair's colour is.

v) We might contrive a concept like 'hedonic tone', such that, just as we can ask what colour something is and get the answer 'Red', we could ask what hedonic tone someone's shoulder was or had, and get the answer 'Painful'; but it would presumably be painful rather than pleasant, itchy or warm, and (a) we do not group these properties together the way we group pink, green and purple as colours, nor (b) is 'painful' used in contrast to 'itchy' or 'warm', but rather in contrast to 'bearable' or 'excruciating'.

I began with a hypothesis about what Wittgenstein might have meant by saying that pain was neither a something nor a nothing. The suggested interpretation was illuminating, in that it provided a way of showing in some detail how nearly all the philosophical perplexity about pain derives from construing the grammar of the words like 'pain' on a typical model of object and name. If there is any unifying thread in the sections of the *Philosophical Investigations* dealing with pain, it seems very likely this is it, and that it is not, for example, the question of the possibility of a private language.

The significance of the concluding deliberations, on the question 'If pain is not a something, is it perhaps a property?', is that we should be wary of moving from one disastrous grammatical model to another. 'Pain' has a distinctive grammar. It is neither an object word nor a property word, but it is more like the former than the latter. There is no telling what perplexities might arise if we all came to speak of shoulders as being jabbingly empained; but rather than inventing new ways of speaking, we will do best to accept the language we have, and protect ourselves from bewitchment by careful documentation of the ways in which it can confuse us.

Fifteen

HOW TO SOUND
DECEPTIVELY LIKE A BEHAVIOURIST

311. . . . But for the private exhibition you don't have to give yourself actual pain; it is enough to *imagine* it – for example you screw up your face a bit.

391. . . . And if I imagine [that people around me are in pain, and artfully concealing it] – what do I do; what do I say to myself; how do I look at the people? . . . I as it were play a part, *act* as if the others were in pain. When I do this I am said for example to be imagining. . . .

450. Knowing what someone looks like: being able to call up an image – but also: being able to mimic his expression. Need one imagine it in order to mimic it? and isn't mimicking it as good as imagining it?

451. Suppose I give someone the order 'Imagine a red circle here'. – and now I say: understanding the order means knowing what it is like for it to have been carried out – or even: being able to imagine what it is like. . . . ?

547. Negation: a 'mental activity'. Negate something and observe what you are doing. – Do you perhaps inwardly shake your head? – and if you do, is this process more deserving of our interest than, say, that of writing a sign of negation in a sentence?

Page 188. What is fear? What does 'being afraid' mean? If I wanted to define it at a *single* showing – I should *play-act* fear.

Page 219. This, however, is the queer thing: it seems as though I did not have to wait on the occasion, but could give myself an exhibition of it, even when it is not actually taking place. How? – I *act* it. – But *what* can I learn this way? What do I reproduce? – Characteristic accompaniments. Primarily: gestures, faces, tones of voice.

WITTGENSTEIN sometimes denied that he was a behaviourist, but often behaved as if he were, for example in the above passages from the *Philosophical Investigations*.

While one could be forgiven for taking anyone who said all these things to be a behaviourist, a closer look at any one of the passages will reveal complications, given which it is very much less clear that such an inference can be drawn.

There is, to begin with the first quotation, something incoherent about suggesting that one can give oneself a *private* exhibition by screwing up one's face a bit. That would be a public exhibition, unless what is meant by calling it private is that it is done when alone. But the alone/in company distinction is not generally the burden of Wittgenstein's use of the word 'private'.

This incoherence would be removed if we supposed that Wittgenstein was making a point in a somewhat, but neither atrociously nor untypically, oblique way here – the point namely that would emerge if the passage were rewritten in some such manner as the following:

> Someone: 'But for the private exhibition you don't have to give yourself actual pain; it is enough to imagine it'.
> Wittgenstein: 'But how do you do that? Surely not by screwing up your face a bit, for that is not private'.

We would then have screwing up the face *rejected* as a possible form of private exhibition; and the supposition that Wittgenstein means to reject it is confirmed by what he goes on to say. He gives two reasons for rejecting such behaviour altogether as a way of exhibiting pain:

> And do you know that what you are giving yourself an exhibition of is pain and not, for example, a facial expression? And how do you know what you are to give yourself an exhibition of before you do it?

There is a connection between grimacing and pain, but grimacing is not pain. One can be in pain and not grimace, or grimace and not be in pain. Certainly if one wanted to *pretend* to be in pain, grimacing would be as good a way as any; but only because we know the connection between it and pain. Hence Wittgenstein can be read as pointing to the role of our understanding of what pain is, an important theme that will be developed further in later passages.

There are two complications to be noted in the second

passage (§391). The first had to do with what the *acting* as if others were in pain consists of. Wittgenstein says 'Perhaps I look at one and think: "It must be difficult to laugh when one is in such pain", and much else of the same kind'. Here the *looking* is partly behaviour, but the *thinking* is either not or (since behaviourists claim otherwise) not so obviously behaviour as to support a behaviourist analysis of imagining.

The second complication is that although one might, certainly, *either* think or say such things as that it must be difficult to laugh when one is in such pain, still the question is, whichever one does, is doing it identical with imagining these people to be in pain? It can plausibly be argued, both that it is not, and that Wittgenstein recognised this.

We can perhaps see the non-identity best through a comparison of imagining that these people are in pain, and believing it. If I believed they were in pain, I might think: it must be difficult to laugh when one is in such pain; but the thinking here would not be identical with the believing. Believing this, I might go *on* to have that thought, amongst other things, and if you only knew what I had thought, you would not know whether I believed or was imagining that they were in pain.

It can be confusing here, that neither believing nor imagining is something *else* that happens. If they were, we could say 'Look, here is the believing (or imagining), and here is the thinking, and they are obviously different. They often occur at different times, and even if they occur simultaneously, there are two different things going on'. Not being *another* occurrence, we may think they must be the same occurrence; but if believing and imagining are not occurrences at all, while having such and such a thought *is*, it is impossible that the former should be the same occurrence as the latter.

But is imagining not an occurrence? The performance of a task is an occurrence, and imagining is task-like in that we can ask someone to imagine something, and he can agree or decline; but it is unlike an average task in that it is either not *done*, or it is done just by agreeing to the request. If I ask you to dig a hole, you may agree, and later dig or not dig, but if I ask you to imagine that the earth is flat, and you say 'All right, what then?', you have done it just by accepting my suggestion. There is nothing you must go on to do in order to comply; and if you say 'All right, what then?', I will not ask

'What! Have you done it so fast?', or probe into what exactly you have done. You may indeed have pictured a vast coin-shaped (or carpet-shaped) object majestically circling the sun, but you need not have done that or anything else; and in some cases, such as that described in §393, there is nothing you *could* picture. But it does not follow that you were assigned an impossible task.

If you agree to imagine that the earth is flat, you will not object when I go on to say for example, 'In that case we could come to the end of it', or 'In that case there would have to be a very surprising explanation of why we can't see things that are more than a few miles away, and can see further, the higher up we are', but these are *consequences* of the supposition we have made, not the supposing of it.

To derive these consequences, we must understand the idea of the earth being flat, but that is not something we *do*. If we understand it, we understand it timelessly, as much before the imagining incident arose as after.

That is a sketch of how it might be shown that what we do when we are imagining something is not the imagining of it. I said it could be argued, both that this is true, and that Wittgenstein would agree: let me turn now to the latter contention. Consider §393:

> 'When I imagine that someone who is laughing is really in pain, I
> don't imagine any pain behaviour, for I see just the opposite. So
> *what* do I imagine?' – I have already said what.

This passage seems intended to describe a case such as I mentioned above, in which it is impossible to produce a representation, but not therefore impossible to imagine. We may not *believe* that it is possible for someone to be laughing naturally, while still in (much) pain, but that is not the question. We can still imagine it, just as we can imagine a cow jumping over the moon, although we do not believe it could ever happen.

Where did Wittgenstein say *what* is imagined here? One might initially suppose that the words 'I have already said what' refer us back to §391, where he said 'Perhaps I look at one and think: "It must be difficult to laugh when one is in such pain"', but there is at the very least an awkwardness in that supposition: I did not *imagine* it must be difficult to laugh when one is in such pain. I *knew* that laughing is difficult when in pain, and thought it because I was imagining he was in pain. No, what I imagined was *that he was in pain*. That is the reference of the words 'I have already said what'.

That is an annoying answer however. One is inclined to rejoin testily 'We *know* that. What we wanted to know is what we produce by way of imagining that someone is in pain'. But since the case is clearly intended to be one in which nothing could be produced, it seems fair to take Wittgenstein's point to be that there is nothing we do by way of imagining this, but that it does not follow that we cannot imagine it. This would be a believable contention if, as I suggested, we can imagine something, not by doing anything, but by going along with the request that we so imagine (at least where we understand what we are asked to suppose).

There is a point that may still need to be added here. It was essential to my argument that in §393 Wittgenstein meant the case to be one in which no likeness of what is to be imagined is possible. It might however have been intended only to exclude picturing behaviour. We might still imagine the laughing person in pain by picturing his pain. On this see chapter 13, above.

When Wittgenstein said, in the section we are considering, 'When I do this [sc. act as if the others were in pain, by doing such things as looking at one of them and thinking it must be difficult to laugh etc.] I am said for example to be imagining . . .', must we not take him to mean that to act in that way *is* to imagine . . . ? No. If I pace the floor, look at my watch, set out cigarettes, and so on, I may be said to be expecting Sally for tea, but doing these things is not what it is to expect her. They are among the things that may happen when I am so expecting, but neither they nor anything else that happens is the expecting. I do not stop expecting her if for a time I become totally absorbed in a book or a crossword puzzle, and I do not expect her more fully if I also reread her letter, or think about the last time she was here (see also chapter 3).

I turn now to §450. Here it is important, and easily overlooked, that it is *being able* to call up an image, or to mimic, that is represented as knowing what someone looks like. This is easily overlooked because, for example, if we say 'If you can jump this hurdle I will give you a prize', we will likely mean

133

'if you *do* it'. We will not see ourselves as bound to award the prize if someone just shows us his ribbons and medals as evidence that he can do it. However, being able to do something is not doing it, or doing anything else either. It is true of us at times when we are neither doing such and such, nor anything remotely connected with it, that we can do it; and it is the ability, not the exercise of it, that Wittgenstein represents as knowing what someone looks like.

It is significant too, that he does not give any preference to mimicking over calling up an image, any more than in §391 he gave a preference to other ways of acting as if someone were in pain over thinking certain things. Both thinking and calling up images could perhaps be given behavioural analyses, but there is no reason to suspect that in fact Wittgenstein has such analyses in mind here.

Section 451 is interesting in other connections for its argument that if understanding an order means being able to imagine its being carried out, there will be a peculiar difficulty about the order to imagine something; but for our present purposes its main interest is somewhat different: whereas the contemplated analysis of understanding an order mentions its being carried out, that is, behaviour, there is even so no actual behaviour required, but only either knowing what it would be like for it to have been carried out or being able to imagine this; and further, following §450, being able to imagine it does not require actually imagining it, even if that were a kind of doing and thus a kind of behaviour.

We should not overlook the fact that in any case Wittgenstein seems to be *rejecting* these analyses of understanding an order. The argument is that, as an analysis of understanding an order, there is no great difference between 'knowing what it is like for it to have been carried out' and 'being able to imagine what it is like', but that the latter (and therefore the former) is awkward when the order is 'Imagine a red circle here'. It comes out as the order to imagine being able to imagine it, which in turn comes out as imagining being able to imagine being able to imagine it, and so on.

This twist lurks also in §547. While the (behavioural) writing of a negation sign is represented as just as deserving of our interest as the non-behavioural inward head-shaking, the point surely is that these are equally *undeserving*. We would hardly accept 'writing the negation sign' as an answer to the question what it is to negate – at least if it were supposed to be a philosophical question – rather than one asked by someone learning English. The philosophical question would perhaps be 'What action is symbolised by the negation sign?'

There are two complications to be noted in the remark about play-acting fear on page 188. The first is that it is only *if* he wanted to define it at a single showing that Wittgenstein says he would play-act it. That is a rather artificial demand, and we sometimes take rather desperate, though not completely useless, measures when confronted with such a demand. Play-acting fear might in appropriate circumstances serve its purpose, just as, when certain other things about the use of the word 'king' are clear, we can explain what a king is by pointing to one of the chess pieces (§31); or just as the meaning of a name can be explained sometimes by pointing to its bearer (§43), although the bearer is not the meaning.

The other complication is that Wittgenstein goes on to say: 'Could I also represent hope in this way? Hardly. And what about belief?' We are not flirting with behaviourism if we note that some words, to walk, to smile, to wince, are behavioural; and we are not fellow travellers if we recognise that 'to be afraid' resembles 'to wince' in this respect more than it does 'to know' or 'to imagine'. In going right on to say that he would hardly explain hope, and presumably belief either, in this way, Wittgenstein was only engaged in his typical practice of noting differences between the uses of various words.

The final passage on my list is also deceptive, but only slightly so. Although Wittgenstein says that one could exhibit the business of looking for the right word by acting it, in the first place he only says this *could* be done. He might have said, along the lines of his remark about explaining fear, that this would be a way of doing it at a single showing, and would not be the only, or necessarily the best way of doing it. More significantly however, he goes on to say that what we thereby reproduce is characteristic accompaniments. The characteristic accompaniments of X are not X itself; and although the accompaniments may be *all* one can exhibit, one is not thereby exhibiting what they accompany. Hence there is some similarity between Wittgenstein's thinking here and

what I claimed he was up to in §391: just as there is a differ-
ence between imagining someone to be in pain and imagin-
ing the various ways in which he may act if he is in pain, so
also there is a difference between the business of looking for
the right word, and its characteristic accompaniments, although of course there is a different *kind* of difference in the
two cases.

Wittgenstein is not more transparent when he is disavowing
behaviourism than when he is (mischievously?) sounding
like a behaviourist. Consider §308:

> How does the philosophical problem about mental processes
> and states and about behaviourism arise? – The first step is the
> one that altogether escapes notice. We talk of processes and
> states and leave their nature undecided. Sometime perhaps we
> shall know more about them – we think. But that is just what
> commits us to a particular way of looking at the matter. For we
> have a definite concept of what it means to learn to know a
> process better. (The decisive movement in the conjuring trick
> has been made, and it is the very one that we thought was quite
> innocent.) – And now the analogy which was to make us under-
> stand our thoughts falls to pieces. So we have to deny the yet
> uncomprehended process in the yet unexplored medium. And
> now it looks as if we had denied the mental processes. And
> naturally we don't want to deny them.

Here one can only guess what would be examples of 'talking of processes and states and leaving their nature undecided'; and we have to guess too, whether it is the nature of
processes and states in general that we think we will some-
time know more about, or the nature of particular supposed
states or processes. It is uncommonly hard to say what
definite concept we have of getting to know a process better,
or in what way the analogy that was to make us understand
our thoughts fall to pieces.
There might be various answers to such questions about
this passage, but the following is a composition out of a set of
answers that may be found believable: We ask for example,
'What kind of a something (a process, perhaps, or a state) is
remembering (or believing or imagining or . . .)?' [Talking of
states and processes, and leaving their nature undecided.] It
seems hard to say, but we feel *that* is the question, and that if
we work on it perceptively we may some day find out. [Some-

time perhaps we shall know more about them.] We must examine what happens when we remember (or believe or imagine or . . .). [A definite concept of what it means to learn to know a process better.] When we do this, the results are disappointing. Sometimes there seems to be no process (or state or . . .), and when there is a process, we find we do not call it remembering. [The analogy falls to pieces.] If we have been looking for a mental process (or state), and get this disappointing result, we will deny that remembering (or . . .) is a mental process, even though, it not being clear what it would like for it to be such, it is not clear what we are denying. [The yet uncomprehended process in the yet unexplored medium.] But here the emphasis will be on whether it is mental, not whether it is a process, and we will be driven to suppose it is some other kind of process. [The decisive move in the conjuring trick that altogether escaped our notice.] Behavioural processes will be the only kind remaining, and we will find ourselves at work trying to make behaviourism believable. [That is how the philosophical problem about mental process and states and about behaviourism arises.] We don't want to *deny* mental processes, as if we knew what they were, just did not think there were any. If we say remembering is not a mental process, it will be a way of saying we as yet make no sense of the idea [The yet uncomprehended process etc.] (cf. §339).

Here we see the behaviourist as much in the thrall of the innocent-seeming question 'What kind of something (process, state . . .) is remembering (imagining, believing . . .)?' as the mentalist. If the question were not taken to be so innocent, there would be no demand for such sophisticated answers as behaviourism.

A person who perceived as clearly as this that behaviourism is one of the ways we flounder in trying to answer questions that it is a mistake to be asking, would not be likely to show behaviouristic tendencies himself; but a person anxious to display the manifold ways in which behaviourism can be tempting might well lull us into accepting views that tend in that direction, and leave us, with the help of some hints, to see for ourselves the mistake we have almost made. That is what I suggest Wittgenstein was doing in the passages with which I began.

Sixteen

CONSCIOUSNESS AND THE CHIEF

419. In what circumstances shall I say that a tribe has a *chief*? And the chief must surely have *consciousness*. Surely we can't have a chief without consciousness!

THERE ARE some very curious things in the *Philosophical Investigations*, but on the face of it at least, this is not so much curious as just daft. What could Wittgenstein be driving at?

One perhaps assumes he does not offer this as in itself a good philosophical point, but rather as something someone might say; but there are limits to the foolishness it is useful to set up for philosophical contemplation, and at least on obvious interpretations, this is well beyond those limits. What is the supposition? – That someone might say it is at least sometimes clear that a tribe has a chief, and since a chief must be conscious, there can be no doubt that consciousness exists? That seems too idiotic to linger over; and yet if not that, what? In the hope of extracting some sense from this strange thing, let me begin by considering various sorts of way in which the question, in what circumstances we might say a tribe has a chief might be answered.

1. We might describe the sort of evidence that would convince us: the fact perhaps that one man was treated more deferentially than others in the tribe, that he sat in the centre at tribal meetings, that remarks at such meetings were mostly directed to him, and he had the last word, that when he gave what appeared to be an order, anyone in the tribe would obey without question, and so on.

2. The 'circumstances' here might be occasions for mentioning that a certain tribe has a chief, for example when he is away on a hunting expedition, and it appears as if there is no chief; or when, owing to the death of the old chief, there has

been a time when the tribe lacked a chief, but a new one has now been installed. Here there is no immediate question of showing or establishing that there is a chief. The speaker is assumed to have information about this that the person he is addressing lacks, and the circumstances are not evidence for what he says, but provide an occasion for saying it.

3. A rather different case of an occasion for mentioning that a tribe has a chief would be if it were a linguistic fact that we do not call anything a tribe unless it has a chief. Then we would *not* say 'This tribe has a chief'; but we *might* say 'A tribe has a chief' (the words Wittgenstein used); and the circumstances in which we might say this are if we were teaching someone this part of the language, or correcting someone who had said that on his recent expedition he had encountered several tribes without chiefs. To this we might, if our language had this structure, say 'No, we call it a "band" if there is no chief. A tribe has a chief. If there is no chief, we do not call it a tribe.'

It is from the first of these senses of 'circumstances' that we might derive the awful argument that some tribes demonstrably have a chief, chiefs undoubtedly have consciousness, so consciousness exists; but not only is this argument too dismal to consider: even if it were being contemplated, it would hardly be necessary to remind us that there are some things that would show that a tribe has a chief. No one would be so contentious as to question *that* part of the argument.

Yet if we therefore move on to the second sense of 'circumstances', it seems equally unnecessary to remind us that there are occasions on which we might mention that a tribe has a chief, or what those occasions are, before saying that a chief surely has consciousness.

There is however some support for the idea that Wittgenstein had in mind the second kind of circumstances, in the fact that he asked in §417 in what situation we say 'I am conscious again' – a question he had in fact already answered in §416 when he said '. . . expressions like "I see", "I hear", "I am conscious" really have their uses. I tell a doctor "Now I am hearing with this ear again", or I tell someone who believes I am in a faint "I am conscious again", and so on'. The circumstances here are when previously one ear has not been functioning, or when someone believes you are in a faint; and they are not evidence for what one says, but occasions for saying such a thing.

Still, there is a difference between 'I am conscious now' and 'I have consciousness', if the latter is not just a stilted way of saying the former – and Wittgenstein might have wanted to contrast the two. If anyone ventured the general observation about chiefs that they have consciousness, then whatever he might mean, he could hardly mean that they are not in a faint, or have come out of a coma, unless perhaps he was expressing the extreme view, hints of which we find in Plato and Spinoza, that most people are living in a dream world. If there is any occasion for saying that chiefs have consciousness, it is not the sort of occasion implied in §416, or described in my second interpretation of 'circumstances'.

We seem therefore to be left with the third alternative, according to which the circumstances are when teaching this part of the language, or correcting someone who has misused the word 'tribe'. If this is what Wittgenstein intended, it is unfortunate that it is not clearly true that only groups of people that have chiefs are called tribes. It would not clearly be a misuse of language to call a group of people who held meetings and acted in concert, but would not let anyone assume the role of leader, a tribe.

However it is only an example we are dealing with, which need not fail because it involves a slightly fanciful supposition about the use of a word which is never likely to be the object of a philosophical investigation. Wittgenstein may either have believed that we would not call anything a tribe if it did not have a chief, or have invited us to suppose for the purposes of his example that this was true; he does elsewhere ask about the occasions on which we would make a grammatical point, for example in §296 (a section which however might be otherwise interpreted).

Although I have not yet settled on a sense for 'to have consciousness', taking the third kind of circumstances in which one might say that a tribe has a chief to be the kind intended, I suggest a rewriting of §419 as follows:

> Just as there are occasions on which we might say that a tribe has a chief, so there are occasions on which we might say that a chief has consciousness. The occasions in both cases however are when we are teaching language. It is linguistic and not political

information we are providing in the first case, and linguistic and not psychological information in the second.

It is a happy feature of this reformulation that, since it is only the fact that we begin by talking about a tribe and its chief that leads us to choose the *chief* as the person we say has consciousness, we cut out the abysmal suggestion that otherwise loomed rather large, that it is more certain that chiefs have consciousness, than that rank and file tribesmen do. We might have said that just as there are occasions for saying that a tribe has a chief, so there are occasions for saying that a tribesman (or a violinist or a gravedigger) has consciousness.

We are not yet out of the woods, however, because if, as was suggested above, there is a difference between being conscious and 'having consciousness', and if it is not a grammatical remark about chiefs or gravediggers that they are conscious, we have not yet set things up in such a way that there could be an occasion for saying, of any class of being, that their members have consciousness. There being no ordinary expression 'to have consciousness', one can hardly teach its use, or correct people who misuse it.

However we can *construct* a use for this expression, and if we do, there will be a nice symmetry in the fact that both the supposed use of the word 'tribe' and the use of 'to have consciousness' are imaginary.

If someone says 'The chair doesn't see me' he will not, except in a fanciful case, mean that it is looking the other way, or that it is blind, poor thing, but rather that it is not the kind of thing that either notices or does not notice, either sees or is blind; and similarly if he says the screwdriver doesn't hear or the hydrangea doesn't feel, he will be recording the fact that neither 'hears' nor 'is deaf', neither 'feels' nor 'is numb' apply to screwdrivers or flowers. Now we could stipulate that we will say anything 'has consciousness' if one or the other of at least some of these pairs of predicates is applicable to it, and that it 'does not have consciousness' if, in the case of none of the pairs of predicates does either predicate apply.

A bus, we would then say, lacks consciousness: it neither sees nor is blind, neither hears nor is deaf, is neither awake nor asleep, neither drunk nor sober, and neither conscious nor unconscious. Including the last of these pairs reminds us that the ordinary words like 'conscious' and 'unconscious' have a different use than 'has' or 'lacks consciousness': a bus is not said to be unconscious, although it 'lacks consciousness'.

When might there be an occasion to say that a tribesman or a violinist had consciousness, or that a bus did not? – Well, if someone said 'Shout a little louder. I don't think the bus hears you', or if someone were to say of a person 'I know he hears me. What I wonder is whether he has consciousness.' We might then say 'We can ask concerning a person whether he hears or is deaf, or whether he heard or did not hear what I said, but we do not ask whether living human beings *have consciousness*. We make no sense of the idea that they might neither have hearing nor be deaf, might neither have sight nor be blind, and so on. It is of human beings primarily that we say that they see, are blind, hear or are deaf. Similarly we make no sense of the idea of a bus noticing something or being blind, hearing what we say or being deaf, and so on.'

We would be representing it as a grammatical truth that human beings 'have consciousness', and buses do not. That, in short, is the interpretation I am suggesting of this mystifying passage. I claim that with a minimum of contrivance it makes Wittgenstein come out as saying something both intelligible and characteristic of him. But given this reading, further problems arise, to which I will now turn.

The first is that if, as I have claimed, 'to have consciousness' does not have an ordinary use, can there be any philosophical gain made by recording the fact that when we have given it a use, it can be a topic of grammatical remarks?

The answer is that, while there is in fact no such English expression, it is an expression that, when given the definition I have assigned it, would enable us to say in an economical way, something that we might very well want to say, namely that the pairs of predicates, 'hears' and 'is deaf', 'sees' and 'is blind', and so on (when 'hears', 'sees' etc. are used intransitively), are applied to human beings in such a way that if a person does not hear, he is deaf, and if he does not see, he is blind – whereas although we can say of flowers and buses that they do not see or hear, in their case it does not follow that they are blind or deaf.

A harder and more important question arises about the status, so to speak, of such a grammatical point. In noting that *we say* of human beings that they 'have consciousness', and do not say it of hydrangeas or gramophones, are we resolving the problem of other minds with a stout affirmation that as for us anglophones (or democrats or what have you?), we take a firm stand on whether people have consciousness, do not tolerate any doubts about it, train everyone to think that way, and come down very hard on anyone who in the least questions this fundamental conviction? Do we further brook no suggestion that carburettors, clouds or eucalyptus trees have consciousness?

Are we in a position like, but opposite to, that of the government and scientists in Z §§528–30, who give it out that the people of a tribe they want to enslave have no souls, although they are in most outward ways just like anyone else? Here a myth that we regard as deplorable is strenuously propagated: do we propagate the contrary conviction, for purposes we think admirable?

No. Given the way we have defined the expression 'to have consciousness', there could be nothing distinct from seeing, not seeing, hearing, not hearing, and so on, as to the existence of which we might have a conviction. 'Having consciousness' is not having something, the having of which explains the fact that we see or hear. It is not, for example, a kind of illumination of the soul, enabling us to see what is going on there. If a blind man's soul is dark, he still 'has consciousness'. The use we assigned to the expression is *only* to mark the difference between beings which, if they do not see, are blind, and those which, although they do not see, are not blind.

We may very much want to suppose that 'consciousness' is the name of something distinct from the fact that we see, hear, smell and so on, perhaps something without which hearing, smelling, thinking would not occur. It is probably in a context of this inclination that Wittgenstein asked (§418) what it would be like if it were otherwise. By this he apparently means, not what would it be like if people who could not see or hear without consciousness lacked it, but what would it be like if we could see and smell and think and remember without this further something. That is why he rejects the answer that we would all be unconscious. If I can see, I am not unconscious. But if I am therefore conscious although, *ex hypothesi,* I do not have a further something we call consciousness, we no longer know what that hypothesis omits, and the sentence 'But I, for instance should not have consciousness – as I now have it' comes across starkly as having been deprived of all meaning. We may want to say that we would be lacking something, but if we could still hear, see and think, we have not the least idea what would be missing. We look for some phenomenon distinct from any visual or auditory experience we may be having, which is called consciousness, and are mystified when nothing seems to fit the bill.

Yet if being conscious is not distinct from the experiences one may be having, it is not clear that it is identical with them either. If I tell the doctor I am conscious now, I do not mean that I have resumed having experiences, even though of course I have. It is not like saying the pain has returned, or the throbbing in the chest. I can report a remission of these things, but could not report a remission of consciousness (see Z §§401–2). It is the fact that I should be speaking at all that impresses the doctor. I might, instead of saying I am conscious now, have asked for a drink or complained that the light was too bright. The fact that I was saying something would be the significant thing, and from that point of view *what* I said would not matter.

We can think of 'I am conscious' as a way of saying something without saying anything in particular – as a way of declining to give any other message, and of drawing attention just to the fact that one is speaking.

There are other expressions that are like this in conveying no information, while yet serving some purpose. 'I am here' is uninformative as to where I am, but from it often another person can tell where I am, by the direction from which my voice comes. When someone calls out 'Where are you?', anything I say loud enough to be heard will serve the same purpose; and 'I am here', like 'I am conscious', serves a purpose without either saying what purpose it serves, or saying anything else.

Yet 'I am conscious' is informative in a sense. From it the doctor does not learn that the patient will have auditory experiences if asked a question (if that means anything), or that he will hear a question if it is put to him (he may be deaf);

but he may learn that either the patient will hear or he is deaf, and will see if he is not blind and feel if he is not paralysed. One could say that the doctor is switched to a different way of thinking. Whereas, as long as the patient remained unconscious, no conclusions were possible about the effect of the operation on his sight or hearing, the doctor can now reason: if he doesn't see this, he is blind; and if he doesn't hear this, he is deaf; if he doesn't feel this, he is paralysed, and so on. In this way we perhaps calculate with an expression like 'He is conscious'. If it informs us of anything, it is that we can 'calculate' in that way. (This chapter is closely related to chapter 10.)

Seventeen

PICTURES AND THEIR APPLICATION

423. *Certainly* all these things happen in you. – And now all I ask is to understand the expression we use. – The picture is there. And I am not disputing its validity in any particular case. – Only I also want to understand the application of the picture.

424. The picure is *there*; and I do not dispute its *cor-rectness*. But *what* is its application? Think of the picture of blindness as a darkness in the soul or in the head of the blind man (see also §§374, 427, 589, 657–8; pp.178, 223).

SINCE the sections of the *Investigations* that precede the above remarks make no mention of things going on in people, the first question will be what we should take 'these things' that 'happen in you' to be. Presumably they are pictures; but we can have a picture in at least two importantly different senses. A picture can be before the mind in such a way that if we had some artistic talent, we could make a likeness of it on paper; but we also speak of picturing things when there is not necessarily a pictorial representation of them with which we would be happy. If I say I picture minds as places where experiences occur, I might be embarrassed if asked to depict an experience occurring in such a place, without seeing myself as therefore bound to withdraw what I said about how I picture minds.

In the first of these senses, but not, or not so clearly, in the second, pictures can *happen*. Although some people, including Wittgenstein on some readings, doubt whether there *are* pictures of this first kind; no one doubts that *if* there are, they can 'happen'; but if in the second sense I picture minds as places where experiences occur, I only mean that it seems

146

right to me to say that about minds. I am not saying that anything ever happens which *is* its seeming right to me. I am using the word 'picture' in the way it is used when someone, having explained something a little complicated, asks 'Do you get the picture?' He does not mean 'Has the picture come before your mind?', but rather 'Do you understand how it all fits together?'

Since Wittgenstein said 'Certainly all these things happen in you', he ought, in view of the foregoing, to have meant that pictures of the first kind occur; but if he did, it is unfortunate in at least two ways: (i) it is hard to suggest that the only example he gives, that of blindness as a darkness in the soul, could be represented pictorially; and (ii) all the interesting examples that we can add to this, of how we might picture mind, conscience, will, and so on, are pictureable in the second, but scarcely in the first sense.

By 'Certainly all these things happen in you', Wittgenstein might have meant 'If you tell me you picture blindness as a darkness in the soul, I am willing to believe you'; but since believing that someone so pictures blindness does not require believing that anything pictorial happens, we would have to say that in that case he wrote carelessly here. Let us make that assumption. It is not gravely damaging to Wittgenstein, and it will allow us a more interesting line of interpretation than might otherwise be available.

A second question is this. When we read 'I am not disputing its validity in any particular case', and later 'I do not dispute its correctness', assuming that no distinction between validity and correctness is intended, what exactly should we suppose is not disputed? There are perhaps three possibilities here: (i) that Wittgenstein is not disputing whether someone has the picture he says he has, or does picture something the way he says he does; (ii) that if someone pictures something as such and such (e.g. minds as places where experiences occur), Wittgenstein is not disputing whether that something *is* such-and-such; and (iii) he is not disputing whether such-and-such is the common or the standard picture of mind, conscience, will, blindness.

i) Wittgenstein might simply be repeating his acceptance that 'these things happen', and that 'the picture is there'. There is after all a curious repetitiveness in these sections, and this might be just one more case of it. Yet (a) 'validity' is certainly not, and 'correctness' is not clearly, a term to use when one is simply accepting the truth of a proposition; and (b) having said 'The picture is there', one would seem to be adding something new in going on to say 'and I am not disputing its validity in any particular case', not just repeating it in different words. It is likely therefore that the correct interpretation will be one of the remaining possibilities.

ii) The words 'in any particular case' suggest that there are at least some of these pictures that Wittgenstein would agree are 'correct' (whatever that means); but it is highly unlikely that he thinks that blindness is indeed a darkness in the soul, that minds are indeed places where experiences occur, or mechanisms responsible for intelligent behaviour, and so on. Since, with the possible exception of the picture of blindness, we are left entirely to guess what other pictures may be contemplated here, it remains possible that he is talking about pictures that may be correct in the sense of describing how things indeed are; but there are no examples of such pictures in Wittgenstein's writings, and that makes it fairly safe to reject this second possibility.

iii) The third possibility is that the picture someone has of an X correctly represents the common concept of an X. It is in this sense that it is correct to say that Santa Claus is a jolly elf who lives at the North Pole and makes a fantastic journey on Christmas eve, although there is no Santa Claus, and no such journey is made. We conceive Santa Claus that way, and it is incorrect that he is a sour fellow who lives in the hills of Bulgaria and makes a foray of terror on Hallowe'en.

In this sense it may be *true* that *will* is conceived as a piece of psychic muscle we have, which directs our physical actions; that conscience is conceived as an infallible and censorious inner sprite, chiding and admonishing some of us mercilessly; that deafness is a silence in the soul, and so on, without it being true that anyone has a piece of psychic muscle, a censorious sprite or an inner silence.

How can the correctness of propositions about how we conceive this or that be ascertained? It comes out in the way we use the words. There is probably no justification for saying that we conceive of blindness as a darkness in the soul; but the proposition that we conceive mind to be a kind of mechanism responsible for intelligent behaviour is supported by the fact that we describe minds as 'powerful', 'small', 'agile', 'frail', 'balanced', 'restless', adjectives we might also use to describe a mechanism, and in the fact that we use these terms in pseudo-explanation of the character of people's performance in discussion, calculation and so on. If someone readily constructs imposing arguments, we say he has a powerful mind; if he is ingenious but not deep we may say he has a small but agile mind, and so on. It is true that we do not have a monolithic concept of mind. No one is clear about the relation between the concept of it as a mechanism, and as a place, but we do also have the latter concept, as is shown by such expressions as 'what do you have in mind?', 'at the back of my mind', 'it brought to mind . . .', and so on. There is however no necessity that our various pictures should be consistent with one another, as long as we are not representing them as depicting how things are, and as long as it is clear which picture we are trading on in a given case.

The likelihood then is that it was this kind of correctness Wittgenstein said he was not disputing. His saying 'in any particular case' allowed him to dispute it on occasion, as perhaps he would in the case of the picture of blindness, while at the same time suggesting that he thought our pictures are often correct in this sense, and ought not to be disputed.

What is meant by the 'application' of these pictures that Wittgenstein wants to understand? Possibly two things:

i) A picture that is 'incorrect' will either not have applications, or not have applications that will be commonly understood. We saw how we 'trade on' the picture of mind as a mechanism responsible for intelligent behaviour as a way of saying various things about the character of that behaviour in different cases; but we neither do, nor is it easy to suggest how we could, similarly trade on the picture of blindness as a darkness in the soul. We do not, as a way of saying he is blind, say his soul is dark, or as a way of saying he is nearly blind, say his soul is dimly lit, although perhaps that imagery might one day catch on; and it is hard to suggest how we could use the picture to say that he is blind in one eye. This shows that we do not have that picture of blindness, but does not show anything about whether people's souls *are* dark if they are blind. Our having a certain picture does not make it true, and our not having it does not make it false.

ii) This can be illustrated in various ways with pictures there is reason to think we do have.

If, as a way of saying that I received numerous or excellent gifts at Christmas, I say that Santa Claus was very good to me this year, you ought not to say in astonishment 'You don't believe in Santa Claus, do you!'; and similarly if I say that Pierre has a very agile mind, you ought not to wonder whether I believe in minds, or press the question whether, seriously now, they are the sort of thing that can be agile. When I say he has an agile mind I may appear to be offering an explanation of how very ingenious he is, as I explain the acceleration of a car by saying it has a powerful engine; but in fact I do not mean to be saying anything at all about *why* he is ingenious, I have just adopted an amusing way of saying *that* he is. You are being inept and sobersided if you either object that minds can't be agile or, since in a sense they can (Pierre's is), wonder earnestly what that shows about their nature. It shows nothing about their nature. There need be nothing that could have some nature or another. It only shows something about a picture we have.

If I see no reason to believe that there is a pyschic entity whose function it is to provide moral advice and exhortation, that is if I think the picture of conscience is not true, I am mistaking the role of that picture if I therefore object to people saying their conscience bothers them, and still more if I become cynical about mankind, concluding that 'no one has a conscience'. In the latter event I am both applying and declining to apply the picture. To say that people have consciences is just to say that they show some concern about moral questions, and in that sense some people do have consciences, even though there may in fact be no pyschic agency with the appointed function of keeping us on the straight and narrow path.

Often a proposition that trades on a picture will be true. I really did have it at the back of my mind that I should leave by four; Pierre really does have an agile mind; Mary's conscience really was bothering her. Here we have a clue to the otherwise mystifying remarks in §427:

'While I was speaking to him I did not know what was going on in his head.' . . . The picture should be taken seriously. We should really like to see into his head. And yet we only mean what elsewhere we should mean by saying: we should like to know what he is thinking.

It is one thing to say that people who use the expression 'what is going on in his head' can be fooled by it into wanting to see into his head, and another thing to say that the picture should be taken seriously, with its suggestion that it is not foolish to want to see into his head. What ever can Wittgenstein mean?

If Descartes were much more widely known than he is, then even if he was not taken at all seriously, there might have come to be in common use the expression 'to want to know what is going on in his pineal gland', which people often laughingly used as an alternative to 'wanting to know what he is thinking'. Some people, when they said 'I wonder what is going on in his pineal gland', would not really be curious about it, but others really would want to know, that is to say they would be genuinely curious about what he was thinking. If 'to wonder what is going on in the pineal gland' is an accepted expression, there can be idle and serious cases of its use, just as there can of wondering what he is thinking, and the serious cases are cases of 'really wanting to know what is going on in the pineal gland', even if we do not take the Cartesian picture at all seriously. It is in that sense, surely, that Wittgenstein meant that 'we should really like to see into his head'. If I am neither uninterested in him nor sure I understand him, I would like to know what is going on in his head. I sometimes say this but do not mean it; but to mean it I do not need to believe that X-rays or surgery would show me what he is thinking.

The 'application of these pictures then is the various ways in which we explicitly trade on them as useful and conventionally understood ways of saying various things we want to say about people. The applications are generally 'pseudo-explanatory', not in the sense that we think they explain, although they do not, but in the sense that they have the form of an explanation, although they are not offered as conjectures or hypotheses, and few of the people who use them suppose for a moment that they explain.

There is no need whatever for the pictures to be true in order to be used as we use them. We can take the most fanciful notion we like, say out of Descartes or a Disney cartoon, and as

151

long as people are familiar with the picture and it has a certain fecundity, we can trade on it to say various other things. We saw that the notion of darkness in the soul was hard to bend to any use, but the notions of mind, will, conscience, imagination, have proved very usable.

We can imagine a group of people who cared a good deal about right and wrong but were often much tempted to do wrong, and whose language did not include the word 'conscience' or anything like it, studying Butler's *Sermons* together and having a good laugh, but later finding that they understood one another very well when they said such things as 'My conscience is bothering me', 'My conscience told me', 'My conscience wouldn't let me'. This would not show that they had been persuaded by Butler, but only that they had seen ways of putting his conscience picture to use in talking about some of the turns of their moral life.

I said just now that we do not use these pictures as hypotheses or conjectures about the explanation of people's behaviour. That may require some justification in view of cases like the following: George has recently done something disreputable, and is now seen looking rather anxious and introspective. Someone says 'I suspect his conscience is bothering him'. A conjecture offered in explanation of his behaviour, surely; but clearly we can divide the thought here into two parts: a conjecture on whether his anxiety is of a moral nature, and a possible conjecture whether, if it is, it is something called a conscience that is giving him that moral anxiety. The former is a fair conjecture, the latter is nonsense. For suppose that George had not merely sat there looking anxious, but had said 'Oh dear me! I shouldn't have done that. I wonder what I can do to put it to rights?': we could not then wonder whether his conscience is bothering him. That is a prime example of 'being bothered by conscience'. So we could say: one wondered whether his anxiety was over what he had done, and was on moral grounds, and expressed it by saying 'I wonder if his conscience is bothering him'. There are not two conjectures here, but only one, and that is not about the theoretical explanation of moral botherment.

When Wittgenstein asked how these pictures are applied he might, as well as what we have already seen, have been asking us to reflect on the kind of application we could expect if a given picture were literally true. In the case of the picture of thoughts as happening in a person's head, we might expect that saying what one was thinking would have the form and style of a description of something that has happened. When a person described his thoughts, he would be careful to say whether they were in words or pictures or what; and if they were in words, he would be misdescribing his thoughts unless he repeated just the words that ran through his head, in just the sequence and with just the pauses with which they had appeared. He would not say 'I wondered why he was doing that', but rather 'The words "Why is he doing that?" ran fairly quickly through my mind, with the intonation, I should say, of a question being asked, and as that happened I had a feeling which I believe to be that of puzzlement'. He might recount these events with the kind of wonderment with which we sometimes tell our dreams; and if we inquired whether he had *asked* himself why Peter was doing that, he could only say that he had described how it was, there was nothing further to report, we knew as much about it now as he did. If we persisted: 'But are you *puzzled* about it?', he could say 'Well I think I am. The feeling I have is either that of puzzlement or something remarkably like it.' If we said 'Do you pursue the question, suggest to yourself possible answers, and try to evaluate each answer?', he might reply 'Soon after I experienced the words "Why is he doing that", the words "Perhaps to make me think he is composing a poem" came along, and then after an interval during which I had that puzzled feeling rather more strongly, the words "But why would he want me to think that?" appeared, in just that order, and again with the intonation of a question. Is that what you would call "pursuing the question" and "evaluating possible answers"?'

Clearly there is no place in the way we talk about people's thinking for this kind of faithful description, or for these doubts whether one was puzzled, asking a question, pursuing it further, and so on; and therefore there is not even the *prima facie* reason for supposing this picture of thinking is true, that there would be if at least the application of the picture conformed to the way we talk about thoughts.

This last thought is, if interesting, still fairly conjectural as an answer to the question what Wittgenstein might have meant by the 'application'. The rest of my interpretive thesis I think I have shown to be at least consistent with everything in these puzzling sections; and to make some clear sense of what would otherwise be extremely baffling.

There is another point which should be mentioned. When Wittgenstein asked us to think of blindness as a darkness in the soul of the blind man, he might have meant either 'Suppose someone were to say that blindness is a darkness of that kind', or 'Imagine that instead of saying people were blind, we said their souls were dark'. Nothing very interesting emerges from taking Wittgenstein in the former way, while taken in the latter way, we would be imagining a form of speech that conforms exactly to the pattern I have described.

There is not a great deal of evidence elsewhere whether Wittgenstein would dispose of some problems in this manner, but in chapter 25 I will defend a similar interpretation of Part II, chapter iv of the *Investigations*; and the following passage may also be cited:

> 112. A simile that has been absorbed into the forms of our language produces a false appearance, and this disquiets us. 'But *this* isn't how it is!' - we say. 'Yet *this* is how it has to *be*!'

The ways of speaking I have described, although I would not call them similes, have been absorbed into the forms of our language in the sense that we use them routinely and matter-of-factly, with no consciousness of their being quaint or in-direct ways of saying what we use them to say. 'She has an agile mind' is often true; and we may think: if it is true, then there must be minds, and she must have one. ('This is how it has to be.') Yet if we ask whether that *is* how it is, we may well conclude either that no, there are not minds and she does not have one, or at least that we do not know what would count as its being true that there are. ('But this isn't how it is!')

Eighteen

HOW SENTENCES REPRESENT

435. If it is asked 'How do sentences manage to represent?' - the answer might be: 'Don't you know? You
certainly see it, when you use them.' For nothing is
concealed.
How do sentences do it? - Don't you know? For
nothing is hidden.
But given this answer: 'But you know how sentences
do it, for nothing is concealed' one would like to retort
'Yes, but it all goes by so quick, and I should like to see it
as it were laid open to view.'

NOT EVERYONE would be likely to pose the question how
sentences manage to represent, and one can need some help
to see how there can be a problem here. §433 is about as
helpful as any. In it we are asked to imagine someone being
given an order, and not understanding at all. It is suggested
that if it is the order to raise his arm, one might explain by
raising one's arm; but that would still leave it unclear that *he*
was to do that. One could try to make that point by pointing
from oneself to him, or by making encouraging gestures; but
whatever we do, it too may need further explanation, and
there seems to be no direct and effective way of making
exactly the point made by the words 'Raise your arm'. There is
a gap there, and no clear way of bridging it; and yet it is
bridged every day by people who have learned English. How
is language so effective when gestures are so inefficient? How
do sentences manage to represent?

You may still not be much troubled by this question, but
given that, for good or ill, it has arisen, we can turn to Wittgenstein's handling of it. He seems to be suggesting that the
answer is not concealed, it is right there for anyone to see, if

155

he will have a good look at cases in which we use a sentence. He offers no argument that it is not hidden, and one might want to take issue with him on that; but let us at least play along with the possibility that nothing is hidden, and see what, if anything, we can find that is open to view and that we could call 'how they do it'.

If I say 'The book is not red', I can point to the book I mean, and also point to something red as an explanation of what colour I am saying is not the colour of the book. The pointing I do might be a visible way in which sentences represent; but if I do point in these ways, one can also ask how the pointing manages to represent; and in any case I would not usually do any pointing or further explaining. I can do that if the need arises, I have that ability; but the ability does not show.

Is it hidden? - No. One can in a sense hide one's ability to do something, but not by keeping it where it cannot be seen; and I am not hiding my ability to explain which book I mean if I simply do not explain it. When an ability is not being exercised, it does not lie hidden. One does not see the ability when it *is* being exercised, but only the exercise of it; and only what can be open to view can at other times be hidden.

Another visible way in which sentences might manage it is that one might say for example 'The book I was just talking about is not the colour I was just talking about'. Such phrases as 'The book I was just talking about', 'The man who just walked by', 'The pen he bought yesterday' *say* which one is meant, and thus manage to represent; but not all sentences are so obliging in this regard, and in any case if there is a problem about how 'Charles is six feet tall' manages it, there is the same problem about how 'The man who just walked by is exactly my height' does. In §433, the difficulty was that the explanations themselves needed to be explained, and definite descriptions are nothing but built-in explanations.

If understanding were a procedure, sentences that manage to represent might do it by providing us with well-chosen material such that, when the procedure was applied to the sentence, we came away knowing what was being said about which object. The material thus provided would certainly not be hidden; but is understanding such a procedure?

People who have learned English have no difficulty understanding most English sentences. We are inclined to compare this to the fact that people who have had lessons from Houdini have no difficulty pulling rabbits from hats. The latter have learned something that they do with great facility, and we would like to know what it is; and similarly we would like to know what it is that we English speakers have learned, that we now do so deftly when we understand a sentence. It is odd, however, that Houdini knows all about how he does it, and could, if only he would, explain it to us. He is not puzzled by how he does it: why, if we have similarly learned something and do it all the time, should it be a problem to us *what* it is that we do? What makes us think that understanding is such a remarkable thing that there must be a trick to it, and that we ourselves must be performing the trick, even though we do not know what it is?

A combination of three things, perhaps: first the fact that the words 'Raise your arm' are so very unlike the raising of an arm that it may appear something needs to be done to get from one to the other; second the fact that language can appear a complex mechanism, when we reflect for example on the very different meanings sentences can be given by making sometimes only minor changes; and third the fact that the word 'understand' has some appearance of being the name of an activity. Things can be hard or easy to understand, can be quickly or slowly understood, and one can try to understand, and succeed or fail.

Normally, unless there are things we do without noticing it ourselves, there is nothing English speakers do by way of understanding an average English sentence. We may have to work laboriously with a dictionary before we understand Swahili sentences, but the fruit of that work is an English sentence, and we do not have to do anything with it in order to understand. When we have established an English equivalent, then we understand.

The word 'understand' may have some, but does not have all the marks of an activity word. 'He understands English' is not like 'He salutes officers'. The latter describes an action that he can be seen performing repeatedly, something that perhaps he has been warned that he must do, or that he has adopted a policy of doing; but we cannot be caught repeatedly in the act of understanding an English sentence, or be warned that we must understand them, or follow a policy of doing so;

157

nor can we forget to understand, or decide against understanding. We say a person understands English, not if there is something he always does, or can do on demand, but if generally he has no difficulty, finds there is nothing he needs to do.

If someone understands quickly, it is not clear that there is anything he quickly executes; and if there *is* something, it is not clear that it is understanding. 'I am now about to understand. I will do it slowly first, so that you can see what it consists of, then quickly, the way I normally do' makes no sense, not because understanding is a private activity that could not be exhibited that way, but because the speaker could perform no activity, even privately, that we would call 'understanding'.

When we do not understand something, there *are* things we do with a view to understanding. If the things we did were the understanding, then we *would* understand, and there would be no need to do them. When Ziff says '"Grandmother is ready for dinner" is ambiguous', one may not right away understand, and ask oneself what words or expressions in that sentence have two senses. Having noted that meat is 'ready for dinner' when it is sufficiently cooked, one may ask oneself whether grandmother could be ready in that sense, and reflect that if we were cannibals, she could. One now understands; but notice that the understanding emerges from and is not identical with the pursuit of these reflections. To say 'I understand' is to say that the sentence has acquired the unpuzzling character of an average English sentence. It is not to say that I have asked myself various questions and answered them, because I might have done other things, or nothing at all, and still understood (§652).

After describing what was done, we could not have written 'Now one is ready to understand, and proceeds to do so'. When it dawns on us that we might be cannibals cooking grandmother for dinner, we already understand; but the understanding is neither something that happens along with that thought, nor identical with it. Saying 'Now I understand' is like saying 'There is no more problem', or 'That is the solution'. It no more describes a further stage in the deliberations that 'Q.E.D.' is short for a step in the proof.

I have been considering cases in which there is some difficulty understanding, sentences that have to be puzzled over;

but the problem of how sentences manage to represent is a problem, if at all, for any sentence: for 'The book is red', 'Supper is ready' or 'He was in a playful mood' as much as for difficult sentences. We make a fundamental mistake if we reflect on our struggles with tricky sentences, on the assumption that what happens there, often slowly and painfully, will happen quickly or easily in the case of sentences that are no problem for us. In the ordinary case nothing whatever, not even understanding, *happens*. We do of course understand, but that is neither an action not an event, does not happen simultaneously with hearing a sentence, nor a split second after.

Do you certainly see how sentences manage to represent when you use them? You certainly see what is in the empty drawer when you open it. Similarly what you see when you use a sentence is nothing. Nothing is concealed, but nothing is open to view either. There is no way in which sentences manage it, because there is nothing there that it is surprising that a mere sentence should do. Sentences are the sort of thing that represent, and do not need additional equipment to carry it off.

In this section Wittgenstein set us to searching desperately for something which is not concealed when we use a sentence, and which would explain how it manages to represent. We did not find any such thing, but that turned out not to be after all so very disappointing, given that sentences do not need anything further, in order to carry out the function of representing.

That Wittgenstein regarded sentences as being capable, just as they stand, of representing, is clear from such sections as 449: '. . . It is as if one were to believe that a written order for a cow . . . always had to be accompanied by an image of a cow, if the order is not to lose its meaning'. Images of cows are not necessary, but neither is anything else – or at least neither is anything else *that might accompany the order*. (The words 'One Hereford cow' must be an expression that is in use [§432], but that is not something that happens when the order is given. Hence Wittgenstein was testing our mettle when he encouraged us to cast around for something unconcealed, that explains how sentences represent.

'How do sentences do it? – Don't you know? For nothing is

159

hidden.' This clearly suggests that it is all there, and we might see it if we reminded ourselves of some actual cases, and examined them perceptively. One must be alert, to decline such enticements, and emerge with the point that, since we are looking for something there is no reason to suppose exists, it will not be hidden, but will not be open to view either.

Nineteen

WHAT IT IS LIKE
TO MEAN SOMETHING?

455. We want to say: 'When we mean something, it's like going up to someone, it's not like having a dead picture (of any kind).' We go up to the thing we mean.
456. 'When one means something, it is oneself meaning'; so one is oneself in motion. One is rushing ahead and so cannot also observe oneself rushing ahead. Indeed not.
457. Yes: meaning something is like going up to someone.

THE ABOVE remarks are surprising in at least three ways:
1. While Wittgenstein often describes temptations one does not oneself experience, one can generally at least understand how someone might be so tempted; but it is difficult even to have some initial sympathy for *this* temptation. If one *had* to answer the question what it is like to mean something, one of the very last answers that would suggest themselves is that it is like going up to someone.
2. It is a distinct departure from one of Wittgenstein's very typical practices, to end up *endorsing* a temptation, as he certainly appears to do in §457.
3. That he should do this here is particularly surprising in as much as he probably does not think that meaning something *is anything*, and therefore ought not to think that it is like going up to someone, or like anything else. Only if anything is some phenomenon or other would one think it could be *either* like or unlike anything.
By contrast with these arresting features, it is only quaint that Wittgenstein should have said it is oneself meaning, and one is oneself in motion, rushing ahead, and not observing oneself doing so. Although the temptation to say such things is also fairly remote, he at least does not endorse such idiocy,

as is moderately clear from §436:

> ... Here it is easy to get into that dead-end in philosophy where one believes that the difficulty of the task consists in our having to describe phenomena that are hard to get hold of, the present experience that slips quickly by, or something of the sort.

Yet if he does not think that in some curious sense one is in motion, what can there be that might be either like or unlike going up to someone?

It will make a difference what Wittgenstein means here by 'meaning something'. He might have had in mind cases where we mean something by a gesture we make; or cases where we say something and mean it – hence mean something; but the fact that in §455 he speaks of going right up to *the thing* we mean suggests that he more likely had in mind cases where we use a word or an expression to refer to something or someone. When we say 'The tree is dead' or 'Peter is coming', we will generally mean a certain tree or a certain man. Let us work with the hypothesis that this is the 'meaning something' that is represented as being like going up to someone. Yet where can the analogy possibly lie, if Wittgenstein does not think that meaning a certain tree or a certain person consists in anything, and so could hardly think there is anything to be either like or unlike going right up to someone?

A rather wild fancy can be generated, given which it could seem right to say something like this. When we think about our explicit references to people or things, they can seem not to take us all the way to the things we mean; while on the other hand it can seem that we do get there, since we do mean a particular person or tree. Our thought does not peter out on the way to the object meant, the way our explanations can seem to do.

Wittgenstein is probably not serious about the failure of our references to 'go all the way', but he does in various places make something of the fact that it can seem that way, for example:

> 689. 'I am thinking of N'. 'I am speaking of N'.
> How do I speak *of* him? I say, for instance, 'I must go and see N today'. – But surely that is not enough! After all, when I say 'N' I might mean various people of this name. – Then there surely must be a further, different connexion between my talk and N, for otherwise I should *still* not have meant HIM.

What is it Like to Mean Something?

Certainly such a connexion exists. Only not as you imagine it:
namely by means of a mental *mechanism*.
(One compares 'meaning him' with 'aiming at him'.)

Wittgenstein is presumably sceptical of the comparison in
the last line of this section, and probably not just because if we
aim at him we might miss, though not if we go right up to him.
He ought to be sceptical of *any* comparison that requires that
we treat meaning something as a phenomenon. Still, we see
him here describing how we can be dissatisfied with the
indefiniteness of explicit references, and can thereby be led to
look for a more definite connection. We are thinking in
similar ways if we sigh over the fact that ostensive definitions
can be variously understood in every case (§28), or over the
fact that there may be no adequate way of explaining what we
mean when we give an order (§§433–4).

Wittgenstein almost certainly did not think that the indefiniteness of references or of explanations of them was a
problem. With regard to ostensive definitions for example he
said (note p.14) 'That it is ambiguous is no argument against
such a method of definition. Any definition can be misunderstood'; and (§87) 'As though an explanation as it were hung
in the air unless supported by another one. Whereas an explanation may indeed rest on another one that has been given,
but none stands in need of another – unless *we* require it to
prevent a misunderstanding. . . . The sign-post is in order – if,
under normal circumstances, it fulfils its purpose.'

He must have thought this indefiniteness could *seem* to be
a problem, otherwise he would not have kept returning to it;
and when anyone does find it a problem, he may be led to look
for the 'further, different connexion' mentioned in §689 – and
may think he has found it in our meaning something, since
however much we may flounder in our explanations of whom
we mean, we are generally not ourselves in any doubt about it.

When we reflect on this – ask ourselves how it is possible
that whereas other people need our explanations and may
misunderstand them, we ourselves manage perfectly without
an explanation – we may be inclined to suppose some hocus-
pocus that the soul performs (§454), that takes us all the way,
by means of which we go right up to the thing we mean.
However, if Wittgenstein does not, and he certainly doesn't,
believe that meaning *is* such a hocus-pocus, he has not yet a

basis for saying flatly that yes, meaning something is like going right up to someone. He does probably think, though, that there is something right about saying that independently of any explanations, we mean a certain person or thing, and are often in no doubt about whom or what we mean. He makes points that are at least similar to this when he says (*BB* 37):

> For how can we wish *just this* to happen if just this isn't present in our wish? It is quite true to say: The mere shadow won't do; for it stops short of the object; and we want the wish to contain the object itself. – We want that the wish that Mr Smith should come into this room should wish that just *Mr Smith*, and no substitute, should do the *coming*, and no substitute for that, *into my room*, and no substitute for that. But that is exactly what we said.

Or again when he says (*PI* §95):

> . . . When we say, and *mean*, that such and such is the case, we.– and our meaning – do not stop anywhere short of the fact; but we mean: *this – is – so.*

What is there then about meaning something, that is like going right up to someone? – Nothing real; just the fancy we build upon the fact that we mean a certain person or thing, and are in no doubt which one we mean. We fancy thought seeking out the thing we mean, wherever it may be, and not being diverted and stopping short by so much as a hair's breadth: going right up to it.

This is of course the wildest of fancies; but what else is there that could carry the analogy? It was naughty of Wittgenstein to write as if meaning something were like going up to someone, when all he can have meant is that one of the dreams of our language bears that likeness. For there is not even always a real object that we mean. When we pretend to be in pain, for example, and then say 'It'll get better soon', or 'It has stopped now', the fact that there is no actual pain to which we can be referring in no way prevents us from meaning the pain by the word 'it' (§667).

Twenty

DISGUISED AND PATENT NONSENSE

464. My aim is: to teach you to pass from a piece of disguised nonsense to something that is patent nonsense.

524. . . . ((The transition from patent nonsense to something which is disguised nonsense.))

WHILE IT may be difficult to give a definition of nonsense as Wittgenstein conceives it (and I will not attempt that task), there is no particular problem about the difference between patent and disguised nonsense. The former is whatever is immediately recognisable as nonsense, while the latter is anything that may sound like good sense but is not, and the absurdity of which may need to be shown.

What Wittgenstein says in §464 of *Philosophical Investigations* about his aim, at least if taken as a general declaration, may come as no surprise, but still it may be difficult to see in just what way he is pursuing that aim in the contexts of the passages quoted; and it may even be more difficult to understand why he would ever want to get from patent to disguised nonsense. The earlier of these passages is preceded by the following sections:

462. I can look for him when he is not there, but not hang him when he is not there.
One might want to say: 'But he must be somewhere there if I am looking for him'. – Then he must be somewhere there too if I don't find him and even if he doesn't exist at all.
463. 'You were looking for *him*? You can't even have known if he was there!' – But this problem really does arise when one looks for something in mathematics. One can ask, for example, how was it possible so much as to *look for* the trisection of the angle?

Here it is not difficult to locate the disguised nonsense in the case of looking for a person: it is the thought that just as we can't hang him if he is not there, we can't look for him if he is not there. The proposition that we can't look for him if he is not there derives some credibility from the comparison with hanging him, and so far remains disguised nonsense; but when we remember that we *can* look for him if he is not there, and even if he does not exist at all, *the same proposition* comes out as patent nonsense. The transition is not from one proposition that is disguised nonsense to another that is patent, but from being tempted by a proposition to finding it preposterous.

The difficulty of locating the nonsense here arises rather in the case of looking for something in mathematics. There would be no problem if we could take it that Wittgenstein was saying that just as it is absurd to say we can't look for a person who is not there or does not exist, it is absurd to say we can't look for the trisection of an angle with ruler and compass; but he at least appears not to be saying this, when he says 'But this problem really does arise when one looks for something in mathematics'. That suggests strongly that this case is different, and that one *cannot* look for the trisection of an angle, or for anything else that is impossible.

Indeed the cases *are* different, in that whereas when looking for a person, we suppose that he is there somewhere to be found, the solution of a mathematical problem is not regarded as being, in that sense, there (perhaps in a cupboard or a drawer), but is something to be *devised*. And further, while we may need some kind of description of a person to identify the one we seek, if we have a description of the solution of a mathematical problem, we have already found what we are seeking. But whether these differences make a difference is not immediately clear.

If Wittgenstein was saying that it is *not* absurd to say we can't look for the trisection of the angle, why would he go right on to say that his aim is to teach us to pass from disguised to patent nonsense?

Perhaps we are misled here by the words 'this problem really does arise'. It is most natural to take this to mean that it is not a nonsense question how we can do it; but it might rather mean that whereas it is fairly obvious nonsense to say we can't look for someone who is not there, in the mathematical case the nonsense is so well disguised that we really seem to have a problem. We can't look unless we know what we are looking for, but if we know this, we have found it.

Wittgenstein aside, *isn't* that a problem? I can suggest at least two reasons for supposing it is not:

i) If a student has been shown how to bisect an angle, and is then asked to see if he can find a way of trisecting angles, and proceeds to try various measures using what he has learned, it seems altogether unobjectionable and by no means nonsense, to say he is looking for a way of trisecting angles with ruler and compass.

ii) Whereas we look for people by matching individuals to descriptions (or photographs or fingerprints etc.), we do not solve mathematical problems by matching would-be solutions to solutions, and therefore what made it seem a problem in the case of searching for something that is not possible – the fact that there will be nothing by which the solution can be identified – is a bogus difficulty, arising from a false analogy with looking for a person.

If, 'Wittgenstein aside', these are good points, it might still be objected that he at any rate saw this as a problem, and not just in the sense that it is somewhat difficult to unmask or that it has a power to beguile: he thought that indeed we can't look for something that is a mathematical impossibility. In support of this objection his treatment of a similar question in §516 might be cited:

> It seems clear that we understand the meaning of the question: 'Does the sequence 7777 occur in the development of π?' It is an English sentence; it can be shown what it means for 415 to occur in the development of π; and similar things. Well, our understanding of that question reaches just so far, one may say, as such explanations reach.

The first sentence of this section will at first appear not to support the objection; but against this it might be emphasised that Wittgenstein says that it *seems* clear that we understand this sentence, and that what he goes on to say should lead us to suppose that this seeming is an illusion. He says it is an English sentence, but then he said that of 'These deaf mutes have learned only a gesture-language, but each of them talks to himself inwardly in a vocal language' – which he did not care to say he understood (§348). And he says that it can be shown what it means for 415 to occur in the development of π, but adds that our understanding reaches just so far as the explanations reach. How far is that? If we take it that the intended answer is 'Not far at all' or 'Not far enough', it will be fair to conclude that it is right to emphasise the word 'seems' in the first sentence of the section.

But now let us ask how far must such explanations reach before we can say we understand? Isn't that far enough? Must they, in the case considered, reach all the way to an actual development of π in which four consecutive sevens occur? That would be as much as to say that one cannot look for a 4 in the development unless it is there and one has found it, which is as true or as nonsensical as the proposition that one cannot look for a man unless he exists.

In sum, I am suggesting that in Wittgenstein's view it is nonsense to say we can't look for something in mathematics. It is disguised nonsense in the sense that it can be made believable by certain comparisons with looking for people, but it is patent nonsense in the sense that it may be *correct* to say of a student working experimentally with ruler and compass, that he is trying to find a way of trisecting an angle, or of a student endlessly calculating π, that he is looking for four consecutive sevens.

Let me now turn to the deliberations in which the indication is that there is a reverse transition. Here we will find the same problem about where the patent and the disguised nonsense lie, and there will be a further problem about why Wittgenstein would want to make this transition – or perhaps about the sense in which it is a reverse transition.

The sections leading up to §524 are mainly occupied with the odd question, what is the sense of a sentence? The question what is the sense of such and such a sentence is not an odd one, even if we do not often pose it in those words, but if we take an answer to this question, a statement of the sense of a sentence, and ask what this latter sentence is *about*, that is a curious question, albeit one we can want very much to press. It is of course about the sense, but what is *that*? We want to find something that is the sense of a sentence, whether it be the act of meaning it, what we imagine in connection with it, or the real state of affairs it records.

Wittgenstein's general approach to this idea that there is something, we may not yet know what, that is the sense of a sentence, is charmingly expressed in §503:

> If I give anyone an order I feel it to be *quite enough* to give him signs. And I should never say: this is only words, and I have got to get behind the words. Equally, when I have asked someone something and he gives me an answer (i.e. a sign) I am content – that was what I expected – and I don't raise the objection: but that's a mere answer.

He rejects the idea that we cannot understand a sentence if there is not something behind the words that we could call the sense or the meaning. It is of course true that if a sentence does not have a meaning, we cannot understand it. That is one of the truisms from which the problem arises; but we misconstrue the expression 'to have a meaning' if we insist that the meaning must be something – we may not yet know what – that is associated with the sentence.

After some discussion of whether the sense of a sentence is the picture it paints, we read:

> 522. If we compare a proposition to a picture, we must think whether we are comparing it to a portrait (a historical representation) or to a genre-picture. And both comparisons have point.
>
> When I look at a genre-picture, it 'tells' me something, even though I don't believe (imagine) for a moment that the people I see in it really exist, or that there have really been people in that situation. But suppose I ask: 'What does the picture tell me then?'
>
> 523. I should like to say 'What the picture tells me is itself'. That is, its telling me something consists in its own structure, in its own lines and colours. (What would it mean to say 'What this musical theme tells me is itself'?)
>
> 524. Don't take it as a matter of course, but as a remarkable fact, that pictures and fictitious narratives give us pleasure, occupy our minds.
>
> ('Don't take it as a matter of course' means: find it surprising, as you do some things which disturb you. Then the puzzling aspect of the latter will disappear, by your accepting this fact as you do the other.)
>
> ((The transition from patent nonsense to something which is disguised nonsense.))

It will be important first to be clear about *what* we are supposed to be disturbed about here. It is presumably not for example signs of deteriorating health, or fears that we will not be able to make a mortgage payment, but rather (a) something that is disturbing because surprising, and (b) something, the puzzlement of which it is the business of philosophy to relieve – something like the fact that there is nothing that is the sense of a sentence.

How is the procedure for ridding us of our puzzlement about this supposed to work? We find something else surprising, such as the fact that pictures and fictitious narratives give us pleasure; but what then? Is the argument that although surprising, it certainly happens, and that if we can accept the surprising character of this, we can equally accept such surprising facts as that there is nothing that is the sense of a sentence? Or is it rather that we can more readily see in the comparison case why we oughtn't to have been surprised, and then apply the pattern of reasoning there to the philosophically troubling case?

The answer to these questions may depend partly on how we would go about finding it surprising that pictures and fictitious narratives give us pleasure. We cannot just turn on surprise (or anyway surprise that is simply turned on is not likely to serve any purpose), we must find some auspices under which a fact at least seems to *command* surprise. Having done that, if we can show that there is some mistake in the reasoning that has made it seem surprising, we may be able to find a similar mistake behind our surprise at not being able to find anything that is the sense of a sentence. (I do not claim to be able to show that this is how the procedure is supposed to work, but only to show that it *can* work this way.)

We can find it surprising that genre-pictures and fictitious narratives give us pleasure by comparing these with photographs and letters. It is what the latter tell us that gives us pleasure. They may tell us that Sarah and David had a lovely time in Venice, and we are glad. So we ask, what news do genre-paintings and fictitious narratives give us, of which we can be glad? And since they do not convey any fact, knowing which we would be pleased, we may be inclined to say that what they tell us is themselves.

Clearly there is a mistake in the reasoning that might make it seem surprising that a novel should give us pleasure, the mistake of supposing that, as with letters and photos, it is not the words and the likenesses that give us pleasure, but what they tell us; and there is perhaps a similar mistake that makes it seem surprising that there is nothing that is the sense of a sentence – the mistake of supposing that understanding a sentence is a matter of getting from the words to something non-verbal that is their meaning or their sense.

It is more conjectural whether there is a further point to be pried out of this business, the point that just as it is absurd to be so much in the grip of the idea that it must be what a picture or a story tells us that gives us pleasure, that we have no recourse but to say that what novels and genre-paintings tell us is themselves – so it is absurd, when we have failed to find anything other than a sentence that is its sense, to be driven to say that it is itself its sense. Wittgenstein does not to my knowledge discuss this imaginable twist, but it is something to which, in the search for the sense of a sentence, one might be driven, and it is also clearly a mistake.

If I am right in my reading of these sections, Wittgenstein here falls well below his usual standard of pungency and philosophical suggestiveness: there is so little inclination to believe either that it is always what words tell us that gives us pleasure, or that a sentence is meaningless if there is nothing that is its meaning, that we are not so much surprised ourselves, as able to imagine someone being thus surprised. However it is uncommonly difficult to suggest anything else that both has some plausibility, and enables us to see a connection between the deliberations about the sense of a sentence that begin around §500, and the curious remarks about what pictures and fictitious narratives tell us.

At the end of §524 Wittgenstein indicates that he thinks a transition has been made from some patent to some disguised nonsense, but leaves us to see for ourselves just where this happened. To the question what the disguised nonsense is, I am inclined to reply 'What the picture tells me is itself'. When we read 'I should like to say: "What the picture tells me is itself"', we are likely, as Wittgenstein appears or pretends to do, to go along with it. If it is nevertheless nonsense, but may be accepted as sense, that it is a good enough reason to call it disguised nonsense.

Where then is the patent nonsense? I suggest it is the same sentence. Anyone overhearing 'What the picture tells me is itself' at an art gallery, or 'What the musical theme tells me is itself' at a concert would go away delighted to have another item of glorious nonsense to add to his collection. In that sense they are the most patent nonsense, although as they emerge in Wittgenstein's discourse they do have the air of sense. He does not immediately mark them as nonsense, but rather lulls us into letting them pass by pressing the (disguised nonsense) question 'What does the picture tell me?' If that is a good question, what can one say, in the case of a genre-painting, but 'Itself'?

Hence, it may be suggested, Wittgenstein was having himself some fun in a rather tricky way: he first gets us to accept 'What the picture tells me is itself' as a fair enough point; later, having been put on notice that there is some nonsense here, we go back and find this sentence to be disguised nonsense; and then Wittgenstein has the last laugh, pointing out what we should have seen all along, that it is patent nonsense.

Explaining the business this way may leave it looking like another transition from disguised to patent nonsense. The sense in which the movement is in the opposite direction is not that we first recognised it as patent, and then came to see it as diguised, but rather that we took something that is patent nonsense, and at first saw it only as disguised nonsense. But what happened in §464 could be described that way too, and hence there is after all no difference between the two transitions, and no problem about why Wittgenstein should want to go from patent to disguised nonsense.

Twenty-One

ON THE QUESTION WHY ONE THINKS

I HAVE suggested more than once that Wittgenstein can in part be regarded as a designer of conundrums, carefully constructed in such a way that, by fighting one's way out of the bafflement they generate, one can make for oneself the philosophical discovery that he might otherwise have imparted. One of his less artful inventions of this kind, but still one that can set us off on some interesting journeys, is the following group of remarks from the *Philosophical Investigations*:

> 466. What does man think for? What use is it? – Why does he make boilers according to *calculations* and not leave the thickness of their walls to chance? After all it is only a fact of experience that boilers do not explode so often if made according to these calculations. But just as having once been burnt he would do anything rather than put his hand into a fire, so he would do anything rather than not calculate for a boiler. – But as we are not interested in causes, – we shall say: human beings do in fact think: this, for instance, is how they proceed when they make a boiler. – Now, can't a boiler produced in this way explode? Oh, yes.
> 467. Does man think, then, because he has found that thinking pays? – Because he thinks it advantageous to think?
> (Does he bring his children up because he has found it pays?)
> 468. What would shew *why* he thinks?
> 469. And yet one can say that thinking has been found to pay. That there are fewer boiler explosions than formerly, now that we no longer go by feeling in deciding the thickness of the walls, but make such-and-such calculations instead. Or since each calculation done by one engineer got checked by a second one.
> 470. So we do *sometimes* think because it has been found to pay.
> 471. It often happens that we only become aware of the important *facts*, if we suppress the question 'why?'; and then in the course of our investigations these facts lead us to an answer.

173

On the Question Why One Thinks

One of the ways in which this group of remarks is less than satisfactory is that the first section, at least on any readily available interpretation, seems to achieve little beyond setting aside some possible confusions, none of which is very likely to arise in the context. The section can be read as making three distinct points:

i) We should not be detained by the fact that it is only in the past that boilers have not exploded when we calculated the thickness of their walls. The question why we calculate in such a case is not a question what reasons we have for assuming that future boilers will not explode if we calculate the thickness of their walls.

ii) If we just do calculate in such cases, and do not consider whether to do so, the fact that we do not review the reasons each time does not show that there are not reasons for calculating.

iii) Even the fact that a well-designed boiler will sometimes explode does not entail that we have no reason for making boilers that way. There might be no design of boiler that would never explode, but we could still have very good reasons for designing a boiler this way rather than that.

If these are the points Wittgenstein was making in §466, not only did he express himself obliquely, but the necessity for these preliminaries is not obvious. It would be too inept altogether if someone were to argue that there can be no reasons for care in the design of boilers, since it is only in the past that certain designs of boiler have proved safe, or since no design has proved absolutely safe. However his words lend themselves readily to this interpretation; and if there is any other business transacted in this section, it is well hidden.

Now why does Wittgenstein raise the question why people think? Is it just so that he can deliver himself of the conclusion that he at least appears to reach, namely that we sometimes do it because it has been found to pay? – That it is not only a dull point, but as I will argue later, a questionable one. Is he perhaps not much interested in that, but anxious to get us wondering about why we think in cases other than where it has been found to pay: whether we have other reasons in other cases, and what they are; or whether we do not generally have reasons, but perhaps are thinkers by nature?

174

On the Question Why One Thinks

The supposition that he wanted to put us onto the various reasons we have in various cases, or possibly onto the fact that we very often have no reasons, is out of line with Wittgenstein's usual approach to a philosophical question. He was not in general a man to *answer* questions. It is more characteristic of him to suggest that there was something odd about the question itself, and that we would be making a mistake if we tried to answer it. One would hardly guess that this was his attitude to the question why we think, in as much as he does venture a partial answer to it, and does not specifically challenge the asking of it; but it *is* an odd question, if only in the sense that we would wait a long time before hearing it asked; and when Wittgenstein said in §471 that it often happens that we become aware of the important facts if we suppress the question 'why?', he may have been suggesting that we do for ourselves what he did not do: try to make clear what is wrong with asking the question. If so, that is another way in which this group of remarks is less than satisfactory, since (a) the word 'suppress' rather suggests not asking the question for the time being, than questioning the asking of it, and (b) when Wittgenstein goes on to say 'and then in the course of our investigations these facts lead us to an answer', it reads as if the answer is to the question we have 'suppressed', and hence as if the question is unobjectionable. However, 'the answer' might be to the question what is wrong with asking the question – or to some other question, like 'Is the word "think" used as the name of a process?'. Let us anyway try treating the question why we think as misbegotten, and see what emerges.

People are asked and can often say why they smoke, play scrabble or study logic, but not why they think; and if the latter question were posed, we should hardly know what to say: I enjoy it? I think it good for my health? I think it is a noble activity?

One might be more inclined to say something more like 'I can't solve problems without thinking', or 'If I think, then I don't say foolish things so often, and I write more interesting letters, and so on'. Such answers can sound right because when we have said something foolish or gauche, we are often said to have spoken without thinking, and that seems to imply that had we thought, we would not have done it.

175

On the Question Why One Thinks

Similarly, interesting letters are often described as thoughtful, as if it was necessarily by thinking that they were composed; and again when we realise that we have made a mistake, we sometimes say 'I wish I had thought of such and such. Then I wouldn't have done that', as if by thinking beforehand we would surely have avoided the mistake.

However, a) people whose conversation is generally intelligent and tactful do not for the most part maintain that standard of performance by thinking before they speak. If Peter does not tell religious jokes in the presence of devout Aunt Elspeth, while Paul sometimes inattentively does, that is not likely due to Peter's having thought 'Since she is here, I had better not tell that one', and Paul's having failed to have any such thought. Tactful people avoid causing offence as it were by instinct, while tactless people, even if they think, are not likely to be very successful at this. Similarly a person who has not taken a lively interest in an incident as it was happening will not likely, by thinking, give an interesting account of it in a letter, while a person who was sensitive at the time to the drama of the incident may not need to think; and a person who has not made the mistake that made me wish I had thought of such and such has not generally had that consideration occur to him: he has just not overlooked it, has quite routinely acted in a way that does not occasion that regret. We might say in general that the learner or the bungler needs to think in order to do what the skilled or artful person does without thinking – and the former even then cannot regularly match the latter's performance.

b) When, after the event, we are expressing regrets about mistakes or gaucheries, we do or can say what we failed to think *of*; but there is a problem what we should have to suppose thinking is, in order that before the event, had we only thought, we would have hit on the considerations that we failed to reckon with. Before the event we cannot just go directly to a fact that is pertinent – or at least if we can, we do not need to bethink ourselves of it: the supposition is that we think, and *thereby* uncover what is pertinent. What magic is it that will thus lead us to what we need? (Does 'I thought of it' say *how* I got on to it?)

To this one might reply that there is no magic about it: we say 'If only I had thought, I would have seen that such and

176

such' only in cases where that consideration and its relevance was known to us, yet we overlooked it. Hence thinking could be like turning on the lights in a dimly lit place, and thereby of course seeing what is there to be seen. Nothing magic about that. That however is only a picturesque expression of how we see it after the event, when we realise our mistake and reflect that we *knew* that such and such was pertinent, and yet acted as if we did not know. When we are thinking hard, trying to write a difficult letter, it does not seem to us as if we are turning on a bright light – or if it does, the scene it is supposed to illuminate remains largely in the shadows. Very often we *are* thinking, and yet we do not think of something that later seems absurdly obvious.

c) If we are to regard 'I think in order to solve problems' and so on as giving a reason for thinking, we could expect it would resemble other cases in which we say we do something for a purpose. In those other cases there is a technique or a routine we have hit on, the particulars of which we could explain in some detail, and which we could compare with other ways of achieving the same purposes, listing advantages and disadvantages. Other people can be surprised on hearing how we do it, and sceptical of its merits, and can either show us other ways or be persuaded after all that ours is best. 'How do you get a finish like that?' 'I put on two coats of shellac, rubbing with fine steel wool after each coat, then three coats of varnish which I pumice stone and finally wax.' 'Oh do you? I use lacquer. It doesn't give such a deep finish, but it is much easier. . . .'

No one however claims to have hit on thinking as an ingenious way of solving problems or avoiding follies; we could not explain to someone who has not heard of it, how it is done; we could not list its advantages and disadvantages in comparison with other approaches; and if anyone is surprised when we say we think in order to solve problems, it is neither because it had never occurred to him to think in such a case, nor because he knows of better methods, but because he finds it logically odd to say such a thing.

'I have a problem and I don't know what to do about it.' 'Have you tried thinking? It takes a while to get the hang of it, but once you do it works very nicely. And it's pleasant, too.' Why is that absurd? Is it because everyone knows that the thing to do about a problem is to think, and there is nothing else one might try, or choose in preference to thinking? – No, there are other things: some people recommend sleeping on it; and in saying I had a problem and did not know what to do about it I *was* doing something else, namely applying for assistance. It is absurd rather because we are not recommending anything when we suggest thinking about it: we could not explain what to do by way of thinking about it. Thinking is neither a specific technique, which serves very well for a number of purposes, nor a variety of techniques, each suited to its own task; and therefore it is vacuous to recommend it, and one cannot have reasons for thinking. One can only have reasons for doing something, the nature of which is specifiable in some way.

Can we not explain how to think? – You might, on learning what my problem is, say *'Think of it this way*: you said you would meet her at the station, but neglected to say which one. Now, she knows there are two stations you can go to from here, and that only one of those is a station she can get to from where she is. She will surely expect you to realise that, and will wait for you there.' Here you would indeed be telling me how to think about it, that is to say offering me a possible solution to my problem; but not telling me what I might have done that would have yielded that (or some other) solution. If I was impressed with your solution, and asked you how you did it, it would be useless to reply that you thought about it.

Yet people can learn to think: how is that possible, if thinking is not a describable procedure or process? What they learn is, for example, that there *are* solutions to various sorts of problem, and what some of them look like. Your solution to my problem about which station to go to might teach me something, enable me to solve some similar problems by myself – that is, I might thereafter find that when I had such a problem, the solution often came to me; but I would still have not learned to think in the sense of learning a procedure by which to generate a solution.

We will see later that although there are sometimes procedures for generating solutions, we are not *thinking* when we apply them. That is not to say that we act stupidly, but only that the word 'think' is not used in such a case.

A question can arise whether, if thinking is nothing in

particular, it is anything at all. One may reckon: it must be something, otherwise how could people think? People do think, sometimes very hard. (But they do not apply a procedure 'very hard').

We of course do think: in different cases we try to remember, try to decide, try to solve a problem or compose a limerick. The question is not whether we think, but whether in saying we think we are saying anything at all about what we do. These 'try' expressions, although they can stand in for the word 'think', do not say what we do any more than does that word. They say what our ambition is, but not what we do by way of achieving it. When we fail in these ambitions, our failures cannot be diagnosed as being due to the fact that what we did was not exactly thinking, or not exactly trying either. When we say 'You weren't really trying' we do not mean that you blunderingly did the wrong thing by way of trying.

There is no process, or no assortment of processes, the normal effect of which is solving a problem or writing an amusing letter. It would be such a process if someone found that after reciting a page of *Alice in Wonderland* from memory, then finding the square root of any number over 1000, his letters were always scintillating; but in doing these things he would not be thinking what to say.

We are thinking what to say when we suggest an opening sentence to ourselves, but that is not a process resulting in the composition of an opening sentence: it *is* the composition of a (possible) opening sentence. If I try several sentences before deciding on one, does the consideration of any one of them have a beneficial effect? Well, the rejection of it does, if it was a dull sentence: but I would hardly make a point of thinking of a dull sentence and rejecting it, on the theory that like reciting a page from *Alice in Wonderland* or like the first few strokes with sandpaper on a rough piece of wood, it will have its effect on the finished product. We say we are thinking when we entertain a possible sentence, not because that is one of the known techniques for writing a good letter, but because we remain undecided. To say that one is thinking is not a description of what is going on, but an indication that whatever we are doing, we are doing with some ambition, which we do not regard as achieved.

There is a sense in which people do often have reasons for

thinking: one can say 'If I don't get busy thinking about his offer, I won't know what to say when I see him tomorrow'. These are however reasons for thinking about the offer now, rather than later or not at all: they are not reasons for choosing thinking about it, in preference to some other way of handling it.

One *can* choose thinking about it in preference to prayer, or sleeping on it; but it is not clear that one can have reasons for doing so. If I say that I think rather than pray because it is more likely to yield an intelligent solution, it is not clear that I am saying more than that I try to be intelligent because I think I will succeed better that way. That may be debatable, but not because 'to try to be intelligent' describes a course of action that is ill-suited to success.

If we cannot have reasons for thinking, it would be a mistake to infer that we must be thinkers by nature, that we just do think, and could no more avoid it than we could stop breathing or urinating. It makes sense to say we breathe by nature, because we can say what breathing is, but unless we can say what thinking is, it makes no more sense to say that we do it by nature than that we have reasons for doing it.

One would hardly say 'I always think when I am designing a boiler'. That one thinks in such a case is not an occasion for surprise, as if other people did it other ways, and might never have thought of thinking. Is that because thinking is such an uncommonly good and well-established policy, and there is none other that anyone might prefer, or might abandon when he learned of thinking? I have been arguing that it is rather because thinking is not a practice at all; but if it is not, how is it that we do often urge a person to think, or complain that he has failed to think?

When a student, having been shown a procedure of some complexity, blunders when he tries to do it himself, we will sometimes say 'You weren't thinking!': or if at some point he does not know what to do next, we may urge that he think. Yet we did not, in explaining the procedure to him, tell him that here you add, here you multiply and here you think. Thinking is not a step in the procedure, which he omitted or executed incompetently. So why do we enjoin thinking, rather than reminding him specifically what is called for at this or that point?

There is something right about replying that it was because he was not thinking that he blundered. This suggests that thinking, though not a step in the procedure, is an over-riding activity that one must perform all the time one is doing such things, and that his fault was to let up on it, and further we do not usually bother to mention it, because if you know anything, you know that it is necessary to think. Yet we could not say *what* he had failed to do, and do not seriously suppose that there was something, over-riding or otherwise, that he was so incompetent as to omit. Generally he could say he *was* thinking. We enjoin thinking when he has blundered just because it tells him nothing whatever about what to do. We have shown him what he is to do, and now he should know: in telling him to think we are declining further advice, and throwing him back on his own resources.

The foregoing line of thought has carried me a long way from anything directly suggested in §§466–71. To see if any of what I have argued might be *indirectly* suggested, let me first consider in what way Wittgenstein might have thought the question why we think is like the question why we bring up our children. The latter can seem beguiling. One may think: it does happen that people will bring up their children because they believe it will pay, but it is a rather special case, and what about the ordinary run of cases? It does not seem right to say that we do it out of love, or duty, or for the sake of some very special kind of satisfaction we get or hope for, so why *do* we do it? There must be some deeper reason, but what can it be?

If we (a) do not doubt there is a reason, and (b) are not satisfied with any of the more ready-to-hand accounts of what it is, the reason will remain a mystery; but if the question whether to bring up one's children does not normally arise, there will not ordinarily be a reason why we do it, and therefore not a deep reason. In this way Wittgenstein might have meant to put us on to the idea that there might similarly be no reason why we think.

His point here would not be that we do it 'for no reason', the way I might, for example, in cleaning my teeth always start at the back. I would be doing something for which there might have been a reason, but I just did not happen to have one. By contrast, I am suggesting that thinking is not (generally) the

181

kind of thing for which there might be a reason, because it is not a specific activity that we might have found valuable.

We might also consider what might be learned from pursuing the question (§468) what would show why one thinks? We know how to answer that question in the case of other activities. We know what to conclude from the fact that a person, when he was being talked into taking up tennis, was unmoved by such representations as that it is fun, or good for one's health, but began to be interested when told that many romances start on the tennis court, and stopped resisting entirely when told that he could meet a lot of important people that way; or we would know what to think if, when he considered giving it up, he was unmoved by the thought of the pleasure he would be missing, or the adverse effect on his health, but could not imagine what he would do with his summer evenings.

We have difficulty however in describing a case in which someone is being talked into thinking, or out of it. This is neither because we are all thinkers already, nor because it is our nature to think, and we have no choice in the matter, but because we cannot say what thinking is. We might imagine a scene in which someone was being talked into thinking, was unmoved by allegations that it was fun or good for the soul, but was all set to think when he heard that it was a noble activity. He might say 'All right, I'll take it up. What is it?' In such a case we would know something about what can move this man to do things, but nothing specifically about reasons for thinking: the persuasion might have taken exactly the same course if one had said 'There is something I would like to see you do, but I will not tell you what it is until you agree to do it. Here are some reasons for doing it . . .'. It would be all the same if we had been talking him into playing tiddley-winks. One needs to know *what* one is considering taking up or abandoning; and in the case of thinking we are unable to say what that is.

It cannot be claimed that these ways of following up §§467 and 468 help much to confirm the correctness of my general interpretive thesis. The most that can be said is that it is interesting and plausible to take these sections this way, and that so read they are consistent with that thesis.

I have argued that there can be no such question as why one

thinks, because thinking is neither a specific activity nor a family of such activities, and hence not something that could be chosen in preference to other ways of achieving the same ends, or whose merits could be argued over, or which we might try as an experiment to see how well it worked.

A question that now arises is, if Wittgenstein meant to suggest anything like this about thinking, how could he say that we do sometimes think because it has been found to pay? If there is no such question why we think, how can it sometimes have an answer?

One way of resolving this difficulty would be to say that although thinking is not generally a describable activity, it sometimes is, and when it is, there can be a question why we do it. It is a specific activity when it consists of calculating, and in that case it is possible to say that sometimes we do it because we have found it to pay. Other times there may be other reasons: in the classroom we do it because the teacher insists, and on winter afternoons we may do it just for fun. Certainly we have various reasons for calculating, but is calculating a species of thinking?

Many people would not doubt it, and Wittgenstein gave every appearance of so believing: in §466 he treats calculating as an example of thinking, and in §§469–70 he treats the fact that there are fewer boiler explosions now that we calculate the thickness of the walls as showing that it sometimes pays to think.

His reasoning is not entirely satisfactory, however. What pays here is not so much calculating as constructing boilers according to certain principles. To do this one must of course calculate, but one can no more say it pays to calculate when using such and such a formula for the thickness of the boiler walls, than that in walking it pays to put one foot in front of the another. It could scarcely happen that people developed a formula for such cases, and only later hit on the idea of calculating its applications. If there is anything that pays here, apart from using a sound principle, it is not calculating, but calculating attentively. Since, if someone makes a mistake in calculating, we can say 'You weren't thinking', but not 'You weren't calculating', it is tempting to regard thinking again as the overriding activity of exercising care in doing such things as calculating. On that basis it could make sense after all to say that thinking pays, but not that calculating does.

However (a) we have seen reason to suppose that the idea that thinking is such an overriding activity is an illusion arising from the fact that we charge people who have performed defectively with failing to think, and (b) the attentiveness with which we may calculate consists, not in something different from and beneficial to calculating, which we call 'thinking', but in further calculating: in doing it a different way to see if we get the same result, or in asking someone else to do it. This could have been what Wittgenstein was suggesting when he said in §469 'Or since each calculation done by one engineer got checked by another'. The 'or' here might be read, not 'or alternatively', but 'or is it rather'. Then the case in which calculating pays is not that in which we calculate, rather than failing to do so, but only that in which, having done it, we do some more by way of double-checking. This would save Wittgenstein from the folly of saying that in applying a mathematical formula it pays to calculate, but not from that of saying that calculating is a species of thinking, if that is not true.

When we teach a person to apply a formula, and he sets about doing it, is he thinking? He certainly is if it is a struggle for him, if he has to stop and try and remember what to do next, or if he has to improvise because there is a feature of the new problem that has not been explicitly covered in the instruction; but when he becomes expert at it, he either does it without thinking or the thinking part of his performance is the effort he puts into such improvising as may always be necessary.

If we ask someone to do a calculation, and shortly he says he is thinking, we would not naturally suppose that he was doing it, but rather that he had encountered some difficulty in doing it. We do not use the word 'think' for times when we are proceeding efficiently and with assurance, but for the breakdown points, when it is not clear to us what to do, but we suppose that the solution lies somehow in using what we already know.

This tends to be obscured from us by our fascination with the fact that thinking goes on, as we say, 'in the head'. We treat as the definition of at least some thinking that it is purposeful activity in the head, and reckon that since calculating can be so described, it must also be thinking. We could cut out the fact that it is in the head by imagining someone who could only calculate on paper. Normally he just writes out his calculations in some clear order, but he sometimes leaves off, and in a separate space on the page writes exclamation points and question marks, rules, or exploratory calculations. Sometimes after writing a rule he will cross it out and write it differently, or write a different one. Normally after making such entries, he returns to his task and proceeds with it in a businesslike way, sometimes transferring entries from the other part of the page. When he is proceeding normally we say he is calculating, but when he breaks off and engages in ancillary activities, he is described as thinking. If we now transpose all this into the head, thinking is not just anything purposeful that goes on in the head. Sometimes when he is purposefully engaged he is not thinking but calculating, and he is thinking when he is engaged in anything intended to enable him to continue calculating. (This of course applies at most only to purposeful thinking, not to thinking what a lovely day it is, or thinking of Aunt Agatha when one sees Margaret Rutherford.)

Hence it appears that Wittgenstein may have been wrong in assuming that calculating was a species of thinking; but whether it is such or not makes little difference to my argument: if it is true that we can have reasons for doing something only if it is a specific teachable action or sequence of actions, it will either be true that it never makes any sense to ask why we think or, if calculating is a species of thinking, it will be true that this question makes no sense except in the case of calculating or any other statable, systematic procedure. It is not in itself particularly interesting, whether we can have reasons for thinking. What is interesting is what we can learn about the concept of thinking by 'suppressing' the question why we think.

Twenty-Two

SUBTRACTING
(AND ADDING) LANGUAGE

491. Not: 'Without language we could not communicate with one another' – but for sure: without language
we cannot influence other people in such-and-such
ways; cannot build roads and machines, etc. And also:
without the use of speech and writing people could not
communicate.

WITH THIS statement in *Philosophical Investigations* Wittgenstein is making a point as obliquely as he ever does.

Let us call the three propositions 'A', 'B' and 'C'. Although
there are obvious differences in wording, we might have been
inclined to say their sense was substantially the same, or if
different, not so different that one could be false while the
others were true. It comes as a surprise therefore that 'A' is
rejected while 'B' and 'C' are accepted; and it is surprising
also because 'A' is a proposition one might well have let pass
as being true. 'A' is rejected; but it is not clear whether
Wittgenstein means that it is false, or that it is unsatisfactory
in some other way, such as being undecidable, or being nonsense.

'A' might be called nonsensical or trivial if we defined
communication in such a way that nothing was communication which was not carried on in words and sentences; or if
we defined language in such a way that anything in which
living beings communicated was a language. Then 'A' would
come out either 'Without a way of communicating, people
could not communicate', or 'Without words and sentences
people could not do what can only be done with words and
sentences'.

The possibility that 'A' is trivial reminds us that we are not
sure what we mean here by 'language' and 'communication'.

These words are not particularly problematic in their ordinary use. The sentences 'Spanish is an easy language to learn', 'He used a lot of foul language', 'He became so upset that we couldn't communicate any more', and 'Complex subjects are better communicated in writing than orally' are not puzzling; but these words are used in an exceptional way in 'A', and we no longer know what is to count as language, or as communication: smiles, gestures, pictures, the chirping of birds, the dancing of bees, might or might not be 'language'; and being cheered by a smile or frightened by a gesture might or might not be 'communication'. (If I shake my fist and snarl at someone, and he runs away as I wished, have I communicated something to him? *What?*)

Even if we take 'language' in its most familiar sense, as at least involving words and sentences, there will be a problem of a rather different sort about what exactly we are called upon in 'A' to subtract. Are we to suppose that certain people who can talk, do not talk on a certain occasion, and so do not communicate – or that there are certain members of a tribe that has a language, who have never learned to talk – or that no human beings talk or write, that no language has yet come into existence? If we make the last mentioned supposition, how much should we subtract from human beings as we know them? Would they understand various fairly elementary concepts, like, 'tomorrow', 'soon', 'as far as that', 'to the left' but just not yet have invented the mechanisms for expressing them? Would they wish, hope, expect, fear, dread, long, believe and doubt, – or are these capacities that they acquire in learning language, and to be subtracted when we subtract language?

In view of questions like these, 'A' might be called undecidable. We are all at sea, and do not know how to answer the questions. It is no use studying apes, for at least two reasons: (i) while it may be clear enough that they desire and fear things, we do not know whether to say they wish or long for them, or that they dread anything. It is not that they clearly do not: it is just that we lose our grip on these distinctions when applied to beings that do not talk. (ii) Even if we could answer these questions as applied to apes, apes are not human beings, and 'A' made a claim about what *we* could not do without language. Some grunting aside, apes do not have a language;

but it is not clear that if they did, they would chat, joke, report, reminisce, discuss – in short that a little language training is all that stands between them and being human.

'A' might be called false if it seemed obvious that children, without either saying or being able to say these things, can communicate that they are hungry, that they do not want to go out to play, that they would like a drink, but not of milk, and so on. Here we would not be working with the concept of people, none of whom had ever talked, but with that of certain members of a talking species, whose members did not yet talk. 'A' would be false similarly if we worked with the concept of people who, having learned to talk, were struck dumb and also forgot how to write. They could clearly communicate a great deal of what they would otherwise have said, in pictures, pantomime, shaking and nodding of the head, and so on. They would have our concepts, and just be deprived of the usual ways of expressing them.

There is no indication at all of which kind of rejection Wittgenstein intended. Perhaps his point was what we might well conclude from what has been said so far: that 'A' leaves altogether too many questions unanswered about what we mean by 'language' and by 'communication', and whether in subtracting language we are supposing people able to speak but not speaking, having learned to talk, but struck dumb, able to learn language but not yet having learned it, or living in a world in which there was no language, and what kind of beings we would then be conceiving.

When we turn to 'B', it may be significant in the first place that where 'A' had 'could not', 'B' has 'cannot'. 'Could not' opens up all the possibilities we have seen of being struck dumb, of never having learned to talk, of being members of a tribe, none of whom talked, and so on; but 'cannot' is a word one would use if one wanted to suggest leaving people just as they are, with the one difference that, say during Lent, they do not talk. During whatever time they did not talk or write, they could not influence people in such-and-such ways or build roads or machines. Depending on what examples we supply of 'such-and-such ways', that does seem 'for sure'.

Why does Wittgenstein give such prominence here to influencing people, and building roads and machines? There is little other evidence that he holds a theory that such are the

Subtracting (and Adding) Language

prime functions of language, and strong evidence, for
example in §§23, 27, 304, that he does not. It seems more
likely that he simply wanted to be more specific about what
one may do with words than 'A' was with the word 'communicate' – and chose influencing people and building
things as two among many specific examples. If that is so, it
would reinforce the suggestion made earlier that part of the
reason for Wittgenstein's rejection of 'A' was that it was not
sufficiently clear what 'communicate' *meant* in that context.

We can perhaps build dirt roads without saying or writing
anything, but not roads designed to withstand frost, to carry
heavy loads and to be safe at high speeds; and similarly we
can encourage people just with smiles and gestures, but not
persuade them that a certain distinction ought to be made, or
relieve psychological problems with tall tales of the machina-
tions of the super ego. It is likely that for 'such-and-such
ways' in 'B', we are supposed to supply examples of fairly
sophisticated forms of influence; and in sum that the point of
'B' is that it disambiguates 'A' by (i) taking the case of people
who can speak, but do not on certain occasions, (ii) being
more specific than 'communicate' is as to the difference not
speaking (or writing) is supposed to make, but not necessarily taking influencing people or building roads as the
specific examples, and (c) excluding from consideration
rudimentary forms of influence, construction or whatever
other uses of language we might take as our specific cases. So
modified, 'A' is 'for sure'.

On first reading 'C', one would not take it to be significantly
different from 'A', and yet it is endorsed while 'A' is rejected.
Given the idea that 'B' and 'C' is disambiguate 'A', it is not
difficult to see what difference is made by the substitution of
'the use of speech and writing' in 'C' for 'language' in 'A'. The
replacement of 'language' in 'A' with 'speech and writing' in
'C' could eliminate uncertainties about whether birds' chirping, bees' dancing or people's gesticulating should for that
purpose be deemed 'language', since whatever these things
are, they are not speech or writing.

The introduction of the words 'the use of' in 'C' might be
intended to settle the question whether we are imagining
people not having a language, or having one, but not using it
on this or that occasion. Obviously if we *refrained* from

189

speaking or writing, we could not communicate, at least not in all the complex ways we do communicate by speaking or writing.

If that is what 'C' means, it is a very humdrum truth, and it is unlikely that Wittgenstein was interested in it for its own sake. The same is true of 'B'. Probably the function of 'B' and 'C' was to help bring out the peculiarity of 'A'.

The most interesting fact about 'A' that has emerged is that while we may incautiously talk of people without a language, or people prior to the evolution of a linguistic capacity, we really are all at sea, and have no idea how much to subtract in order to imagine people without language: whether to conceive them having the same natural capacities we have, but just not having learned a language; whether to suppose that they can think, believe, guess and hope; whether to reckon that they will have the concept of giving things names, but just no names; and so on.

When do we have occasion to substract language? When we are wondering what language is and what it does for us, it seems plausible to pursue a program of imagining that we had no language and then considering how we could establish one, what needs it would satisfy, what relations it would bear to our surroundings and thoughts and feelings.

In the very statement of this program we have assumed that our thoughts and feelings would remain when language was subtracted; but let us look first at how we might work out some of the relations between language and our surroundings.

We suppose that long ago it occurred to a few people that it would be useful to have a way of saying where game was to be found, and what sort of game, and that they might do this by establishing relations between various noises and deer, stags, pheasants, and so on. Here again we have assumed that we could have this thought, without yet having any words in which to express it. We go on from there to imagine our primitive people calling *these* things 'stags', *these* 'deer', and so on. These? *What*? – Well, they call *deer* 'deer'. We are supposing, that is, that they have the concept of an animal species of which this animal will serve as a paradigm, they only need to attach a word to it.

If we go on to suppose them calling the direction of the

rising sun 'east', that of the noonday sun 'south', that of the setting sun 'west' and that opposite to that of the noonday sun 'north', and that they call the distance to yonder hill a 'mile', and they repeat that word twice for two miles, three times for three miles, – we are supposing that they have the concepts of direction, noonday, opposite, distance, number and same.

We are likely to think that there will be no difficulty here, because after all we do not teach young children at least the rudiments of language without relying on their having a prior understanding of any of such concepts? Why then could not a whole language, or at least the rudiments of one, come into being without anyone having a prior understanding of its basic concepts? The answer to that is because the teachers of children understand the concepts they teach, and can chivvy, correct and encourage children until they get things right. We are trying, as it were, to imagine learning a language without anyone to show us the way, and even: without there being a way to be learned.

If, in subtracting language, we incautiously subtract just the words, we will be apt to suppose that, just as there are deer, directions and distances to which we can give names, so also there are beliefs, hopes, expectations, fears, memories. The words for these things will each name a familiar state of affairs, and when another person who has learned the words hears them, he will know that a state of affairs of an appropriate kind exists.

We then, not doubting that there is a distinctive something called a belief, a hope, a memory, press the question *what* distinctive something it is, and thereby bring upon ourselves all the intractable problems of traditional philosophical psychology. The problems arise, not because the phenomena are elusive or hard to describe, but because we never doubt that there are phenomena, and that it is in view of their existence that we say hope, believe, and so on.

A rather different offshoot of the incautious subtraction of language is the idea that words are just noises or marks on paper, meaningless in themselves, and deriving their meaning from the connections we make between them and our hopes, wishes and doubts, or deer, stags and the rising sun, or both. This gives rise to a search for a general account of what the meaning of a word is. The problem here is not to specify the meanings of various words, but to say what we are specifying when we specify meanings. The word itself seems dead. To understand it we must go from the word to its meaning. So much seems clear. It is when we ask *what* we 'go to' that puzzlement and disagreement arises. No answer seems to satisfy us, but we persist with the question because it seems so clear that words are something we have devised to stand in for meanings, and would be nothing without the meanings they express.

I have now shown how the idea of subtracting language may be connected with a number of different philosophical problems. The suggestion of course is that the problems to which this idea gives rise are false problems; but since their fascination derives only in part from this source, it would require a great deal more than what has been done here, to establish this proposition.

There are more detailed applications at a number of places in the *Investigations*:

In §§2 and 6 we are asked to conceive the description of the use of the words 'slab', 'block', 'pillar' and 'beam' as a complete primitive language. That would mean among other things, that these people would not have sentences or questions or explanations of the meanings of words; but we easily forget this, and ask (§10) that the expression 'This word signifies this' be made part of the description; or (§19) whether 'Slab' is a sentence or a word, or whether it means 'Bring me a slab'. We had subtracted these features of language, but then we proceed as if they had not been subtracted.

In §25, the person who is inclined to say that animals do not talk because they do not think is treated as supposing that people, by contrast, being thinkers, had some use for a language, and so developed one. When he subtracted language from people, he incautiously failed to subtract thought.

In §32 Augustine is accused of having subtracted language from children without subtracting thought: of treating them as if, without language, they could figure out the linguistic behaviour of adults, much as an anthropologist does that of a tribe with a language he does not know (see also §206).

In §51 it is suggested that in setting up the primitive colour language in §48, while we thought we were connecting the letters R, G, B and W with colour patches, we had in fact connected them with our colour words. In subtracting ordinary colour language, we just subtracted the words, and failed to subtract our ability to use them.

In §§257, 261 and 270 it is suggested in various ways that we are forgetting how much 'stage setting in the language' is presupposed in the act of naming: that in §258, although we were supposing a language being created from scratch, we called 'S' the *name* of a *sensation* the diarist *has*, using words from our language which would not yet exist in the diarist's language.

If we reflect that language did get started, somehow, it will be very puzzling *how*, if not in the kinds of way just now described. The question will be best divided into two: how did the human race come to have any language at all, and how do children learn a language?

Wittgenstein did not have much to say about the former question, the answer to which in any case is not likely to be of great philosophical interest. In §18 there is in the background a suggestion that languages evolve; but what probably interested Wittgenstein about this was not their first beginnings, but their further development once they have somehow got a foothold. If languages evolve, there will be little reason to expect that at any stage in their development they will have a particularly elegant or orderly structure. However it is perhaps a further implication of an evolutionary view that there is no reason to suppose that the first beginnings of speech bore any extensive resemblance to language as we know it. If there were encouraging and discouraging noises that people made in teaching the fashioning of hunting tools, we could not yet call them words, or identify them more with 'yes' and 'no' than with 'good' and 'bad'. If they occurred initially along with smiles and frowns of pleasure and disgust, it might be a long time before (a) it became quite standard in the community intentionally to make a particular noise along with these smiles and frowns, or (b) anyone used the noises just by themselves, without accompanying demonstrative behaviour, and was understood, or (c) they were used in situations other than those in which they first made their appearance. If 'yomp' were an encouraging noise, and had initially occurred only in teaching the fashioning of tools, but one day it was used when someone responded appropriately to gestures intended to mean 'look over there', a large step would perhaps have been taken towards having a language.

Wittgenstein had a good deal more to say about how children learn to speak, and here, as is well known, his primary emphasis was on training, as distinct from explanation (see for example §§1, 2, 5, 6, 9, 143, 199, 208). While explanations *can* be used in the course of training, some training is done without explanations – (we train dogs, as well as soldiers and logicians) – but the primary notion of training is that, with or without explanations, we bring it about that people behave in various complex ways *automatically*. Thus for example Wittgenstein writes (§198):

> ... What has the expressions of a rule – say a sign-post – got to do with my actions? What sort of connection is there here? – Well, perhaps this one: I have been trained to react to this sign in a particular way, and now I do so react to it.

(See also §§201, 211, 217, 219, 228.)

Wittgenstein was not much interested in *how* this training is carried out. In §1 he writes 'Well, I assume that he *acts* as I have described. Explanations come to an end somewhere'; but in §208 he does describe what may sometimes happen:

> I do it, he does it after me; and I influence him with expressions of agreement, rejection, expectation, encouragement. I let him go his way, or hold him back; and so on.

One may also use inventive, individualised methods, for example when we find a student making a systematic mistake, and teach him our way as an offshoot of his (§143). In such ways we work with a student until he does what we are trying to teach correctly, that is, as we do it (§§145, 190). At this point there is a congruence between what the student does 'automatically', and what masters of the business at hand do automatically.

In this connection Wittgenstein uses the word 'custom' in a way that initially sounds strange. He says (§199) 'To obey a rule, to make a report, to give an order, to play a game of chess, are *customs* (uses, institutions)'. This will sound strange if we suppose it implies that, for example, a tour guide might say 'Among the customs of these people are obeying rules, making reports, playing chess . . .'. In the tour-guide sense, it might be a custom to play chess only in the early afternoon, or always when the moon is full, but hardly just to play chess;

and there could not be a custom of disobeying rules, because in that case the concept of a rule would not be understood (§§204, 345).

Hence Wittgenstein is surely using the word 'custom' in a special sense; and we might get some feel for this sense if we wrote 'the art of', or 'skill in' obeying rules, making reports. . . . Then, it might be suggested, 'custom' means 'habituation to or in something cherished as standard in the community'. It is ambiguous, and unlike most employment of ambiguous words, it is here being employed at the same time in both its senses. On the one hand it has the sense it has in the expression 'being accustomed to' ('being used to'), while on the other hand it is a matter of being accustomed to a custom, that is, to do something the way it is done. The way it is done, however, is not something that could be fully described, the way most customs in the ordinary sense can, but it is the way people do it who are themselves 'accustomed' to doing it.

The term 'custom' might have been borrowed from Hume. In the *Treatise*, Book I, Part I, Section VII, Hume explains our grasp of general words, saying

> When we have found a resemblance among several objects . . . we apply the same name to all of them, whatever difference we may observe in their degree of quantity and quality, and whatever other differences may appear among them. After we have acquired a custom of this kind, the hearing of that name revives the idea of one of these objects. . . . But as the same word is supposed to have been frequently applied to other individuals . . . the word not being able to revive the idea of all these individuals . . . revives that custom which we have acquired by surveying them. They are not really and in fact present to the mind, but only in power . . . we . . . keep ourselves in readiness to survey any of them.*

A 'custom' here is equated with a *power* and with a *readiness*, and later with a *habit*. In Hume, there is nothing social about this. It is a disposition or a capacity one comes to possess, and can exercise when the need arises. Whereas Hume, we could say, takes a private enterprise view of the acquisition of these capacities or customs (see the first sentence quoted above), Wittgenstein's view is that we come to have the same disposition, capacity, habit or custom as is possessed by other mem-

* Hume, *Treatise of Human Nature*, ed. Selby-Bigge (Oxford, 1967) pp. 20-1.

bers of the community.

We come to agree in the way we use language (§241), that is, to have the same linguistic dispositions, capacities or customs as other people. The word 'in' in §241 is worth dwelling on. We do not agree *on* ways of speaking, or work out agreements *how* we will use words. There are not in that sense conventions established. Most of us cannot say what we know about the use of most words, and yet we are very sensitive to odd or incorrect uses (compare Z §§111, 114, 119). A departure from the usual use, Hume might have said, 'revives the custom', and sets us to correcting, or for example to contrasting the normal implications of what someone has said with what we take it he meant.

It is as a result of rejections, in countless cases, of our initial blundering ways of speaking, that the complex propensity, custom or habit of using a word as other people do takes shape. A misunderstanding arises from our having innocently misused a word, and thereafter we avoid using it in that kind of case, or avoid using it in just that way; while on the other hand if we try out an application of a word in a case that is new to us and no difficulty or confusion arises, an addition is thereby established to our habitude with regard to that word.

This all seems scarcely controversial: if it is (fairly) obvious, why might Wittgenstein see fit to harp on it? Because we can easily be befuddled by the problem: How can it be that (a) we can understand a word at a particular time, (b) in understanding it, we know something complex, but (c) it is not evident that anything suitably complex runs through our minds?

Wittgenstein poses this and similar questions repeatedly:

> In saying 'When I heard this word, it meant ... to me' one refers to a *point of time* and to a *way of using the word*. (Of course this is the combination we fail to grasp) (page 175).
> 338. ... in order to *want* to say something one must also have mastered a language; and yet it is clear that one can want to speak without speaking. Just as one can want to dance without dancing.
> And when we think about this, we grasp at the *image* of dancing, speaking, etc.
> 627. 'I know exactly what I was going to say!' And yet I did not say it. – And yet I don't read it off from some other process which

took place then and which I remember.

Nor am I *interpreting* that situation and its antecedents. For I don't consider them and don't judge them.

692. Is it correct for someone to say: 'When I gave you this rule, I meant you to . . . in this case'? Even if he did not think of this case at all as he gave the rule? Of course it is correct.

139. . . . Can what we grasp *in a flash* accord with a use, fit or fail to fit it? And how can what is present to us in an instant . . . fit a use? (See also §§138, 191, 197, 318–20.)

For some of these cases, Hume had the answer: the word revives the 'custom'. In other cases, when we suddenly understand (i.e. understand something we have not previously understood), we perhaps make a connection with an already established 'custom', for example when it dawns on us that this word has the same meaning as that. If there is a habitude already established for the second of these words, we can then use the first, in the ways we know how to use the second.

In such cases as that of saying what one had wanted or intended to say, or that of saying what one had meant another person to do in such and such a case, we are exercising abilities of somewhat different kinds; but concerning all these cases Wittgenstein's point is that a person possessing the relevant ability simply exercises it. He knows what to do and does it; but this knowledge does not consist in a likeness of what he does (or a description or a set of instructions) being lodged in his head or running through his mind.

Perhaps the most arresting analogy Wittgenstein offers here is that of the string of beads being drawn from a box through a hole in the lid (*BB* §40). We naturally suppose that the beads were already strung together this way inside the box, but Wittgenstein suggests that they might have come into existence at the hole in the lid. In the case of the beads coming out of a box, this is an unlikely possibility, but in the case of speaking, it is not. There is no doubt a wonderful lot of neural equipment in our heads that enables us to say things, but when the equipment is in good order, appropriate and grammatically correct sentences form *on our lips*.

When, having subtracted a language, we set about restoring it, great care must be taken if we are to avoid restoring, not language but a monster of our own devising.

Twenty-Three

SUBTRACTING THE FACT THAT
ONE'S ARM GOES UP

> 621. Let us not forget this: when 'I raise my arm', my
> arm goes up. And the problem arises: what is left over
> when I subtract the fact that my arm goes up from the fact
> that I raise my arm?
> ((Are the kinaesthetic sensations my willing?))

THE ABOVE quotation is a much-pondered passage from
the *Philosophical Investigations*. The sentence in double
parentheses suggests that Wittgenstein thought that when we
raise an arm, we *will* it to go up. In the surrounding sections
he said nothing that clearly indicated the contrary, although
it would not be surprising to find that he did not himself make
this assumption, but was portraying one of the ways our
deliberations may run if we do make it. He did, in *RPP* i.51,
say: 'How is "will" actually used? In philosophy one is un-
aware of having invented a quite new use of the word'. Do we,
in the normal case of doing something, will to do it? Do we
even know what this means?

In general, and excluding technical terms, we understand a
word when it has an ordinary use with which we are familiar,
and its current use is one of its ordinary uses; but 'to will' has
no perfectly ordinary use. There are noun forms of 'will', as in
the expression 'against my will', 'will power', and 'last will
and testament', but it has an ordinary use as a verb only when
we talk of willing another person to turn left, or of willing a
stone to move. Although we are sometimes asked to do those
things, and sometimes do something in response to such
requests (like picturing the stone moving and grunting as
with effort at the same time) – we have no idea whether we are
doing the right thing, or whether there is a right thing for
these purposes. Moreover even if there were something to be

done in these cases, that would not show the applicability of the verb 'to will' to the case of raising one's arm or wiggling one's toes. If, by adeptly executed mental gymnastics, we could make stones move, and called that 'willing', then by analogy we would get our toes to wiggle by willing, not in the case in which we wiggled them, but in the case in which we pictured them wiggling and whistled softly, and lo, they wiggled.

If it is therefore doubtful whether the difference between raising an arm and having it go up is that in the former case we will it, it is correspondingly doubtful whether what we find when we subtract that fact that an arm goes up from the fact that we raise it will be the phenomenon of willing; but that is not to say there is no problem here. There is surely a very important difference between raising an arm and having it go up, and it is a puzzling question what the difference is. If we found what it was, we might not choose to say that we had thereby discovered what willing is, but we could still suppose that we learned something else, perhaps something about what it is to *do* something.

How then should we perform this bit of subtraction? A procedure that will naturally suggest itself is that of considering cases in which the arm does not go up. That would certainly take away the fact that it goes up. We could fix an arm down with straps and then try to raise it, reckoning that what we then observe will be what we do by way of raising it. What we observe in such a case is chiefly bulging muscles and a sense of great strain; and since it seems fair to treat the bulging muscles as part of the effect of what we do, and not the doing itself, it may appear that the sense of strain must be the doing – perhaps that what we do is play this feeling over our muscles, and the greater the resistance to be overcome, the more we have to turn up the intensity of the feeling. (After all, the harder we try, the more intense the feeling is.)

Some such reasoning as this might explain the popularity of the notion of trying as a kind of psychic strain; and yet it is surely a misbegotten idea. There is no better reason for treating the strain we feel, when an arm will not go up, as the cause of the bulging muscles, than as the effect of the fact that they are bulging; nor is there any explanation given of what we do by way of turning on the feeling of strain. Worse than that, we are examining the wrong kind of case. We are trying to see how we raise an arm by studying a case in which we do not raise it.

This last may have been Wittgenstein's point when he said 'Let us not forget this: when "I raise my arm", my arm goes up'. It is odd that he should say this, in as much as you would think it would be the last thing we would forget; and odd too that he should say it first, and then pose his question, rather than saying something like 'When we ask what is left over when I subtract the fact that my arm goes up from the fact that I raise it, let us not forget that when I raise it, it goes up'. Yet this is just what we did forget in the preceding line of thinking; and it is surely a mistake. We cannot find out what happens when I raise it from studying cases in which it does not go up.

We were trying to subtract physically, one might say, as we might subtract the effect of light on plant growth by keeping plants in darkness and seeing what happened. It is now clear that we need a different kind of subtraction, one in which all the elements remain precisely where they are, but we as it were cross out some, and focus on what is left. We want to stick with everyday cases in which we raise an arm, and just find what they contain, apart from the arm going up.

There is a problem now that scarcely arose before, of what exactly to take away. Do we just subtract the spatial relocation of the arm, or do we subtract with it the various sensations we might have – a slight feeling of the motion of air, slight pains in the joints if we are a little rheumatic, scarcely noticeable feelings of muscular strain?

These questions are not difficult, but the reason they are not may be significant: we are not prepared to accept just any remainder. We could not accept the slight draught we feel, because it is the effect, not the cause, of the arm going up; and the same for the slight pains and muscular sensations. Nor would we accept some random thought we happened to have at the time, or the grief we happened to be feeling. We are guided in what we accept by the idea of the cause of the arm going up.

What is wrong with that? We are slipping back from a case in which we raise an arm, to one in which we do something and it goes up. It is indeed a special case of its going up, special in that it is in accordance with our own wish and machination that it rises; but not more special than the case in which something has gone wrong with my arm and I find that the only way to make it go up is by certain manipulation of the shoulder. When I do that and it rises, it is not an ordinary case of raising an arm.

Something like that was perhaps Wittgenstein's point in §616 when he said 'When I raise my arm, I have not wished it might go up. The voluntary action excludes this wish'. The wishing here is treated as what we do that has the effect of the arm rising; and when Wittgenstein says 'The voluntary action excludes this wish', he can be taken to mean that wishing and thereby making the arm go up is no more a case of raising one's arm than pressing the arm against a wall and then standing away and having it go up. We can make arms rise that way, and we might have been able to make them rise by wishing, but in neither case would we be raising them.

The point is clearer in §627, where *deciding* to raise an arm is treated as a candidate for what we do in order to make the arm rise. Wittgenstein says that the correct description is not 'I form the decision to pull the bell at five o'clock, and when it strikes 5, my arm makes this movement', – but '. . . when it strikes 5, I raise my arm'.

The point here has nothing to do with the special character of wishing and deciding. It is not that neither wishing nor deciding is what we do, and therefore it must be something else, but that whatever we put into that slot will have the consequence that the arm goes up, rather than that we raise it. Hence there is nothing we do by way of raising an arm, and it will be no use sifting through what remains when we subtract the fact that the arm goes up, looking for something that is an action and makes the arm rise.

This is not of course to deny that there is a difference between raising an arm and having it rise, but only to deny that the difference lies in anything we do that brings it about that the arm goes up. There is certainly a difference, and that is the fact that haunts us. What does remain when we subtract the fact that the arm rises?

Here we must remember to stay strictly with ordinary cases in which we do things: point to an object in the distance, shake hands with someone, reach for a cup on a shelf – not allowing any of the various things we are predisposed to expect, to creep into the picture, unless they are clearly to be found in the ordinary cases. Because in the ordinary case it is not against our wishes that we do something, we are predisposed to expect a wish or a desire; yet in the ordinary case of getting a cup down from the shelf we will look in vain for a yearning or a craving, or even a slight yen, to perform that action. We just do it; and its being not against our wishes comes out in our not being surprised or vexed at having done it. Wishing and craving is much more characteristic of cases in which we cannot and do not perform an action.

When something queer happens and our arm goes up when we have not decided to raise it, we are predisposed to expect a decision in the case of raising it; but again we will look in vain for a decision in the ordinary case of pointing something out or of shaking hands; and as we saw, even when there is a decision, the action when it comes is not different from what it would have been if it had been done in the ordinary course of events.

We are not *trying* to raise an arm when it mysteriously goes up, and therefore we are predisposed to expect endeavour; but we do not *try* to point at something, shake hands or get something down from a shelf (§623). We can try to do those things when we are weak and feverish or the shelf is very high or the object pointed at can only be glimpsed occasionally, but it is not only or even chiefly in those cases that we do something.

If we thus exclude wanting, wishing, deciding, trying, the sense of effort, and of course random thoughts or incidental feelings of grief or excitement, there will appear to be nothing left as a remainder when we do this subtracting, and the difference between raising the arm and having it go up will again threaten to disappear. There is perhaps, as Wittgenstein pointed out (§628), an absence of surprise in the case in which we raise an arm; but if he meant to offer that as the arithmetical remainder, he was saying that the remainder is zero.

Then after all is there no difference? When I raise my arm there will not be drugs administered or electrodes fastened or experiments under way such as that involving pressing the arm against a wall and then standing away. Those are real

202

differences, and are enough to relieve any anxiety about whether we might be involved in denying the obvious fact that there is a difference; but they are not differences we get by subtracting the fact that an arm rises. In that operation we were looking for a positive feature that remained when we eliminated the motion of the arm. Such a fact as that no experiment was under way is not such a feature, and we have found no other.

The position we reach is perhaps similar to what Wittgenstein suggests in §183. He says that 'we must be on our guard against thinking there is some *totality* of conditions corresponding to the nature of each case (e.g. for a person's walking) so that, as it were, he *could not but* walk if they were all fulfilled'.

It is normal for people to raise their arms, and abnormal for their arms to go up. We can explain why the abnormal event occurs, but there is no totality of condition in which the normal thing will happen. It is something like that totality we have been looking for, and have not found.

Twenty-Four

DEPTH GRAMMAR

664. In the use of words one might distinguish 'surface grammar' from 'depth grammar'. What immediately impresses itself upon us about the use of a word is the way it is used in the construction of a sentence, the part of its use – one might say – that can be taken in by the ear. – And now compare the depth grammar, say of the word 'to mean', with what the surface grammar would lead us to suspect. No wonder we find it difficult to know our way about.

HERE WITTGENSTEIN introduces a new notion, 'depth grammar', with only the sketchiest of explanations of what he means by it, and immediately asks us to put it to work, promising that the results of doing so will be interesting. While he has elsewhere used the word 'grammar' often enough, he appears to attach an unconventional sense to it, which he nowhere explains; and we do not even know, although perhaps we could figure it out, whether by grammar *simpliciter* he means surface grammar, depth grammar, the whole of which surface and depth grammar are parts, or something else. We are asked to compare the depth grammar of 'to mean' with what its surface grammar would lead us to suspect, without being given any examples of surface grammar leading us to suspect anything, or any examples of the kind of thing this is to be compared with. No wonder indeed we find it difficult to know our way about.

Let us anyway review the clues we are given, and some assumptions it is fair to make:

1. If Wittgenstein is not completely perverse in his use of the word 'grammar', there ought to be something in common between what we all know as grammar, the grammar we learn

204

in school, and what he is calling grammar – although the connection might for all that be rather remote.

2. Surface grammar, whatever it is, is somehow very patent – can be taken in by the ear; but beyond that it is by no means clear *what* it is. It does not seem very likely that it is a matter of whether a word is a noun, a verb or some other part of speech. (a) That is not likely to be philosophically interesting. (b) It is not easy to see what that would lead us to suspect, if the suspicion must be of a grammatical kind; and (c) most words would be nouns or verbs wherever they appeared, whereas it is the way they are used in the construction of a specific sentence that is represented as the surface grammar.

3. Since depth grammar is distinguished from surface grammar, it is unlikely that the former does *not* have to do with the way a word is used in the construction of a sentence. However we must be careful here: It might be a question of which sentence we are talking about. The depth grammar might be a matter of the way a word is used in the construction, not of a particular sentence on which we are reflecting, but of other sentences, for example the generality of sentences in which the word is also used.

4. It may be beneficial to note that the expression 'the way a word is used' can, in philosophical parlance, include the way it is not used. 'The use of the word ———' includes the fact that we do not say '———'.

5. There is a kind of bridge between surface and depth grammar: surface grammar leads us to suspect certain things, and depth grammar confirms, or perhaps more often conflicts with these expectations; but it is not immediately evident how the expectations arise, or what further findings that can be called 'grammatical' will confirm or disconfirm them.

6. It would be fair to expect that, having suggested we compare the surface and depth grammar of 'to mean', Wittgenstein would help us out by doing some of that; but if any of his points in succeeding sections constitute such help, we need some explicit interpretive hypothesis in order to see at all clearly just how they do.

Although the clues I have listed are by no means sufficient to lead us to such a hypothesis, the following is a philosophical operation that may be found to be Wittgensteinian in flavour, and can be described as one of checking out expectations arising from something it would be fair to call surface grammar, by explorations of something it would be fair to call depth grammar. Following the suggestion in §664, the verb 'to mean', or one kind of use of it, will be taken as an example.

We say 'I said it and I meant it'. Here there is a striking surface similarity between the use of the words 'say' and 'mean'. Since saying it is something we do, this similarity might lead us to suppose that meaning it is likewise an action. Now it is part of the grammar of action verbs that, if 'X' is such a verb, we can intend to X, remember or forget to X, set about X-ing at the appointed time, be busy X-ing, interrupted while X-ing, know or not know how to X, and so on. If 'to mean' is an action verb, we can expect that it will have these constructions. However we do not say 'I intend to mean it this afternoon', 'I forgot to mean it', 'I got busy meaning it', 'I was interrupted before I got it meant', or 'I never learned how to mean it'.

The following is a general description of the sort of investigation of which the foregoing is an example:

1. The procedure involves a pairing of two grammars. It is the grammatical analogy between 'I said it' and 'I meant it' that gets the investigation going, and the grammatical disanalogy between other constructions with the verb 'to say' and other constructions with the verb 'to mean' that disconfirms the suspicion arising from the similarity of surface grammars.

2. Contrary to some uses of the expression 'depth grammar' by other people, depth grammar is not something further we find out or maintain about the same sentence of which we have noted the surface grammar: we move to a different set of constructions with the same word; and it is not something new or deep about these constructions, but just their surface grammar, that is significant.

3. *Which* other constructions we move to, that is to say *what* we suspect, is determined by what other constructions there are with the word with which our problem word is paired. In the example, 'to mean' was paired with 'to say'. We noted that one can intend to say something, remember or forget to do so, set about and be engaged in saying, and so on, – and hence we ask whether similarly one can intend, remember, or forget to mean something, or set about meaning it. Should we find that

there are these grammatical constructions with 'to mean', we have good reason to say that *meaning it* is an action; but if, as was suggested, there are none of these constructions, we have good reason to take the contrary view.

4. A proposition of depth grammar will take such forms as 'We say (or do not say) "P"', 'It is correct (or incorrect) to say "P"'. In practice it will very much more often be the fact that we do not say something, that proves significant.

We can see that this interpretive hypothesis is consistent with the clues I have noted:

1. There is at least this much affinity between these propositions and the grammar we learn at school: in school grammar we learn various things that is incorrect to say, or that we do not say, as well, of course, as what it is correct to say; and the decisive propositions of depth grammar have the same form. Also, it is not because of how things are outside of grammar that we do not say, for example 'There are a very large number . . .', and similarly it is not because no one puts off meaning what he says, or meaning something by what he says, that we do not say 'I intend to mean it later' or 'I intend to mean something by it later'. However, while it is at least not clear whether a construction that is ungrammatical in the ordinary sense is therefore meaningless, Wittgenstein, as we will see later, says 'We say such and such' if it is meaningful, and 'We do not say it' if it is not.

2. There *is* something altogether patent about what I have designated surface grammar, and it is something about the way a word is used in the construction of a particular sentence, rather than something general, such as that it is a verb. What is patent about it is not, however, something conforming to any of the clues Wittgenstein here provides, but rather its similarity to another sentence; but that is something of which he speaks elsewhere, for example in §90, where he speaks of 'misunderstandings concerning the use of words, caused, among other things, by certain analogies between the forms of expression in different regions of language'.

3. While depth grammar, being also a matter of the way a word is used in the construction of sentences, might appear to be insufficiently distinct from surface grammar, its distinctness lies in the fact that it is not the grammar of the sentence with which we begin. This is also the justification for the use

of the word 'depth' here: the fact that certain sentences are not used, or in the confirmatory case, the fact that they are, is not before us when we contemplate a sentence as 'I meant it'. We must probe for depth-grammatical propositions, and it can require some know-how to list a sampling of the sentences that ought to be used, given any striking feature of the surface grammar.

4. Although what I am calling depth grammar tends in practice to be more concerned with the ways a word is *not* used than with the ways in which it is used, given the peculiarity of the expression 'the use of a word' that I noted, that is all right.

5. We have just the kind of bridge here between surface and depth grammar that was indicated in the fifth clue: the surface grammar generates certain expectations, and the depth grammar tests them.

6. There is a further confirmation of this interpretation in some of the things Wittgenstein does in the sections surrounding §664. He did not specifically designate any of his points there as depth grammatical, but we can see him as either pursuing the method above described, or at least providing leads which can without great contrivance be taken in that way. Consider for example §661: 'I remember having meant *him*. Am I remembering a process or a state? – When did it begin, what was its course, etc?' The first sentence is an ordinary remark, the surface grammar of which, because of its resemblance to 'I remember having followed him', might lead us to suspect that what was remembered was a sequence of events; but now if it were a process it could have a beginning and a describable course. However we do not say 'My meaning him began just after lunch, went rather slowly for the first thirty seconds and then picked up speed ...', not because that is not the kind of course that meaning a person ever takes, but because it does not take a course, or start or end either.

A case in which a grammatical proposition is not a representation of what we do *not* say is in §667: 'Imagine someone simulating pain, and then saying "It'll get better soon". Can't one say that he meant the pain? and yet he is not concentrating his attention on any pain'. The fact that 'I mean the pain' is in order even when one is simulating pain, and therefore there is no pain on which we could focus our attention, is the grammatical proposition that shows it to be a mistake to suppose that meaning the pain (or anything else) is focusing one's attention on it.

If meaning the pain were something we did, we might have to do it in the right way. However (§674): 'Does one say, for example: "I didn't really mean my pain just now; my mind wasn't on it enough for that"?' We do not bungle the job of meaning it, either by not having our minds on it enough, or in any other way.

A rather different point is made in the same section: if meaning something by a word were something that *happened* we might sometimes not know what had occurred, and thus what we meant, because we were distracted and did not pay careful heed to what was happening. However: 'Do I ask myself, say: "What did I mean by this word just now? My attention was divided between my pain and the noise – "?'

If meaning were something that took place, one might further expect that 'I was meaning . . .' would be accepted as an answer to the question 'What went on in you when you said. . . .?' However (§675): '"Tell me, what was going on in you when you uttered the words . . .?" – The answer to this is not: "I was meaning . . ."!' There may be the construction, 'I was meaning . . .', but it is not used in answer to the question what was going on.

A somewhat quaint item of depth grammar appears in §680, where it is claimed that even if cursing were thought to be *effective* only when one had a clear image of the person cursed, or spoke his name out loud, we would not say 'The point is how the man who is cursing *means* his victim'.

If we had to do something the right way, there could be a doubt whether we had succeeded in meaning *him*, but (§681) there is no place for the question 'Are you sure you cursed *him*?'

Finally, another case in which it is the grammatical expectation that is negative, and the grammatical proposition that is affirmative: We might suppose that if we did not at all think such and such, we could not have meant such and such, but (§692) it is correct to say 'When I gave you this rule, I meant you to . . . in this case', even if one did not think of this case at all as one gave the rule.

I did not, in every one of those examples, show how the

expectation arose from the surface grammar, but this is generally not difficult to work out. Sometimes there is an extra step. For example in the last of the cases, the supposition that meaning something is an action arises from the surface grammar, but that in turn gives rise to the question 'Which action?' It is a possible answer to that spin-off question that Wittgenstein is considering in §692.

My hypothesis about how Wittgenstein conceived surface and depth grammar has now been shown to be richly supported by the textual evidence. It not only conforms neatly to all the clues provided in §664, but also shows how Wittgenstein can be read as carrying out some investigation of the depth grammar of 'to mean', in the nearby sections. This is something he certainly owed us, and which, without this hypothesis, he could not be seen as having delivered.

If I am right, Wittgenstein's conception of depth grammar is entirely different from Chomsky's, but since neither man holds a patent on the expression, that is no problem. It is not as if depth grammar certainly was some one thing, and Chomsky and Wittgenstein had conflicting theories on what it was.

Twenty-Five

ON THE SOUL

'I believe he is not an automation', just like that, so far
makes no sense.

My attitude towards him is an attitude towards a soul. I
am not of the *opinion* that he has a soul.

Religion teaches that the soul can exist when the body
has disintegrated. Now do I understand this teaching? –
Of course I understand it – I can imagine plenty of things
in connection with it. And haven't pictures of these
things been painted? And why should such a picture be
only an imperfect rendering of the spoken doctrine?
Why should it not do the *same* service as the words? And
it is the service which is the point.

If the picture of thought in the head can force itself
upon us, then why not much more that of thought in the
soul?

The human body is the best picture of the human soul.

And how about such an expression as 'In my heart I
understood when you said that', pointing to one's heart?
Does one, perhaps, not *mean* this gesture? Of course one
means it. Or is one conscious of using a *mere* figure?
Indeed not. – It is not a figure that we choose, not a
simile, yet it is a figurative expression. (*PI*, ɪɪ, iv)

SOME OF THE fairly hard questions this passage suggests
are:

1. Why does it 'so far make no sense' to say 'I believe he is
not an automaton'? The words 'so far' suggest that there are
conditions under which it *would* make sense. To find these
conditions we may make a distinction between the literal and
the figurative use of 'He is not an automaton'. Wittgenstein
fairly clearly took the view that there is absolutely no question
of a person really being an automaton. This comes out when
he asks, just before the passage quoted, what information

211

could be conveyed by 'He isn't an automaton', as applied to a human being one has met in ordinary circumstances. We do however use such expressions figuratively. 'The man's an automaton' can be a way of saying how peculiarly mechanical his behaviour is, or how humourless and unfeeling he is.

If we believed a person to be humourless and unfeeling, but had only hearsay to go on, might we say 'I believe he is an automaton'? No, the figurative expression would be out of place in such circumstances, and we would be better to speak more plainly. We do not naturally say we suspect, believe or are sure when we are using a figurative expression, because these words too strongly suggest a literal interpretation.

However, if we were watching a film in which there were human beings and very artful simulations, and it was often hard to tell which was which, we might say of a particular character 'I believe he is not an automaton'. Here, unlike the ordinary case, there is some question of a character's actually being one.

2. What is the 'attitude towards a soul' that Wittgenstein says he has? Does it involve believing that someone has a soul, and therefore adopting an attitude appropriate to that supposition, an attitude that would not have been adopted, given the contrary belief?

Suppose the attitude included expecting that he might be hurt by unkind remarks, intrigued by subtle points, touched by sad stories. It is part of a picture of a soul that we have, that it is through having one of them that a person may be affected in these ways. This comes out in our descriptions of people as soulful, and soulless. When we use these words, are we expressing the *belief* that someone has or lacks a soul, or is describing people as soulless just another way of saying that they are cold or insensitive?

In the juxtaposition of ' "I believe he is not an automaton" ... so far makes no sense', and 'I am not of the *opinion* that he has a soul', there is a strong indication that Wittgenstein would answer the latter question affirmatively. Saying he is not an automaton comes to about the same as saying 'He has a soul, you know'. Believing and being of an opinion come to about the same, and just as it ('so far') makes no sense to say 'I believe he is not an automaton', so, we may infer, Wittgenstein was saying it (so far) makes no sense to say 'I believe he

On the Soul

has a soul'. He is not saying he doesn't merely believe it, he knows it, nor is he saying he disbelieves it. None of those words is applicable when we are using a figurative expression like 'He has a soul, you know'. (In Z §§528–9, the case of the tribesmen who are cast by the government and scientists as having no souls, although in every detectable way they are just like people who are thought to have souls, is perhaps meant to bring out the emptiness of the idea that it is the literal possession of a soul, rather than having feelings and sensibilities, that commands one attitude rather than another.)

3. What about the religious teaching that we have souls, that can continue to exist when the body has disintegrated? Is Wittgenstein, in saying that 'I believe we have souls' so far makes no sense, saying that 'We have souls' is in all cases a figurative expression, in connection with which it is incorrect to use words like 'believe', 'know', 'suspect', 'doubt' (or their negations)? Certainly we do not *have* to take him that way. He might just be making a distinction between the secular, figurative use of 'He has a soul', and its religious use, where for the former purposes the sentence need not be literally intelligible, still less believed, while for the latter purposes it is at least taken to have a literal meaning, and to be a proper object of belief, doubt, uncertainty and so on.

It is not very likely that he was expressing the view that religious believers, in saying that we have souls, can only be taken to mean some such thing as that we live in people's memories after we die, or we live on in the lasting effects through the ages of our actions. If he did mean anything like that, he would certainly be wrong:

i) It is characteristic of figurative expressions, like 'to have an agile mind', that they have settled into the language, and there is no controversy as to what they mean; but it is a controversial theory that a believer's 'We have souls' is a figurative way of saying that we live on in people's memories, or anything else of that sort.

ii) While some not very scrupulous believers might gratefully accept such a suggestion, because it seemed to make what they believed clear and uncontroversial, (a) the fact that they were grateful should show that it was news to them, whereas it is not news to us what we mean by an expression

213

we understand, and (b) most believers would say it is not what they mean. They expect that after they die they will experience joys or torments, and may be reunited with people they have loved and lost. These expectations are not reconcilable with the suggested account of what affirmations like 'We have souls' mean.

The fact that Wittgenstein would be wrong if he took this stand does not of course show that he did not take it, but he was not at all given to propounding positive theories of that kind; and whatever his attitude towards religion, it was one of greater respect than would be expressed in such a theory.

4. How could Wittgenstein, who in general seemed to find theology mystifying, so flatly say that of course he understood the teaching that the soul can exist when the body has disintegrated?

He could say this of figurative expressions 'He has a soul, you know', because they are in everyday use and are as well understood as an average expression in a newspaper or a novel; but if, as I have just argued, he was not offering that kind of analysis of religious teachings, we cannot take that route in answering this question.

In the *Lectures on Religious Belief* (ed. Cyril Barrett, University of California Press 1966) Wittgenstein took a somewhat complicated line on whether he understood religious teaching: (i) he said that he understands it in the sense that even as a child he could answer questions about it, and understood questions when they were put in different ways, and knew that certain things were mistakes (p.59). (He did not give examples of the mistakes, but perhaps he knew that heaven is not in the sky and that God is not a patriarch with a long beard, and does not hear prayers better if they are shouted.) (ii) Although he had certain scruples, both about saying that he does not believe and that he does not understand religious teaching, he is clearly altogether unwilling to say that he does believe or does understand it – except presumably in the foregoing sense (pp.55, 58). (iii) Perhaps mainly because of the above mentioned scruples, Wittgenstein preferred to say that he *does not think that way*. He seemed to mean by this that the Last Judgment, the soul's survival of death, and so on, are *no* part of his thinking: they are not even excluded from it. He thinks in an *entirely* different way.

If in the *Lectures* Wittgenstein was at least not prepared to say that he did understand key items of religious teaching, then unless he changed his mind, why would he say in the *Investigations* that of course he understood about the soul existing when the body disintegrated?

It would resolve this difficulty if we supposed that the sense in which he understands it is the sense in which, even as a child, he understood: he can answer questions about it, and knows what it does not mean. However, being able to imagine plenty of things, or knowing what paintings there are, is not part of understanding in that sense, unless his understanding consisted in knowing that the imaginings and the paintings showed what the teaching did *not* mean.

Christians say that Christ sitteth upon the right hand of God, and paint pictures accordingly; and they sing of the

... rapture it will be,
Prostrate before his throne to lie,
And gaze eternally.

But if I say I do not believe that God sits on a throne, before which I might lie and gaze upon him, they will reply that they do not believe that either, and that there is no disagreement here. They will say 'You don't understand, if you think that's what we mean'; and Wittgenstein knows this. He knows that the pictures do not represent the meaning of the teaching, because he writes (*Lectures*, p.55): 'And then I give an explanation: "I don't believe in . . .", but then the religious person never believes what I describe'. So why does he say of course he understands, he can imagine plenty of things? Does he mean to say that, disavowals notwithstanding, the pictures do represent the meaning?

Hardly that: one cannot except ironically tell a person what he means, and certainly not insist on it in the face of his denial; but it is possible to suppose that something like the following was what Wittgenstein had in mind: one of the cases in which we can say we understand is when we have seen through something, and there is a way of seeing through some religious teachings that starts, as Wittgenstein does, with what we imagine in connection with them, and the paintings we may be shown. We can imagine Christ ascending into heaven, descending into hell, or coming from a place at God's right hand to judge the quick and the dead, and we can imagine God sending down his holy spirit or making his face to shine on us; and pictures have been painted of such things, many of which have a place of honour in cathedrals and chapels. When anyone says he does not believe that God sits on a throne or has a face, or that heaven is above and hell below, devotees say they do not believe these things either. Defenders of religion must at every turn disavow crude interpretations, but while we can make a very long catalogue of these things, we never seem to come to what is true. One can say that 'sitting on the right hand of God', 'descending into hell', and so on are metaphors, but they are unlike an average metaphor in that it proves impossible to say what they are metaphorical *for*. While sophisticated theories of religious meaning are sometimes contrived, their intelligibility tends to be no improvement on what they purport to interpret, and they can rarely be said to represent what the man in the pew, or in the pulpit either, believes. Even more rarely are they such that, if they were believed, it would any longer make sense to continue the eternal round of prayer and praise.

The suggestion then is that Wittgenstein was saying that while the imaginings and pictures by common consent do not explain the meaning, nothing else does. This might have been the point of the far from transparent remark, crudely reported one supposes, in *Lectures*, p.59: 'The word "God" is amongst the earliest learnt – pictures and catechisms, etc. But not the same consequences as with pictures of aunts. I wasn't shown [that which the picture pictured].'

I suggest taking this to mean that whereas with pictures of aunts, there is here the aunt and there the picture, with religious pictures there is never anything corresponding to the aunt. If that is the point intended, the analogy is not well crafted, because it suggests too strongly that not believing that God created Adam is not believing that an event occurred quite like what the picture by that name depicts, while people who believe that God created Adam do not believe that an event occurred of which the picture is a fair likeness.

There is an example in Z §127 in which, although the word 'understand' is not used, Wittgenstein might say he understood, and mean that he had seen through the teaching:

> The soul is said to *leave* the body. Then, in order to exclude any similarity to the body, any sort of idea that some gaseous thing is

On the Soul

meant, the soul is said to be incorporeal, non-spatial; but with
the word 'leave' one has already said it all.

5. When Wittgenstein says 'Why should [a picture] not do
the *same* service as the words? And it is the service which is
the point', what might he mean by a 'service', and what
service could he assign to these words and pictures?

I can think of at least three possible answers to this question:

i) A *figurative* expression might be said to 'do a service': it
conveys something different from what it appears to say, and
it would be fair enough to call what one is conveying by using
the figure 'the service'. However, as we have seen, religious
teachings are not figurative, either in the sense that they say
something quite ordinary, such as that we will be remembered after we die, or that they say something less ordinary,
that could be explained in some other way. There is no well-
understood point the words or pictures make that is different
from the representations they appear to make, even if both
with figurative expressions and religious teachings, the
apparent representation will be denied. We say 'I understood
in my heart', but deny that we mean that something called
'understanding' occurred in the organ that pumps blood; and
similarly as we saw in Z §127, people say both that the soul
leaves the body and that it is incorporeal, non-spatial, and
hence should deny that it goes anywhere; but whereas we can
explain what we meant by 'I understood in my heart', we
cannot make the idea of the soul's departure from the body
any clearer. In this sense of 'service', there is therefore no
service performed by the words or the pictures. They might
still, however, perform the same service: none (cf. chapter 18
above).

ii) Being told about the soul's survival, the last judgment,
the mansions of heaven or the torments of hell will serve to
comfort the bereaved, threaten the sinner, or reassure the
virtuous. However, threatening sinners in this way is not like
threatening rapists with imprisonment, and comforting the
bereaved in this way is not like assuring someone that her son
is still alive, unless we can say what is threatened and what
will suffer it, or what still lives when someone has died; and
that is what I have been supposing cannot be done. In the
absence of explanations of what it means to say for example

217

that the soul exists when the body has disintegrated, we are therefore faced with a choice, if we treat the 'service' of the words and pictures as that of comforting and threatening, between saying that a hoax is being perpetrated, which relies on simple people's supposing that the teachings have a meaning like ordinary threats and assurances, when in fact they do not mean anything – and saying that the teachings just are soothing and disturbing, the way music can be, not because of what they say, but perhaps because they have been intoned repeatedly in ways that condition us to shudder or relax on hearing them.

It is not likely that Wittgenstein would take either of these courses. While as noted above, he appeared profoundly sceptical of religion, his scepticism was never so lacking in respect as to verge on accusations of fraud; nor did it tend in such psychological directions as that of treating the teachings as a kind of soothing incantation.

iii) More sophisticated accounts of the 'service' of the words and pictures might be contrived. For example it is not absolutely implausible to say that religious pictures and doctrines give us something, the contemplation of which or the repetition of which is a specifically religious act, an act deriving a peculiar pathos from the fact that we know we do not understand the words, or know that God is not as depicted in the paintings. Our religious wonder can focus on the painting, make it do duty for God, just because we feel the absurdity of believing that this is all that human beings can do by way of depicting the divinity. It is a striking fact that a painting like Michelangelo's of God creating Adam, although ridiculous and known by believers and unbelievers alike to be ridiculous, should, surrounded as *it* is by disclaimers of its verisimilitude, nevertheless have a place of honour on the ceiling of the Sistine Chapel.

While this possible account of the 'service' is respectful, and in that way not un-Wittgensteinian, it requires that we take the idea of an underlying mystery more seriously than Wittgenstein showed the least sign of being ready to do. The account requires us to say that 'God created Adam' means *something*, it is just mysterious, and probably impossible for us to say, *what* it means; and all the indications so far have been that Wittgenstein would not accept this.

In the case of each of these interpretations, there is something against attributing it to Wittgenstein, but nothing very conclusive; and nothing much that counts in favour. Perhaps he had no particular 'service' in mind, and his aim was to set us to thinking about what service, in any sense, the words and pictures performed, or whether indeed they performed any; because it is at least clear that any service they perform will be of a peculiar nature.

6. In what way does the picture of thought in the head force itself upon us? And when Wittgenstein asks 'why not much more that of thought in the soul?', does he mean to suggest that the latter might force itself upon us, or does he just want to know why not?

I suggest that the way a picture can force itself on us can be explained in terms of my interpretation of §§423–4 (see chapter 17 above). If it is sometimes true that a person has an agile mind, then (we think) there must be minds, and there is a question what they are; and if wanting to know what is going on in his head is wanting to know what he is thinking, then (we think) thinking must be something that goes on in the head. Since these expressions have settled into the language, and seem to be among the primary, plain ways we have of expressing ourselves, we may use them without any awareness of their figurative character (compare the remark about similies at the end of the passage quoted), and good-heartedly become puzzled for example about what minds are, or about what it is that goes on in his head that leads him to say he was thinking of such and such. In this way pictures, figures of speech, may force themselves upon us. (The word 'force' here is perhaps too strong, and 'insinuate' might have been better.)

Might the picture of thought in the soul insinuate itself in that way? Clearly not, because there is no question 'I wonder what is going on in his soul', that might fool us. We would be wrong to think: 'Wondering what he is thinking is wondering what is going on in his soul, hence thought goes on in the soul', because these two questions are not interchangeable. If someone said 'I wonder what is going on in his soul', we might guess what he meant, but it is important first that we would have to guess, there is no settled sense that the question has acquired; and second that our guesses would run to 'What is he feeling?', not 'What is he thinking?'.

219

7. It is not at all obviously true that the human body is the best picture of the human soul: why might Wittgenstein have said this? Some possible answers are:

i) If I wanted to make a picture of my grandfather's soul arriving at the gates of heaven, I would probably do a likeness of him, otherwise I would be at a loss how to make him identifiable as my grandfather; and similarly if I wanted to depict souls, not clouds, arriving at the gates of heaven, it would be best to make them humanoid, at least in the way ghosts will generally be given a roughly human form. They may be translucent, and it may not be clear whether they have legs, arms or pot bellies, but they will at least have faces, and a roughly human stature. It is not very clear whether it is appropriate at all to represent souls pictorially, but it is clear, if not very interesting, that in this kind of case at least, *if* one does so, one is best to give the soul human features.

There are other cases however. If I wanted to depict the soul leaving the body, the identification of the soul as human would be provided by the body it was leaving; and if I were to do the soul animating the body, it would at best be a joke to show a little person in the head or the heart, manipulating a set of controls.

ii) In a community of believers, a picture of someone riding a bicycle could be entitled 'Man with Soul', and one of a person in his coffin 'Man without Soul', but in neither case would the soul be depicted. 'We have souls' does not just mean we are alive, even if the person who believes it is sure that anyone without a soul is dead.

iii) Might Wittgenstein have had in mind secular uses of the word 'soul'? We say 'He is (not "has") a gentle soul' or 'a timid soul', though interestingly we do not speak in this way of vengeful or boring souls; we speak of certain activities as being soul-destroying; and we say of some people that they have no soul, meaning that flowers, music and poetry mean nothing to them, or that they are blind or unresponsive to other people's fears, ambitions and joys.

We could draw a picture of a timid soul, that is, of a timid person, but that would not be, just simply, a picture of a soul. The picture of a sadistic person would not be one of a sadistic soul, or of a fat person that of a fat soul. Souls in this sense are not tall, fat or rosy-cheeked, even if a timid soul may be any of those things. Before-and-after pictures of a person who had done soul-destroying work might, but would not necessarily show the difference the work had made; and even if they did, if all the life had gone out of the face, the liveliness of the face in the 'before' picture would only by straining language be called the soul, and in any case it would be an aspect of a picture of a body, not just the picture of a body, that was the soul.

It would be a rare picture of a person who 'has no soul' that showed he had none; but if a film of his behaviour in a number of cases showed it, here again it would be aspects of the picture of a body that showed the want of a soul. In this figure of speech we make as if we inferred the absence of something from the behaviour, but we could no more depict what we pretend is lacking than we could depict the mind, in the back of which someone had the intention to write a letter. The soul here is conceived as the agency, having which a person will have a certain sensibility; but if we depict the sensibility, for example showing a person registering delight over a desert landscape, we will not thereby have depicted the agency figuratively responsible for his delighting in such things. Hence if pictures of the human body may illustrate secular uses of the word 'soul', it is still not true that the picture of a body *is* a picture of a soul.

iv) It would seem from the first two paragraphs I am examining that Wittgenstein opposed 'He is an automaton' to 'He has a soul', and regarded the latter as making sense if used as a reminder that someone is human, capable of hoping, fearing, believing, understanding, remembering, suffering. Another way of saying this would be 'He is a person', and one of the best ways of explaining what we mean by a person is with pictures of people, sad, wistful, joyful, angry, puzzled, intent.

If it was in this context Wittgenstein said the human body is the best picture of the human soul, we could see what he means. The *service* of 'He has a soul' could be brought out very well in such pictures; but still the pictures do not show the soul that we would be pretending is responsible for the joy, anger or puzzlement, any more than the picture of a man playing chess depicts the powerful mind we would say he had if he played masterfully.

On the Soul

Unless Wittgenstein was only saying that, for example, a picture of my grandfather's soul will hardly be recognisable as such unless it looks in some way like him, he was speaking carelessly in saying that the best picture of the human soul is the human body.

Even Wittgenstein can't be right all the time.

Twenty-Six

GETTING RID OF THE IDEA
OF THE PRIVATE OBJECT

> Always get rid of the idea of the private object in this
> way: assume that it constantly changes, but that you do
> not notice the change because your memory constantly
> deceives you. (*PI*, p.207; see also p.222)

THIS READS as if Wittgenstein conceived the procedure
described to be a self-sufficient device for doing this job – as if
it provided all we needed to know or do, to achieve this
supposedly desirable purpose. The word 'always' reinforces
that impression, making it sound as if the idea of the private
object were a well-known psychological nuisance that kept
coming back, but could be banished as often as it reappeared,
in this simple and effective manner.

Suppose that some people gratefully reported that the
technique worked every time, while others said it often
works, and some that it never does. Are we misunderstanding
the procedure if we are inclined to do a survey on its effective-
ness?

The device is not a kind of mumbo-jumbo for disposing of
annoying mental states, like getting rid of an evil desire by
reciting a psalm. The idea of the private object is not that kind
of nuisance. People do not complain of it as they do of head-
aches or hallucinations. What is needed is not a way of con-
tending with an obvious but persistent ailment, but a way of
showing that our thinking has gone wrong if it involves the
idea of a private object. The trouble is that it is by no means
obvious how the procedure is supposed to achieve that
purpose.

Part of the reason this is not obvious is that it is unclear just
what we are getting rid of, and whether it is desirable to rid
ourselves of it. In the case of pain for example, are we getting

rid of the idea that when we say we have a pain, we are talking about a disagreeable sensation we have, that no one else can experience? Would we *want* to be rid of this idea, and would Wittgenstein's procedure do the job for us? Is it not true, both that we are talking about a disagreeable sensation, and that if it is in the elbow, no one else experiences the pain I have in the elbow? If that idea is true, we would not want to be rid of it; and in any case it is not clear that *that* idea could be banished in the way described. If I assume that the sensation constantly changes, but that I do not notice this, must I not conclude that, whether I realise it or not, I have not been in pain during *all* the time when I thought I was?

Perhaps this depends of what kind of changes we are supposing to occur here. It is not clear whether it makes sense to suppose that a sensation changed from being disagreeable to being agreeable without the change being noticed, but if such a change did occur, I would certainly not be in pain as long as what I felt was agreeable. *If* it changed from nice to nasty, and when it was nasty, my memory played a trick on me and I thought it had been nasty all along, that might be a way in which the change could occur without it being noticed, but it would not be a case in which the change would make no difference. The assumption that this change had occurred would be an assumption that I was wrong in thinking I had been in pain all along.

Does this show that Wittgenstein was wrong, and we cannot (always) get rid of the idea of the private object in the way he recommended, or does it show that the conception of a private object with which we have been working is not the conception Wittgenstein intended?

We *could* try various senses of 'the idea of the private object' until we found one on which Wittgenstein's riddance procedure worked, and conclude that it was the sense he intended, but from the point of view of evaluating its merits, this would be unfortunate, because its workability would then be a foregone conclusion. However if it was a sound method, and if what it rid us of was an idea that made for trouble, the fact that the soundness of the method was a foregone conclusion would not be an objection.

Let me suggest then that in the case of pain at least, the idea of the private object may be the conception of pain I described chiefly in chapter 14. It is the idea that there might be various sensations that were disagreeable and gnawed or jabbed or streaked, and that amongst these, the sensations properly called pains are identified by essential properties, that can be recognised, but not described. The sensation is private in the sense that its identifying properties are indescribable; when two people have a frightful jabbing sensation in their shoulder, they never know whether it is the same, and hence never know whether they both have pain, or even whether either of them has.

Can we get rid of this idea by supposing that the sensation constantly changes unnoticed, and finding that it makes no difference?

When we supposed that the sensation changed, unnoticed, from being nice to being nasty, the method did not work. What difference is made by the present supposition? Now it is not whether it jabs or is disagreeable that is supposed to change, but rather the character of *what* jabs or is disagreeable; and we can see that *this* supposed change makes no difference, from the fact that it is no part of the way we decide whether to say that we are in pain, or that someone else is, to ask questions about the character of what jabs or is disagreeable.

One may however think: *of course* we don't ask questions about the peculiar quality of the sensation itself. We can't, because, it being private, we have been unable to develop a language in which to pose such questions. But that does not show that there are not important questions to be asked, if only we had a way of framing them.

This might be a good point if, in our own case, we took whether we had a pain to be a matter of whether what we felt had a certain indescribable but recognisable quality, and regularly distinguished pains from other sensations that jabbed disagreeably by whether they had that quality. Over the years we might have found some important difference between nasty sensations that felt *like so*, and others, and reserved the word 'pain' for the former, and we might have found that other people made (or seemed to make) a similar distinction. 'It jabs most frightfully, but it is not a pain' might be something we frequently heard people say, and any of us might explain that we could tell it was not a pain by the way it

Getting Rid of the Idea of the Private Object

felt, even though we could not describe the peculiar feel that a pain has.

Even so, saying that a sensation we had was a pain would not be saying that it had that distinctive feel, but rather that the important difference we had come to associate with the special feel of the sensation obtained. Suppose that some frightful sensations would soon pass, while others were sure to require some kind of medical treatment, and the two felt different and we only called the latter pains. Calling a sensation a pain would be saying that it was going to require medical treatment. Even if, by the age of fourteen, everyone came to be a reliable judge of whether a sensation was a 'pain', on the basis of how it felt, they would not, in so describing it, be saying how it felt, and it would be possible that my treatment-requiring sensations felt different from yours. [It would be possible, too, that it was not actually how they felt that led us to call them pains: we just came to be able to say which sensations would need medical treatment (cf. chapter 9 above; also §§322, 625.)]

We do not need to rely on these last considerations to show that it is no part of the concept of pain that it should have a distinctive feel. The fact that, even in our own case, we do not distinguish pains from other nasty sensations on the basis of their feel, the fact that no one says 'She is clearly in great agony, but it may not be pain she has', is enough to show that it makes no difference if the feel of the sensation changes without our noticing it.

Here one need not deny that pains *have* a distinctive feel, only that the feel they have, if they have it, is not essential to their being pains.

An analogy: it is said that in the early days Henry Ford refused to produce cars in any other colour except black, but it would not be essential to a car's being a Ford that it be black, the way it might have been if he had produced two lines of cars, one red and one black, and called the red ones Henrys and the black ones Fords.

My argument that Wittgenstein's riddance procedure works, in the case of pain, given the conception of pain as 'a something', that is, as defined by indescribable properties supposed to be those of the sensation itself, as distinct from the fact that it jabs or gnaws or is nasty or excruciating. I have

226

not shown, and do not propose to show, that this is the only conception of pain on which the procedure will work, but the fact that it works here, the fact that this is a conception of pain that there are *other reasons* to think Wittgenstein thought was at the root of a lot of our perplexity about pain, and the fact that it is of some philosophical value to be rid of that conception, – add up to a fairly strong case for this interpretation.

Wittgenstein said 'Always get rid of the idea of the private object in this way . . . '. If the word 'always' does not, as I suggested, imply that he thought of this idea as one that annoyingly keeps reappearing, he might have used the word because he thought the idea of a private object is at the root of *various* philosophical troubles. It may be useful to consider at least one other example.

Sometimes our troubles in philosophy arise from supposing that *there is* an object we are talking about in using this or that word, when in fact there is none. We then press the hapless question *what* object is it, and of course become hopelessly mired. I would list the words 'believe' and 'intend' as prime among various examples, but it is not uncontroversial whether that is the problem with them, and I will not argue the point. (But see e.g. Z §50.)

Given anyway that there are words of this kind, it is not clear whether the mistaken fancy that there is an object they are used to talk about is a case of an idea of a private object, and could be got rid of in the way Wittgenstein prescribes. There are behaviouristic analyses of these words, which do not involve a concept of privacy, and mentalistic analyses do not, just as such, require us to suppose that the object is private either, at least in the sense of being inherently indescribable. At some point we may in desperation say they are indescribable, but in the cases in which that point is reached, it is not clear whether we can be asked to imagine the object changing, when it is so unclear what the object is, that is supposed to change. 'Believe' is not like 'pain', where there is no doubt what to focus one's attention on, as the pain one is now having.

There are other cases however that resemble that of pain in this regard. In some of its uses, 'to think' is one of them. (i) If I was thinking about his problem all morning, there was something real going on, that was the thinking I was doing. (ii) If I said I had been thus thinking, and someone asked 'How do you know it was thinking you were doing?', or if I were to suppose that in saying I had thought about his problem, I was recording the peculiar character of my exertions over the problem – that I had (you know) *thought* about it, rather than anything else – we might again have an idea of a private object. Just as in the case of pain we may think that a sensation is not a pain unless it has a certain indescribable quality, so in the case of thought we may come to suppose that there is something recognisable but indescribable about the way we go about our mental exertions, that entitles them to be called thinking. Thinking then is a special kind of mental zapping we do, that has such effects as helping us decide, putting us in a better position to discuss, enabling us to devise useful suggestions, and so on; and whatever someone has done, if it does not have the distinctive quality this zapping has, he has not been thinking. The object here is private, not in the sense that other people have to guess what has been happening, whereas I know, but in the sense that it is defined by its possession of a distinctive character, that cannot be described.

Wittgenstein may well have had this idea in mind when he wrote (§328):

> ... If I say I have thought – need I always be right? – What *kind* of mistake is there room for here? Are there circumstances in which one would ask: 'Was what I was doing then really thinking; am I not making a mistake?'

Clearly we are all at sea when taxed with the question 'Are you sure it was thinking?' It is not part of the language-game, not a question we learn how to answer in learning to use the word 'think'; and therefore it is no part of the concept of thinking that mental exertions are not thinking unless they have a distinctive experiential character. Hence if the exertions changed unnoticed from having one such character to having another, it would make no difference. The riddance procedure works as well here as in the case of the word 'pain'.

There seems to be something different at issue in the following passage (p.222) in which the riddance procedure is fairly explicitly invoked:

> Let us assume there was a man who always guessed right what I was saying to myself in my thoughts. (It does not matter how he manages it.) But what is the criterion for his guessing right?

228

Well, I am a truthful person and I confess that he has guessed right. – But might I not be mistaken, can my memory not deceive me? And I might not always do so when – without lying – I express what I have thought within myself? – But now it does appear that 'what went on within me' is not the point at all. (Here I am drawing a construction line.)

The question here is not one of whether this person was *thinking* ('exactly'), but of *what* he was thinking; and also it is not a question of a quality of, or a manner in which, something ran through his mind, but (apparently) of whether it is necessary that *anything* (or is it anything describable?) has run through his mind.

I confess I am uncertain what to make of this passage. It is difficult to see how one could be truthfully reporting 'saying something to oneself in one's thoughts' if in truth such and such words had not run through one's mind, but rather other words, with a different sense; and I am initially inclined to say the riddance procedure is being carried too far here.

However the following is believable, and there is some evidence that Wittgenstein believed it. It is possible to maintain that what is important is what one is willing to go on record as having thought. If I have seen a skit in which people repeatedly say 'What a ridiculous concept!', and those words have been echoing in my mind, and one of the occasions on which this happened was just after I had read a passage in the *Investigations*, I would not report this in the words 'I thought, what a ridiculous concept', unless that was my estimation of the passage I had read. And I might say 'I thought, what a cunning idea!', even if the words 'What a ridiculous concept' had run through my mind, and the words 'What a cunning idea' had not. Here 'what went on within me' is indeed not the point at all.

The idea that it is what we are prepared to go on record as having thought that is important might be gleaned from Z §656: 'To be ashamed of a thought. Is one ashamed of the fact that one has spoken such and such a sentence in one's imagination?' No, one is ashamed that the sentence should have expressed one's opinion, or one's inclination at the time; but (given some of the foregoing reasoning), there is nothing that shows that it did better than one's readiness to go on record as having so thought.

The idea that one can truthfully say one thought such and such whatever ran through one's mind might be taken from Z §100 (cf. *PI* §330). Wittgenstein imagines someone constructing an appliance out of various bits of stuff using a given set of tools. The tinkerer makes some noises, but does not say anything, either aloud or to himself. Wittgenstein asks:

> If the worker can talk – would it be a falsification of what actually goes on if he were to describe that precisely and were to say e.g. 'Then I thought: no, that won't do, I must try it another way' and so on. . . . ?
>
> I want to say: may he not later give his wordless thoughts in words?

Here we *might* suppose that he had had the thoughts in some other medium, and later translated it into words, but since none of us knows what this medium is, or can explain how to translate it, that would only be a desperate measure to sustain the idea that to have thought such and such, something must have occurred, recognisable as having that thought.

While I think there is something right about the points I take from these passages, and while they provide a way of seeing how 'what went on in me' need not be the point at all, I do think that here getting rid of the idea of the private object requires much more than just imagining that the object changes without one's noticing it.

In the other cases, such as that with which I began, more is required too, but what is additional there is not argument, but just coming to see what the 'private object' is conceived to be. Once that is clear, the procedure Wittgenstein prescribes seems to be all that is required to do the job.

Twenty-Seven

ON BEING HIDDEN

NOTORIOUSLY Wittgenstein had various and persistent misgivings about saying that pains, thoughts, dreams, internal speech, intentions, beliefs, motives and so on are hidden; but he was not at his clearest when he was explaining these misgivings; and it seems so right to say, at least of some of these things, that they are hidden, that he may appear to be setting himself an impossible task in questioning it. He could surely not maintain that pains, for example, are open to view.

He presumably does not mean to deny that people sometimes conceal their thoughts, intentions or sufferings. It is not the possibility of such ordinary judgments as 'He concealed his intentions from me' that he is questioning, but the philosophical contention that intentions, thoughts and so on, as distinct from the expression we give them, are always hidden. He was making a distinction similar to this when he said:

'I know what I want, wish, believe, feel ...' (and so on through all the psychological verbs) is either philosophers' nonsense, or at any rate not a judgment a priori. (PI, p.221)

What he can be taken to mean here is that although we can, with sudden insight, say 'I know what I want!', it is not in contemplation of such cases that we say in philosophy 'only he can know what he wants'. It is propositions like the latter that Wittgenstein calls 'judgments a priori', and it is these and not the ordinary judgments (or exclamations) that are in question.

We can disqualify some, but not all, of the psychological candidates for hiddenness by applying the principle that only a discriminable object can lie hidden. There must be an answer to the question 'What is it that is hidden?' when we ask that question about pains, there seems, at first blush at least, to be a good enough answer: it is for example this nasty jabbing sensation I have in my side; but in the case of my intention to buy a shirt, or my belief that Wittgenstein died in 1951, I am quite at a loss to say *what* the intention or the belief is. I may be in no doubt that I do so intend or believe, but even so I can find nothing upon which I can direct my attention, or features of which I could describe, that is my intention or belief. Hume, notwithstanding, a belief cannot be vivid; nor can it be pulsing, undulating, or anything else. We do describe beliefs and intentions as 'firm', but the description of them as 'flabby' is not in common use, even if we might guess what a person meant; and it is not on grounds of observation that we describe them as firm. The word 'firm' here is a picturesque expression of our reluctance to be shaken.

If there is nothing that *is* the intention to buy a shirt, there is nothing that might lie hidden. Any psychological word that similarly does not have a discriminable object can right away be struck from the list of what may lie hidden; but it is not easy to decide in every case whether in fact there is a suitably discriminable object. Even in the case of intentions and beliefs there is room for disagreement, if one is prepared to say that they do have objects, which however are indescribable.

We could however give a rough rating of the debatability of the question whether a psychological word has a discriminable object. The least debatable cases might be pains, itches, clutching sensations in the throat, burning sensations in the chest, the feel of wind on the face, after-images and hallucinations. Next might come dreams, mental picturings and internal speech. The inclination to say there is a discriminable object in these cases is very strong, but not so strong that any doubt will seem absurd and hyperbolic.

With thoughts and other mental endeavours, doubts get more of a foothold. These do have a fairly definite time of occurrence, and it is not particularly obscure to us what we are thinking; but on the other hand it is not clear that we can read our thoughts in the experience of thinking, or that there are descriptions of thoughts. They are not filmy, bulgy, jagged, lithe or anything else. Such adjectives as 'dismal', 'ingenious', 'alarming', and 'tentative', which we do apply to them, are evaluative, rather than descriptive. We can often say a good deal about what we have been thinking, but our doing this has more the character of carrying on in the same vein than that of describing a process that has occurred.

Yearnings and desires have much the same in-between character; but motives, reasons, hopes, fears, wishes and expectations are at least as clearly lacking a discriminable object as are intentions and beliefs.

Disagreement is possible about all these cases, and I will not rely heavily in any particular case on the claim that there is no discriminable object. It is obvious however that *if* there is not, the word 'hidden' will have no application; and it is clear too that I would be winning too easy a victory if I were to concentrate much on such cases as intentions, beliefs and expectations, rather than on the harder cases of sensations, after-images, internal speech, and so on.

How could anyone deny that pains are hidden? Would that not be as much as to say that they are open to view, and is that not clearly false? It is true that *the fact that* a person is in pain is normally not hidden. We can see the winces and wounds, and hear the moans; but if pain behaviour is open to view, that is not to say that pain is, for the two are not identical. The pain is perhaps in the shoulder and gnawing, but the behaviour is neither in the shoulder nor gnawing.

Hence Wittgenstein was either wrong or he was not *deny-ing* that pains and so on are hidden. He could refuse to say they are hidden and also refuse to deny it if his claim was that the word 'hidden' has no application to psychological states or processes: they are neither hidden, open to view, nor something in between. When we say that thoughts are not round, or intentions are not brown, no one takes us to mean that they do not happen to come in those shapes or colours, but if we say that pains are not hidden, it is not so easy to see that it is the intelligibility, not the truth, of the application of 'hidden' to pains that is the question. We dwell on the fact that when he is in pain. I do not feel it, and so require to be persuaded that nevertheless it is wrong to say that his pain is hidden from me.

What is the justification for ruling out the word 'hidden' here?

1. There are hidden reefs and hidden grottos, but if some-one said his friend had a hidden pain, we would not know

what to make of it. There are labour pains, chest pains and jabbing pains, but not hidden pains. A person might adopt the usage 'hidden' for pains when they are temporarily relieved by some drug, or for pains he only notices when he is not pre-occupied with other things, but this would not be the happiest of linguistic devices, because it implies what is at least not obviously true: that a pain may exist when it is not felt.

One might agree that there is something odd about the concept 'hidden pain', but argue that it is not senseless, but rather pointless, to describe another person's pain as hidden: we do not need to mention this, since it is *always* true. If it is always true that other people's pains are hidden, the concept at least makes sense.

Yet it is not just that it never happens that I feel your pains: I have no idea what it would be for me to feel them. I would not care to suppose that a pain was something physical that might migrate from your body to mine; and if I found one day that in the same way that people can feel pain as being in an amputated foot, I felt a pain as being in your foot, then even if you had a pain in your foot and we each described our pain in the same way, my pain would be in your foot and so would yours, but I would no more be feeling your pain than you would mine. Clearly its location in your foot does not make it your pain: if I felt a pain as being in your foot, and you felt nothing, I could not inform you that you have a pain in your foot. I could as well say that a stone had a pain, if I felt a pain as being in a statue. We want to say here that one pain exists full-blown in your foot; that although normally you perceive it and I do not, it is quite possible that both or neither of us should perceive it, or that I should perceive it while you do not; but this implies that a pain might exist and be frightful although no one was suffering from it, and also that suffering from it is a matter of perceiving, noticing its frightfulness. The former implication is patent nonsense, the latter, disguised. In '2' below, an attempt will be made to remove its disguise.

2. There are two ways of setting up the hidden/open-to-view dichotomy. In one of them it is possible for psychological phenomena to be hidden from or open to the view of the same person. That is the schema we have just been considering. In it, we want it to be conceivable, even if it never

happens, that your pains should be open to my view, although normally hidden, and equally that my pains should be hidden from me, although normally open to my view. In the other, it is enough if what is hidden from me should be open to somebody's view. That is, we want to say that your pains being hidden from me makes sense even if it is inconceivable that they should be open to my view, because they are at least open to yours; and correspondingly that my pains being open to my view makes sense even if it is inconceivable that they should be hidden from me, because they are at least hidden from you.

The reasoning here is circular: we relieve our doubts about whether 'hidden from me' makes sense by saying that 'open to your view' is possible; and then we relieve our doubts whether it makes sense to say that your pains are open to your view, by saying that they are hidden from me.

Clearly we need to break the circle. Let us consider whether my pains are indeed 'open to my view'. This suggests a relation between me and my pains like that between me and things that happen around me, things that I notice or fail to notice, attend to more closely or turn away from, like or dislike, and having first disliked sometimes come to like. However I do not *notice* or *witness* my pains, I *have* them; and it is not a matter of taste that I dislike them, I would not call anything a pain that was not frightful. I cannot say, as I might in a horror gallery, 'Oh, there's a nasty one. I didn't notice it until now.' The monsters in a horror gallery are mostly open to view, but not always in view. One's gaze wanders from one to another; and one experiences the horror of any one only so long as one attends to it, and experiences it more fully by attending more closely, and by getting oneself in a receptive frame of mind. Although it can be a little like that with mild pains – if we busy ourselves with other things we scarcely notice them, and if we attend to them and get in a self-pitying frame of mind they seem worse – with pains of any intensity there is no such thing as their not being experienced until we direct our attention their way, and no such thing as dwelling on or savouring features of the pain that a less observant person might not have noticed.

Some of the horror exhibits, unlike some of our pains, may be hidden in odd corners, where one can come upon them by surprise; and hidden or not, there can be monsters one has not yet come upon, although they are here, open to view. However, there are no pains there, waiting to be felt. One can *find out* what is in the horror exhibition, or not find out, by not going there, or not looking around much; but one cannot find out what pains one has, or fail to find out, by not being sufficiently inquisitive to discover the hidden pains.

Someone might object here that I am using the wrong analogy: that having a pain is not like seeing a frightening beast, but like being mauled by one. We could hardly not notice the mauling, and our experience of it is not a matter of being observant, inquisitive or receptive. There is something right about that; but then neither is the mauling open to the view of the victim. Peter might have been mauled in full view of someone else, but hardly in his own full view – as if he might have undergone a hidden (but not a figurative) mauling.

3. Let us now consider some uses and misuses of 'hidden', contrasting these with its use in connection with pains, thoughts, and so on.

i) If I make a sly remark, we say my words have hidden meanings. Is there something called the meaning, which is normally open to view, but sometimes artfully concealed? In straightforward discourse, the meaning is clear, but only the words are open to view; hence if we say the meaning is not open to view, it is hidden, even when my words do *not* 'have hidden meanings'. That absurdity is a consequence of taking 'hidden' literally; but it is used figuratively here; and it is appropriate because when anything is hidden, it can be found, and I have not made a sly remark if it is not soon clear to some of my hearers what I mean. We do not mean to be using 'hidden' figuratively when we make the *a priori* judgment that a person's thoughts or pains are hidden from us. We picture something very real lurking there, inaccessible to us; and we do not worry about the fact that what is hidden can be come upon.

ii) If I am guessing the meanings of a list of Russian words, they all have meanings, but only the words are open to view. Are the meanings hidden? We could say this, if each word was written on a piece of paper, on the reverse side of which was written the meaning, or if words and meanings were written in two columns, and the meanings column was covered over; but we could not say 'Here are the words. I will keep the meanings hidden in my mind', nor could we say 'All these words have hidden meanings', if we just meant that the meanings were to be guessed. Here we meet again our principle that hiddenness requires a discriminable object. When the meaning is written out, it can be hidden. Otherwise, unless we use the word figuratively, 'hidden' does not get a foothold.

iii) A person, as I noted before, can hide his thoughts and his sufferings from us, but this is a departure from the normal case in which they are not hidden; and *what* is normally not hidden is the misery we read in his face, or what he has to say about a problem we have posed. While he can hide his sufferings, he cannot hide his pains, or show them either; and while he can hide his thoughts, he cannot hide the inner process of thinking them, or show it either. Moreover he hides thoughts and sufferings, not in the sense that he says something, but inaudibly, or looks miserable, but invisibly, but only in the sense that he does not let himself say or show things in the way he is naturally inclined. We can imagine a compulsively demonstrative person who could hide things only by keeping away from people whenever there was a risk of them showing. His thoughts and sufferings would always be open to view, although sometimes hidden.

iv) Some people are an enigma to us. If there was a tribe of such people, could we say that something about them was hidden? Suppose we learned their language, and that we knew what they were thinking at least as often as we know what people we understand are thinking, we might still not understand them. It is not through not knowing what goes on in their heads that we do not understand them. We might know, for example, what they will think if we spread a pile of wood out on the ground: that there is more wood now, and one must pay more for it. We might also know what answers they would give to our expressions of puzzlement about this. Our difficulty need not be that we do not know enough: it may be that what we know does not add up. Hence we could not say that there was anything hidden here (cf. *PI*, p.223).

v) If a person says he is going to learn Sanskrit and we do not understand why he would do that, we do not know his reasons yet. Are they hidden from us? They are not open to view; but the things he will say or could say are not floating full-blown in his mind. When he explains his reasons he will compose (though not invent) the explanation as he goes. It is the fact that he does not *invent* the explanation – that those have been his reasons all along – that is puzzling here. We think there must be something lying hidden that makes his explanations not inventions, but truths; but he does not himself know what it is; and all that is necessary is that he would have explained his reasons in those ways all along. The fact that he *would* do something is neither hidden nor open to view.

vi) If there is a sign on the road saying 'Hidden Curve', and we proceed along and find no curve, one could not say 'Of course not, it is hidden'. What is hidden can be come upon; but we do not regard ourselves as able to come upon the pains or thoughts that we say are hidden from us.

vii) The future could be said to be hidden from us if we could coherently suppose that future events and actions are all taking place now, but have not yet floated down the river of time to where we are, and can never be seen until they arrive; but if I wonder if my cold will be better by Friday, I am not wondering if it is already better, only its betterness has not reached me yet.

If an astronomer does not find the future hidden when he calculates an eclipse of the sun, he does not find it open to view either. It is by calculation and not by perception of coming events that he makes his prediction (p.223). It is the crystalball gazer who can purport to find the future open to view. Similarly it is the idea that if I could see into his head I could say what he is thinking that persuades me to say that his thoughts are hidden; but it is not what *he* sees in his head that enables him to say what he is thinking (cf. p.217).

4. In the ordinary run of events, if we want to know what a person's motives or intentions are, what he believes, what he wants, what he is thinking or where his pain is, we ask him. It is not true that we can never know these things without asking him, nor is it true that he knows the answers to these questions (p.221), and when he replies honestly there can be no further doubt; but asking him is a business-like and generally reliable way of finding out. It is plausible to explain this

by saying that his psychological states and activities are open to his view, but hidden from us. We now have some reason to doubt this, but if that is not the explanation, then why *do* we ask him?

When a person has said something odd or paradoxical we may ask him whether he means it. We would be mystified if he answered that he did not remember or did not notice himself meaning it, or that it is hard for him to tell because there were so many distractions at the time when he said it (§674). We ask him, not because if he meant it, that fact will be open to his view, but in recognition of his right to determine how the conversation will develop: whether we laugh about his remark and play around with it, or take it seriously, ask for further explanation, require him to reply to our objections, and so on,

We ask a person whether he *intends* to do the dishes, rather than saying 'When are you going to do them?' or 'Will you do them?', to make it clear that we are neither expecting nor asking him to do this, it is entirely up to him. We are not asking him whether he notices something with the special marks of an intention: the word 'intention' can be used entirely to express *our* attitude, although grammatically it is *his* intention that is in question. Similarly if we ask 'Will you do them?', he may reply 'I intend to, later', defiantly, to indicate that he will not be doing them to oblige us, or because we asked him. Whichever of these questions we have, we address it to *him* for no deeper reason than that he is one of the people available for the task. In other cases we ask a person because we may not get a profession of intention without applying for it, and certain consequences attach just to the fact that a person has said he intends such and such. We may then in appropriate circumstances have a right to expect that if he changes his mind he will let us know. When we complain of his failure to let us know, it is no defence to say 'I only *said* I intended to do it. I didn't intend that at all'. Our right to expect that he would let us know derived, not from the intention, but from the profession of it. His having been set on doing something, so that he might have told us of his intention, although he did not, would give us no rights.

Why do we ask a person what his motives are? Partly to put him on notice that we find something unusual and needing explanation in the fact that he should have done the action whose motives we are inquiring about. We ask for the motives of immoral actions, and sometimes for those of virtuous acts, but cutting the lawn, going to work, having some wine with a meal, raise no questions about motives, unless it is surprising that such and such a person should have done them, or should have done them when he did, or in the way he did. Hence we are not expressing a hunch that a distinctive psychological event has occurred when we ask for a motive, but only expressing an opinion that an act was immoral, or that it was out of character for this person to have done it, or to have done it in the circumstances in which he did it. Sometimes it is very clear to us what a person's motive is, and yet we are inclined to ask him: is this to confirm our hypothesis? We would not always be much shaken from our previous supposition about his motive if he gave a conflicting account of it, or be materially reinforced in our belief if his account agrees. What we may want is not to know his motive, but that he should confess it. Confession, even when what is confessed is already known, is a significant act, to which various consequences attach. A father, who will have to pay for it, can confess that his child broke the window, but he cannot confess that a neighbour's child did it, unless what he is confessing is for example that he knew all along, but said nothing. The consequences of confessing a motive are not so clearcut as those of confessing that one broke a window or told a lie. They are roughly that a point about my character becomes common ground between us, and is no longer a topic for insinuation, allegation or tactful avoidance. Before my confession, you might know, and I might know you knew, and you might know that I knew you knew; but a new plateau is achieved by my confession, in which there is no longer a place for any of that web of thoughts. Nothing new is known, nothing that was hidden revealed. A relationship is altered.

The question why we ask a person what he is thinking is like the question why we ask him to a party: the answer is that we are interested in him, we want to know what *he* has to say. If someone's face darkens sceptically as we talk and we ask him what he is thinking, we are saying 'Have I blundered? Has something gone wrong here?' All we want is an answer, and of course we ask the person whose face has darkened. We take him to have something useful to say, but we misunderstand having something to say if we think it is something going on inwardly, where it is hidden from us. It is not going on inwardly, or outwardly either. It is not going on. If someone has a sceptical thought, there is something he can do that he has not yet done, even inwardly, and we ask him to go ahead and do it. One's ability to do something is not hidden before one does it, and is not open to view when one does it. The expressing of a doubt may show, but it is not identical with, an ability to express that doubt.

We do not ask a person who is wounded and writhing whether he is in pain. If we doubt it, we would have no reason to believe his answer. However we may ask a person who looks miserable whether he is in pain, and we ask a person who is in pain where it is, how bad it is and whether it is gnawing, jabbing or leaden. The reason we ask him is not that he perceives it, while we do not, but that he has it. When he says it is in the shoulder, he has not ascertained its location, as one might locate the source of a puzzling sound in the basement, and when he says it is frightful he has not had a look and seen it to be so. His descriptions of it as jabbing or leaden are not like his descriptions of an object as making thrusting motions or as heavy: there is something that thrusts and might cease thrusting without being a different something, but nothing that jabs; and when the jabbing ceases there is either no pain or not that pain. He could fail to notice the thrusting, but not fail to notice the jabbing, or notice it either. There is as it were nothing but the torment. The fact that we say 'The pain jabs' suggests a tormentor, and it is the tormentor that we fancy he sees and we do not when we say that pains are hidden; but if what does the jabbing is hidden from us, it is hidden from him too. We of course do not experience the jabbing, and he does; but we do understand him when he says that it jabs, whereas in thinking of the pain as hidden from us, we are ready to say that we do not understand him when he says he is in pain – that what he calls 'pain' might be entirely different from what we call pain. We do not similarly suppose that what he calls 'jabbing' we might call 'leaden'. We have no reason at all to suspect that his linguistic competence might so fail him when it comes to pains. He can describe such severally different things as sounds, light effects and bodily organs as 'pulsing': why should this ability fail him in the case of pains?

I have now reviewed an array of different reasons for withdrawing the application of the word 'hidden' from pains, thoughts, beliefs, intentions, motives, at least where its use is supposed to express a judgment *a priori*. Because my one question has been 'Can we call psychological states and processes hidden?', it might appear that I am merely being fussy here about the choice of word, and someone might say 'All right then, I will not henceforth speak that way; but what difference is that going to make?'

Appearances notwithstanding, the usage is of no interest for its own sake. What is important is the false picture of psychological states and processes, of which this use of the word 'hidden' is one of the more salient marks; the picture of them as discriminable somethings, the familiar but indescribable properties of which lead us to say that we intend, rather than plan, or that we believe, rather than suspect, and also to say *what* we intend, plan, believe or suspect. It is not a foolish picture: it arises reasonably from a considerable array of facts: from the fact there is a distinction between pain and pain behaviour, between having a thought and expressing it, between believing something and saying what one believes; from the fact that many times we do not know what kind of pain a person has unless he describes it, or what he is thinking or why he did something unless he tells us; from the fact that we can say falsely what we were thinking, what we believe, expect or intend, or why we did it; and from the fact that we all have such enormous difficulty describing the having of a thought, for example, or the day in, day out believing, in such a way as to make it clear that it is specifically a thought or a belief we are describing.

We misconstrue these facts however if we suppose that pain is so entirely distinct from pain behaviour that we could have a pain that left us altogether unaffected, that expressing a thought is a repetition in public of having a thought, that saying what one intends or believes is informing another person how it is with one inwardly, that we survey ourselves to decide whether and what we are expecting, hoping or thinking, or that the reason we cannot usefully describe a

242

pain, as distinct from its jabbing, or the having of a thought as distinct from expressing it, or day in day out believing as distinct from saying what one believes, is that these things are indescribable.

Here, as in many other cases, it is not the conclusion we reach, but the considerations we assemble in the course of defending it, that are of primary interest.

INDEXES

Index of Topics

Indexes

somebody, something, 161ff.
  to do something, 31
meaning it, 206
meaning something, 207
meaning what one says, 207, 239
minds, 22, 146, 149
motives, 239-40

names, 7, 9, 10, 12, 15
naming, 193
nervous system, 38, 39, 40
nonsense, 121,142,165ff., 234

occurrences, 131, 146, 147

pain, 22, 25, 26, 64, 66, 67, 101,
  103, 241
  language, 104, 107, 108, 109
pictures, 112ff., 146ff.
  forcing themselves on us, 219
  of psychological processes,
    242
'post', 18, 21, 25, 26
private object, 223ff.
  concept of 224, 225

reasons, 47, 237
  for thinking, 175ff.

resemblances, family, 53ff., 61ff.
rules, 38, 79, 81, 82, 83

sensations, 90, 91
  disagreeable, 84ff., 95
sense, 20
  of a sentence, 168, 169, 171
service
  of words, 217, 218, 219, 221
signal, 76
soul, 212ff.

talking to oneself, 33
thinking, 28, 29, 32, 34, 35, 36,
    37, 64, 153, 173ff., 192, 219,
    227, 228, 232-3, 340
training, 73, 194
trying, 199, 202

understanding, 28, 29, 34, 36, 41,
    49, 156, 157, 158, 159, 171,
    198
use, 7,9,12,19
  of a word, 40

voluntary action, 201

will, 148, 198, 199

Index of Passages Cited or Discussed